RAVEN C

JOURNAL, VOL. 25

BALANCING
ACTS

RAVEN CHRONICLES
JOURNAL, VOL. 25

BALANCING
ACTS

Editors

Phoebe Bosché

Anna Bálint

Matt Briggs

Paul Hunter

Doug Johnson

RAVEN CHRONICLES PRESS
SEATTLE, WASHINGTON

FIRST EDITION

ISBN 978-0-9979468-3-3
Library of Congress Control Number: 2017960225

Cover Art: "Raven Blue," watercolor and gouache painting,
28" x 20", August, 2017, by Jeannie Grisham.

Book Design: Phoebe Bosché, using 11/14 Palatino typeface.
Cover Design: Tonya Namura
Raven Press Logo: Scott Martin

Established in 1991, *The Raven Chronicles* is a Seattle-based
literary organization that publishes and promotes artistic work
that embodies the cultural diversity and multitude of
imaginations of writers and artists living in the Pacific Northwest, other regions of the United States, and abroad.

Raven Chronicles Press
15528 12th Avenue NE
Shoreline, Washington 98155

editors@ravenchronicles.org

http://ravenchronicles.org

THINK OF HOW TIGHTROPE WALKERS TRY TO
MAINTAIN BALANCE. ONE STEP TOO FAR TO
THE LEFT OR RIGHT AND THEY FALL DOWN.
THAT'S JUST LIKE THE ENVIRONMENT.
ALL THE ORGANISMS IN AN
ENVIRONMENT (PLANTS, ANIMALS,
INSECTS, AND EVEN BACTERIA)
HAVE TO LIVE TOGETHER
IN BALANCE.
BIODIVERSITY IS THE RINGLEADER IN
THE ENVIRONMENTAL CIRCUS.

—STEPHANIE VERA

Dimensions

Avis M. Adams

The steep ascent was nothing.
It was the looking
that hurt—for snakes.

I found birds.
He once read to me
from an aviary.

I was the bird he would not cage,
while I perched on the ledge
of his knowledge,

on the gyration of his words.

No arms can hold you,
he said, yet I wanted
to hold him forever.

An osprey rises from her
nest, describes an arc
in three dimensions.

I watch her cut over the valley
as I scale the ridge,
understanding well my

marriage to gravity.

TABLE OF CONTENTS

VII Featured theme: *Balancing Acts*

VIII Rants, Raves & Reviews

Preface

For Raven's Vol. 25 Journal, we chose the theme "Balancing Acts." We asked writers and visual artists to think about and address the following: How do you live your life, fully, and maintain your relationship with the planet and the diversity of life on it? Biodiversity is balance in the dance of nature. Where do you fit in that dance. Can nature, sensate creatures like chimps, be granted legal rights? If you could be an animal or a tree or a work of nature, what would you be and why?

Here is what our editors have to say about editing this particular theme:

Anna Bálint (Safe Place Writing Circle):

In Safe Place Writing Circle we explored the theme of "Balancing Acts" over a period of several weeks. This resulted in some beautiful and original writing. I was intrigued by the number of people who gave expression to balancing acts in relation to their ongoing and invisible struggles of living with mental illness, and periods of frightening chaos and instability as part of that. People also wrote about their inner turmoil as a reflection of, and impacted by, the overall state of the outside world, with its intensified upheavals and dangers of war, and ecological and political disasters.

Alongside this, the inner turmoil and challenges people wrote about also give rise to more absences from class due to illness and personal crisis during this same period. This, in turn, led to less work being typed up, edited, and submitted than for other issues of *Raven Chronicles*.

But for others, including the two poets included in this issue, the theme was an invitation to move beyond the day to day realities of life and to plunge into a more celebratory, cosmic, and majestic view of the planet. In recalling the earthquakes of her childhood in Chile—vivian linder levi writes of "the clamor of the earth, its deep movement," and "I had the time of my life . . ." Later on, her poem transforms trauma survival into a spirit of resistance. In Dana Nelson Dudley's poem, "Magic Tree," the Milky Way becomes part of the tree, ". . . its myriad branches / with a multitude of leaves, flowers and fruit." "Endless River" both moves and sings the praises of water, while also pausing to note "how good it is to be a rock."

Phoebe Bosché (Managing Editor):

The U.S. contributors in this Balancing Acts-themed issue live in seventeen states—Washington, Nebraska, Pennsylvania, California, Oregon, Illinois, New Jersey, , Virginia, Idaho, New York, New Mexico, Colorado, Texas, Alabama, Wisconsin, Florida, Washington, D.C.; and 52% are from Washington State. Contributors, particularly visual artists, also hail from ten countries—U.S., Germany, Colombia, Russia, Australia, New Zealand, Spain, Canada, Chile, Singapore.

We are especially pleased to present the work of a selection of established and emerging writers from New Zealand as part of the Sister Cities Program, a collaboration between Seattle and Christchurch, New Zealand. Talk about synchronicity! Just as we were getting ready to go to press with this journal, we heard the announcement on October 31, 2017, that Seattle had been designated as a UNESCO City of Literature, after all the hard work by the folks at Seattle City of Literature! Congratulations to Stesha Brandon, Bob Redmond, et al, and Ryan Boudinot—who did the heavy lifting early on and produced a vivid book of "Reflections From A Community of Writers," *Seattle City of Literature*, Sasquatch Books, 2015. This is good news for the international cooperation and exchange of ideas between writers on a global scale—even though, under our current fear-mongering U.S. administration, our government has withdrawn from UNESCO as a full member effective December 31, 2018. Despite that setback, as this issue of *Raven Chronicles* will attest, individual artists and writers continue to reach across the miles, and collaborate in lively and substantial ways.

Matt Briggs (Fiction Editor):

In reading the stories for this issue of *The Raven Chronicles* I was mindful of the "Balancing Acts" theme. Balance is unavoidable. When you trip, you are caught by the ground. When you fire a rifle, the stock recoils into your shoulder. The bullet finds rest in the target. I was pleased to find stories by Anna Reaney and Willie Smith. Reaney's story, "There Was Always Something Wrong With Her," captures the balancing act of a narrator who is always watching herself, and her articulation of state is simultaneously unsettling and calming. Willie Smith finds balance by rooting his stream-of-consciousness with labiodentals.

Paul Hunter (Poetry Editor):

We love to watch the precarious in motion—captivated by tightrope walkers in rosined satin slippers, or by plates spun atop wobbly flexible poles—and always the more the merrier. Maybe we just love the tension built into aerial shows, that flimsy anxiety that something, anything, the dishes or Flying Wallendas, might come crashing down, since that's what so often happens in our lives. We're like Mickey in *The Sorcerer's Apprentice*, we itch to play with awesome powers, but when things get out of hand we can never quite catch up and put things right, though we know it's only a click or a keystroke away, and all at once the castle is under water, the dinner ends up burnt or raw.

So when we ask to hear about your balancing acts, we all know what that means both personally and generally. In this topsy-turvy moment each of us seeks a place to stand, some existential footing that will make sense of the insinuations and provocations that seem to rain down every day. You didn't need a writing prompt, but many of you responded with a lovely balancing of the trivial and monumental in mood and motion—the small things where we have an illusion of control, and the huge and sometimes no more meaningful events that afflict us. As the King in *Hamlet* says, "When sorrows come, they come not single spies, but in battalions." So we catch the spider in a cup hoping to do a good turn for us both—try to shake it loose on the night wind without giving it a ride to bed with us, up the sleeve of our bathrobe, in our hair.

Doug Johnson (Nonfiction Editor):

In considering the theme of balance, the body of work presented itself in two distinct categories. Many people took it to mean they should provide a memoir of direct experience out of their own lives. Others took it to mean it should be an essay. The essays addressed theories, much looking like a college book report . . . sometimes politics. Politics speak nothing of balance, at the moment, choosing to be more absurd than comedic fiction. That narrowed my decisions to the first group that decided to take the memoir strategy. In this subgroup there was a fine line between revealing to the reader a piece of their lives and placing the reader in the box as priest confessor as they wrote more in a blog / therapy / diary manner. In the end I chose writing that was invisible to the reader because it did not put moral pressure on them to absolve the lives of the writer. The reader and writer are in constant relationship. The nonfiction writer, especially, needs to think of their reader first, the craft second, and their own needs for reconciliation last.

I

BRIDGES NOT WALLS

Bridge Over Center, photograph by David Anderson

The Immigrant Called Moon

Anita Endrezze

Moon crosses the river
without any papers.
Moon dies of thirst in the desert.
Moon scrubs your toilets,
plucks oranges from trees.
Moon hides her Otherness under a bright scarf.
Moon eats food you can't pronounce
but you decide you like it anyway.
Moon is a doctor who saves you.
Moon is a singer who desires you.
Moon is a stranger in your own house.
Moon walks your uneasy streets.
Moon is murdered under the stars
and lies there, dimly glowing til dawn.
Moon is frightened by the knock at the door.
Moon marries your son and lives in bicultural compromise
    forever.
Moon becomes part of your family and you kiss her cheek
    at bedtime.
Moon dies one day, and suddenly, everyone realizes how
    life is darker
without Moon's fluid syllables and strange ways.
The light that was her eye
is the light that shines from each of us:
little orbs, little souls, crossing over, without boundaries.

The Daily News

Anita Endrezze

Bombs leveraging the sky.
The choppy sea and its fulcrum of clouds.
A child face down
on the shore.
A man cries.
That woman stares into the bone of grief.
The TV is on, and there is war
in between ads. Some of us
want to cradle the wounded
in our arms. Others want to be
the teeth of the Beast.

Raven In Eden, detail of collage by Anita Endrezze

II

THE FAMILY CORVIDAE

Neighborhood Crows

Edward Harkness

In lazy flight this afternoon, they resemble
scraps of crepe blown aloft above the sunlit
crowns of firs. They're my aloof neighbors.
All their guttural utterances are black, cynical,

feathered with irony. *The point is*, they mutter,
there's no point. They clean up our messes.
In the corner of a field they hop to a scrap
of burger still in its silver wrapper.

Tolerant as Lao Tzu, plain as nickels, they gather
on wires in squads of nine. Earning a living,
they know, depends on luck, a canny eye
and magic, which explains their sorcerer's robes,

glossy as lacquered shadows at twilight.
Like the universe, they do not judge.
They have no comment on the divorce rate
or the attendance of gangsters at church.

Instead, they're the lamplighters of old, lighting stars
to signal day's end as they pass over power lines.
Imponderable, ordinary, like night itself,
they spread their wings to shelter their young,

invite their friends to dinner in a ditch
or near an upturned garbage can. When threatened
by a hawk they call in reinforcements to harry
the intruder, distracting hunter away from the hunted.

At dawn they reappear, routine as soot
but wiser. For crows are learned monks
in vacant lots, beggars who take the vow
of poverty and then take over the city.

Crows have nothing to teach, nothing to sell.
They joke, cajole, bicker and tend
to their families. They are Zen masters
of the art of blending in, always making the best

of a bad situation, as poets do who know
it's hopeless but go on anyway with their crow visions
and dark pronouncements, feigning nonchalance
when we fail to understand their off-the-cuff

commentaries, those suggestions they offer in order
to survive the coming apocalypse. If we paid attention,
we might even learn something—not merely
how to face the day when the comet strikes or the missiles

rise from their silos, but how to live in the now,
how to start anew, how to be better than we've been
and, despite the madness of our time,
how to get along with our neighbors, how to thrive.

Women's March, January 21, 2017, Seattle, photograph by Anna Bálint

III

WORDS FROM THE CAFÉ

The Recovery Café

An Introduction

The Recovery Café sits on the corner of Boren and Denny, in downtown Seattle. It is a unique and remarkable place. "Recovery Café and its School for Recovery serve men and women who have suffered trauma, homelessness, addiction and/or other mental health challenges. In this loving community, men and women experience belonging, healing and the joy of contributing. The Café and School for Recovery help participants develop tools for maintaining recovery and stabilizing in mental/physical health, housing, relationships and employment/volunteer service."—*Excerpt from mission statement, Recovery Café website.*

Writer/teacher, Anna Bálint, joined the Café community as a volunteer, teaching writing classes with the School of Recovery. Over time, her classes evolved into "Safe Place Writing Circle," an ongoing and fluid group that has met weekly since Fall, 2012. Its purpose is to provide a "safe place" for Café members to creatively explore many different aspects of their lives through writing, give voice to their beliefs, hopes and fears, and discover the power of their own voices. Raven Chronicles Press published *Words From the Café, An Anthology*, edited by Anna Bálint, in 2016. It includes ten featured writers, many Other Voices, and a CD of the featured writers reading a selection of their work. Check our website to buy a copy.

Some amazing stories and poems emerge, on a regular basis, from everyone involved in this writing circle. Here are a few of those voices.

Earthquakes

vivan linder levi

As a child of the Holocaust
taking refuge in Chile
I and my cousins
played on the top of mountains,
the majestic Andes.
Naked, we played with mud,
put colors on our bodies
when suddenly a grumble
and the rumble of boulders,
the force of the earth penetrating
the soles of our feet.

I had the time of my life,
and fell in love with earthquakes—
the clamor of the earth, its deep movement.
I only lamented the tragedies they left behind,
houses swallowed whole, villages in ruins.

Now living here,
in this north American city,
in the middle of this pollution
that is killing me with every breath,
I am on my knees dusting,
everyday dusting
this thick dark dirt that invades
everything, that accentuates
my migraines. I accumulate
every piece of wet paper towel
as evidence that I am under the threat

of eviction from planet earth,
from the slow burning of toxic fumes
with no respite from the assaults
on air and water,
on the sacred territories
of Native American Peoples.

Wealth has become the only voice
and that is an earthquake,
a social-political earthquake.
I miss the real earthquakes
where neighbors helped each other.
Here I might die,
but I come from people who trace
persecution back to the Inquisition.
So swallow me, earth.

Endless River

Dana Nelson Dudley

Our lives pass like rivers
sometimes from little trickles of snowmelt
sometimes from fresh water springs
sometimes from magnificent glaciers
seeping underneath from its many small melting parts
gathering into a torrent, a raging violent surge
from the mouth of the glacier
from where it touches ground below.
Canyons are carved by these rivers,
water tumbles down them,
leaving us trembling with fear.

How good it is to be a rock.
The water passes by and settles down
to irrigate peaceful fertile plains and fields.
Cattle graze and peasants plow and till
nurture and harvest the fields.
Such is the passage of time.
There may always be a war or conflict somewhere
but life will still depend on water
from where it all began
when the Nordic fish man rose out of the sea.

Magic Tree

Dana Nelson Dudley

There is a tree somewhere
a magic tree.
This wishful sitting tree
is the nature of humanity.

Or have I got it upside down?
Space is like a tree,
the burl root is our earth.

The trunk leads to the North Star.
The pendulum of the big dipper and the little dipper
circles round the two main branches.
The Milky Way, its myriad branches
with a multitude of leaves, flowers and fruit.

They produce whatever is called for
in this needy greedy world,
our confused paradise
messed up by praise and blame
our wonderland full of challenges
and benefits beyond belief.

Chief Sealth Trail, Pea Patch, Seattle, 2017, photograph by Anna Bálint

IV

THE ENDLESS SENTENCE

The Endless Sentence, Monroe State Reformatory, 2003,
drawing by Jeff Niles Hacking

Daniel Carter's Two Stories, One Thousand and Three Nights

Matt Briggs

Tales like the two that Daniel Carter has written here evoke for me the contradictions of reading. When I first learned to read, these contradictions were familiar to me. The entire sensation of seeing marks on a page that put a voice in my head was bizarre, but at five years old I didn't know from bizarre. These marks made a sound, but I was the only one who could hear them. The sound was not my voice, it was the voice of the author, even if the author was someone who had died a long time. The voice that was in my head knew things about the world that I could never know. For anyone who has read *One Thousand and One Nights*, the merchants, beggars, and princes in Carter's two stories are familiar. Tales like Daniel's feel like there are things working under the surface just beyond comprehension. I find they make me receptive to the things I don't really understand.

The Wise Shaykh and the Bedouin

Daniel Carter

O ne day a Bedouin arrived at a caravansarai on the Old Silk Road leading to Samarkand. Upon entering he heard the laughter of children. Following the sounds he found a gathering of young boys and girls in the majlis of an old man. The elder had a long wispy white beard that matched the color of his turban and thobe. One of the boys sat right in front of the Shaykh in the center of the circle and was trying hard to look stern while the elder stuck out his tongue and made funny faces. The rest of the children laughed hysterically.

"This man is a fool," thought the Bedouin. "Though he has the look of a learned man, he is sitting there acting like he's crazy. When he is finished with this buffoonery I will test his knowledge."

After the midday prayer was finished and the children went back to their parents, the Bedouin returned to find the Shaykh reciting the Qur'an.

"Shaykh, what is your name?"

"My name is Isma'il ibn al-Qasim."

"Are you not an Alim?"

"I am a traveler like you."

"Don't speak in riddles and rhetoric old man. I am no child and care not for games. 'Speak straight to the point,' the Qur'an says."

"Sadaqa Allaahu al-'Azeem," said the Shaykh, touching his breast with is right hand.

"Uff! What kind of learned man sits around with children laughing and making a fool of himself all day? What do you know of the teachings of the Prophet, upon him be peace?"

The Shaykh stood up and smiled. "Salaam," he said and walked away while reciting the Qur'anic verse, "The servants of the Most Merciful tread lightly on the earth; And when the ignorant ones address them they simply say, 'Salaam.'" 📖

* * * *

Majlis: Arabic term meaning "a place of sitting, used in the context of council."

Thobe or Thawb: An ankle-length Arab garment, with long sleeves.

Alim: a scholar; a Muslim learned in religious matters.

Salaam: Peace.

The Merchant and His Sons

Daniel Carter

One day the merchant from Al-Maghreb was leaving the masjid with his sons. Outside the courtyard an elderly man covered in dust sat next to a dirty young boy. Beside the man was a discarded wine vessel.

"Alms for the needy?" asked the man as the merchant and his sons passed by.

"Uff!" said the eldest son, turning his nose up in disgust and hurrying along. His brothers followed him, laughing under their breath as they went. The merchant followed them a few paces then paused. He pulled out his purse from a sash around his waist and took out a few dinars.

"Father, don't give that man anything," said the second eldest son. He pointed to the wine bottle. "Look, he's a drunk. If you give him the money all he will do is buy more khamr."

The merchant told his sons to wait for him. He walked back to the beggar and spoke to him. The old man looked down at the vessel and pointed to the sky. The boys couldn't hear what was said between them, but they were all astonished as they watched their father hand his entire purse over to the beggar. The old man stood up and the two men embraced.

"Who was that man father?" asked the eldest son when the merchant rejoined them. "Why did you give him all of your money?"

"Never mind; let's go home. Tomorrow I need you to go on an important journey for me."

"What about us father?" said the youngest son.

"Don't worry; you will all make the journey this year, inshaa' Allah."

The following morning after the Fajr prayer, upon the instruction of his father, the eldest son set out to the east to locate a female pistachio tree. After a long and arduous trip in the winter, the young man found the tree. With money from his father he purchased the tree from a farmer and took note of its condition.

When he returned the merchant ordered the eldest son to tell his brothers how to find the tree. When spring arrived the merchant sent his next oldest son to go check on the pistachio tree and inspect it. Then in the summer he sent his third son and in the fall he sent his youngest.

After his youngest son returned home the merchant ordered his sons to meet him in the masjid. When they arrived he asked them to describe the condition of the pistachio tree. "It was barren when I saw it in the winter," said the eldest son. "When I saw it the leaves were bright green and small reddish-orange flowers were beginning to blossom from the ends of its branches," said the second eldest. "When I got there the tree was full of clusters of yellow fruits," said the third son. "In the fall the tree was full of fruits that looked like little mangos," said the youngest. "In the center of the fruit were ripe pistachio nuts."

"Your descriptions are different," said the merchant. "Which description is the right one then?"

The boys paused to think about the question. "All of us are right, father," said the third son. "We each saw it in different seasons so what we saw was different, but not wrong."

"Ah, that's right my son. Very good! Because you each only saw the tree in one state, your descriptions differ, yet no one can say any of you are wrong. But if you had thought that only your own description was right, then you would be wrong, Sah?"

"Correct," said the eldest.

"So you all understand that there are more to things than what meets the eye?"

The boys agreed.

"Very well, do you remember when we were all here last year and that elderly gentleman asked for alms?"

"You mean that dirty drunken beggar in front of the mosque who you gave your purse to?" asked the second eldest son.

"All of you assumed he was a drunken beggar. But there was more to him than met the eye. In truth, that man was Isma'il ibn al-Qasim, the wise Shaykh. The boy next to him was an orphan. They had just arrived in the city after being stranded in the desert for three days. The caravan they were traveling in was attacked by brigands and everything they had was stolen from them."

"But we saw his wine bottle, father," said the youngest son.

"When I greeted him I asked if that vessel was his. He looked at it in surprise. Apparently, through his fatigue he hadn't noticed it. He pointed to the sky and sought refuge in Allah, swearing he never saw it before. That was when I recognized him. 'Aren't you Isma'il ibn al-Qasim?' I asked him. 'Yes,' he replied. 'And you are Suleiman the merchant.'"

The merchant pointed at his sons. "Never forget the words of your Lord, 'And avoid much suspicion, for verily in some cases suspicion is a sin.'"

"My sons, just as you all found the pistachio tree in different states, so too will you find people. Therefore, do not rush to judge others because oftentimes you do not know the full reality of things. Always give your fellow brothers and sisters the benefit of the doubt and make excuses for them rather than jumping to conclusions and assuming the worst of them. To remind us of this lesson we will keep the pistachio tree in our family as long as we are alive."

And so it was that the sons and grandchildren of the merchant kept the pistachio tree, generation after generation, to remind them to not be judgmental. 📖

* * * *

Masjid: Arabic word for mosque.

Dinar: The main currency unit in seven mostly-Islamic and two mostly-Orthodox (Serbia and Macedonia) countries.

Khamr: An Arabic word of wine.

Inshallah or Insha'a Allah: If Allah wills; Allah knows best.

Fajr: The Fajr prayer is the second prayer of the five daily prayers offered by practising Muslims.

V

ODES TO PERSONS, PLACES & THINGS

Budapest, District 8, Forbidden Pea Patch, Hungary, 2017,
photograph by Anna Bálint

Left To My Own Devices

JT Stewart

Dishes stack up
in the sink

Rust collects
on the stove

Bacon turns green
in the fridge

Newspapers yellow
on the porch

I nap intending
to wake up tomorrow

Tomorrow comes soon
I sleep past it

Left to my own devices
I cheat

Leaving town
is too simple

Juan Rulfo: Sombra de Arreguín, pen & ink drawing by Doug Johnson

Brettler Family Place 3

—In Memory Of Charleena Lyles

Anna Bálint

Not a good place to be a family
this Father's Day, 10am under cloudy skies.

Not a good place to be a mother of four
with number five on the way.
Not a good place be black and poor
with no-one around to keep you safe
from the man who keeps coming around
with fists and fury and a whole lot more.

No one around to keep you safe
from the demons inside your head
talking about how your kid gonna morph
into a wolf and you better look out for the KKK.

No one around to protect you or your kids,
your baby crying and crying—hush baby hush.
No denying someone's been in here,
someone came in and messed with your things.
No denying someone's messing with your head,
wants you dead, your head spinning . . .

Cops the ones supposed to keep you safe, right?
Except . . . they never do, they never do.
What you supposed to do when the voices in your head
won't let up long enough to let you think?
What to do? What to do? What to do?
Not a thing you can do except call 911 . . .

Listen!
Hey kids, turn down that TV.
Listen!

Someone's knocking on the door.
Someone's out there knocking.
You better look out, Charleena.
Girl, you know this place ain't safe.
Someone's out there knocking.
Someone's out there calling your name.
Someone's out there knocking
and there's no telling who
or just what they might do to you . . .

Note: Brettler Place 3 is a low income housing facility in Seattle, Washington, where Charleena Lyles lived with her four children. On Father's Day, 2017, Charleena, who was in need of mental health care, made a 911 call to the Seattle Police saying her house had been broken into. Within two minutes of arriving at her apartment door, the responding officers shot and killed Charleena in front of three of her children.

La Llorona: Sombra de Arreguín, pen & ink drawing by Doug Johnson

The Real Uncle Sam

Thomas Hubbard

After the last "good war" . . .
GIs came home, raised hell for a while,
then found a wife and looked around for a house.

Markets provided prefabricated house kits, delivered to your lot.
Prefabs. Buy them on the GI Bill. Put them up in a few days.
Crackerbox houses.

Square, plain, two bedrooms, kitchen, bath and living room.
Plywood. A few of them are still around. Crackerbox houses.

Tonight . . .
Somewhere in an american suburb,
maybe in a midwest town,
on the gravel drive of a ramshackle crackerbox house,
an aging beater car stands among tall weeds, waiting.

Sometimes late at night,
an old man steps out of that house, and
he looks up at the distant stars in a bruise-colored sky, then
he carries a paper bag to the car and climbs inside.

Sitting in the driver's seat of his beater car,
he opens the bag and removes the first of a six-pack, and
he opens the can, and sips, and from far across the evening
wafts the sound of a brass band blowing,
"Stars and Stripes Forever."

That same brass band played while history unfolded, while
governments offered cash bounties for dead ndns, while

humans were kidnapped in Africa and
brought across the sea and sold as slaves
to help build the USA on this stolen land, and

That same brass band played on while
andrew jackson gave tribal land to slaveholders, while
seventh cavalry murdered those ndn families, while
secret agents trained central american death squads,

That band was just jammin' while
crooked voting machines put a bogus president in office,
    while
chickenshit police at protests taped over their nametags,
    while
secret torture chambers produced phony evidence, while
cops murdered unarmed men, women, even kids, and

The band kept on blowin' "Stars and Stripes" while
cockroaches carried tiki torches in the bloody streets, while
the country that old man once fought for
became the next third reich . . . .

And now, floating through the polluted evening air
comes the sound of that same old brass band,
broken-hearted and way out of tune,
faintly blowing "Stars and Stripes Forever,"
slow as a funeral dirge, and

That old man sits behind the wheel of his beater car, and
he opens another can of beer, there along a midnight street
in a fading neighborhood, and right there behind the wheel
of that car sits the real uncle sam, way past middle age,
six pack besides him, cigarette in hand, chain-smoking,
wondering how in hell it ever got this way, but

Realizing, deep down inside, nothing much has changed.

Ghost Print, by Judith Skillman

VI

ACROSS BORDERS: WRITERS FROM SEATTLE'S SISTER CITY CHRISTCHURCH, NEW ZEALAND

Seattle, USA, and Christchurch, New Zealand. On the surface they don't hold many similarities, geographically and culturally, but they both have a proud tradition of literature, a uneasy history of colonisation, and proximity to mountains, the Pacific Ocean, and a major fault line. They are also officially Sister Cities. Sister Cities programmes, according to the Christchurch City Council website, "foster communications across borders—a mutual exchange of ideas, people, and materials in cultural, educational, youth, sports, municipal, professional and technical projects."

In 2015, I travelled to Seattle in search of people and organisations working in the literature sphere with which to build relationships. My goal was to find great Seattle writers to invite to the WORD Christchurch Festival, and to promote the idea of an exchange that would send a Christchurch writer to Seattle on alternate years. I landed in time for Lit Crawl, and was welcomed warmly by an array of Seattle writers, booksellers, and organisers. I met Bob Redmond of Seattle City of Literature, and through that connection invited Seattle writer Elissa Washuta, of the Cowlitz Indian Tribe, back to Christchurch for our festival in 2016, funded by the Sister Cities programme. Elissa was able to showcase her work, and make important connections, especially within Ngāi Tahu, the Māori tribe of the South Island. Along with

Ali Cobby Eckerman, an Aboriginal poet from Adelaide, Australia, another sister city, and Nic Low, a writer of Ngāi Tahu and Pākehā (European) descent, we put together a panel called "Sister Cities / First Nations," and ran a workshop for indigenous writers.

This year, thanks to further funding from the Sister Cities programme, and with support from Seattle City of Literature, we were able to send a Christchurch writer back to Seattle. Nic Low participated in Lit Crawl and continued to forge connections with Seattle writers and organisations.

In 2016, *Catalyst*, a Christchurch-based literary journal, published a group of Seattle writers, and this year *Raven Chronicles* is returning the favour. Here you will find a selection of established and acclaimed Christchurch writers such as Fiona Farrell and Frankie McMillan, alongside emerging talent such as Erik Kennedy and Heather McQuillan. Readers will note many of the works are united by the most defining event in recent Christchurch history—the earthquakes of 2010 and 2011, in which 185 people lost their lives and which flattened the inner city. We are in the process of rebuilding and it's been slow and painful, but the city's artistic and grassroots communities have provided pockets of vigour, agitation, and hope along the way. At WORD Christchurch, we aim to bring life back into the inner city as it recovers, and to provide a platform for discussion and meaningful work.

I am grateful to Phoebe Bosché for commissioning the work, Stesha Brandon of Seattle City of Literature for her enthusiasm for the exchange, and to Doc Drumheller, for helping with the submissions. We look forward to welcoming a Seattle writer to Christchurch in 2018, and it is our hope that the Sister Cities Committee will continue to fund the initiative for a long time to come, and that we find new and innovative ways to connect and collaborate with your fine city.

—*Rachael King*
WORD Christchurch

Founded in 2013, to manage Seattle's bid to join UNESCO's Creative Cities Network, Seattle City of Literature is a nonprofit organization dedicated to serving our city's literary community by connecting it to the world. Seattle was designated a UNESCO City of Literature in October of 2017. For more information, please visit www.seattlecityoflit.org.

—*Stesha Brandon*
Seattle City of Literature

Proposal for the Garden City

Doc Drumheller

Before the earthquakes crumbled our buildings
fields of orchards were bulldozed to build houses.

Now that they're gone volunteer potatoes
self-seed abandoned backyards of the red zone.

Wild lettuce sows itself into vacant lots
parsley rises in-between pavement cracks.

Empty car parks transform into greenhouses
for the homeless to sleep with tomatoes.

Watercress sprouts in construction site streams
beans grow beside the river to fuel the rebuild.

The four avenues turn into an orchard
granny smith apples grow in the gutters.

Peel back the concrete to sow a new CBD
let the garden city reclaim its name.

My Father's Fingers

Doc Drumheller

Days after my father died I felt a sense
of urgency to take care of his hot house.

It was early spring and his tomatoes
were already five feet tall and rising.

Small green fruit poked out of yellow flowers
protruding like an outie belly button.

His cucumber vines began to climb
his banana peppers were small but sturdy.

Then came the frosts that spread like cancer
then came the aphids acting like assassins.

But there will be no sprays on his tomatoes
no poisons on his peppers and cucumbers.

I washed each leaf by hand as I couldn't bear
to lose the final things his fingers touched.

The Swamp of my Childhood

Doc Drumheller

Catfish whiskers twitch stirring memories
as my sons fish in the swamp of my childhood.

Alligators bathe in the fountain of youth
where Ponce De Leon searched for immortality.

My brother's speed boat races to his honey holes
black crappie creep underneath the lily pads.

The fertile cattail reed beds spawn large-mouth bass
while white ibis taste minnows in the marshes.

Red wiggler worms writhe in Styrofoam cups
yellow bobbers sink with bream on hooks.

Snapping turtles hide inside their shells
cane poles, rods and reels clash all afternoon.

Back at the camp fishermen compare their catch
telling tall tales as bass sizzles in the pan.

Ode to a Turkey Buzzard

Doc Drumheller

New world vultures
gathered at a wake
you were the tormentor
of my youth
huddled in masses
around the scent
of the swamp's decay
your pervious nostril
gave me the impression
you were evil.

It is easy to be misunderstood
when the sight
of your wingspan
invokes images
of mortality
as you soar
almost motionless
sensing the thermal density
of the dearly departed.

Your bald red head
resembles a friar
from the order
of Cathartiformes
frilled feathers
on your neck
ruffle like the collar
of plumed black robes

worn in display
of your vow to live
a life of poverty
performing the last rights
to carrion before tearing away
traces of their existence.

You are the coroner
of the condors
astute incisions
of your scalpel blade beak
extract the truth
buried down deep
in our gizzards
results of your autopsies
unveil the secrets
of life and death
laid bare for all to see
it may be dirty work
but somebody has to do it.

Cobden, 2013, digital photograph by Bridget Reweti

Decline and Fall on Savage Street

Novel Excerpt

Fiona Farrell

This novel is made up of one hundred small chapters, recording the tumultuous history of the 20th century through the story of a single house until its demolition following the Christchurch quakes of 2010-11. Interleaved with human history is the history of a longfinned female eel in the river across the road. She also lives one hundred years before setting off one night on the immense journey north to tropic waters somewhere off Tonga. There, at last, she releases her millions of eggs and dies, and the whole miraculous cycle begins again.

. . . this house, with its ridiculous turret, its inglenook and aging roof, and nighttime creakings, delighted her. It was scuffed and layered. When they stripped away the wallpaper in a back bedroom it was to find four different kinds of paper, a pale blue floral over ochre stripes over a pattern of green acanthus, and at the bottom, against the sarking, a layer of newspapers dating from 1910, with pictures of women wearing long skirts and enormous hats. It reminded her of a book she'd read as a child, about a little house that was built upon a hill where it could see the sun and the moon and stars. And steadily, season by season, the world about it changes, from horses and buggies to cars and the city edges nearer until the little house is engulfed by tall buildings blocking out the sun and the moon and stars. It becomes sad and derelict. And then a woman comes by and buys the little house and moves it on a truck far out into the country where it can see the sky once more and is happy. She'd loved that book, with its illustrations of trees in all seasons and the house whose windows were eyes and whose front door was its nose. She'd loved the idea of the building living through change.

And now here she was, living in just such a house, a place that had seen many people come and go, perched on a rise above the river. She loved it for itself. She did not want to restore it to some notion of authenticity, with flowery Edwardian friezes and lumbering antiques. She did not want to retain the off-white good taste of its previous owners. She wanted to play, fill its ample shell with colour, dress it up, a garish old lady with wonky lipstick. There was room for that here. For silliness. For happiness.

So they drink their pinot as the house settles into the dark. It is late, after midnight, when Rob reaches out and touches her hand, the way he does. It's the familiar question to which she feels the familiar response, the bubbling excitement, and they are kissing, they are fumbling on the retro sofa and she is a little drunk, her head somehow not quite attached to the rest of her body which is tumbling somehow or other onto the mat in front of the fake fire and both of them are laughing, but quietly. Tom is staying with his friend VJ somewhere in town, but Poppy could blunder in on them at any time, in flight from some dream, so half-undressed they stumble across the hallway to their bedroom and shut the door. The curtains have been taken down and the windows left wide open to let out the smell of undercoat. The carpet is covered in drop sheets and there are ladders and trestles. It does not look like their bedroom at all. It is strange.

Strangeness has always done it for them. Hotel rooms, for example, where in hushed anonymity, several floors above a city street filled with cars driven by people they did not know, to places they did not know, it was as if they too became strangers. Rob became the man in the fantasies they sometimes murmured to one another, the man she has just met at a party, or on a beach: the one who picks her out among the crowd, the one whose shadow falls across her as she lies sunbathing naked among the sandhills. That's the man she meets in the hotel room, not Rob who wonders if he should get back into surfing, get another job, lose a few kilos, slams in from work, rumpled and fed up, dragging off his shoes without undoing the laces, kicking them into the corner, saying, "God, I'm buggered. Bloody commissioners. I need a drink." Rooting in the cupboard above the fridge where they kept the whisky.

Not that man. On the hotel bed's 500-thread white linen, he is a stranger, someone she picked up ten minutes earlier in the lobby downstairs.

And now, in their bedroom, their bed waits, and it too is strange, though they have made love on it on average three times a week for fifteen years allowing for interruptions following the birth of each child when she had sat in the dark, feeding, Rob passed out from exhaustion, managing somehow to sleep through the crying. She had leaned against the headboard as first Tom and then Poppy had sucked mightily, while her own body clenched the way it had previously done only at the point of orgasm. And with that clenching came such a surge of love: not the ordinary soppy Valentine's card love, but an all-pervading, fierce attachment to this little creature whose steady slurping relieved the pressure that had built within her breasts. Then there was the time of the wakeful toddler clambering between them at odd hours, squirming into the nest and resisting all attempts at eviction until one of them, usually Rob, gave up and left the child in full possession, chattering away at 2 am, while the adult squeezed into a vacated bed among the stuffed toys.

But that time passed. Now the children sleep alone behind doors firmly closed with signs warning off intruders and two or three times a week through the tangle of jobs and deadlines and assignments and meetings they find their way back to one another. Sometimes a brief coupling before sleep, sometimes a more elaborate business of strangers on a beach or the fiddle of the black lacy outfit Rob had brought back from a trip to Sydney, with suspenders, for gods sake. It slid over stretch marks and cellulite and the scar where Poppy had been cut from her in haste, the ring of masked faces looking down at her as she lay, high as a kite on Pethedine. The lacy outfit slid over it all and Rob's hand moved up and under and they were off again.

Tonight they navigate their way over the drop sheets between ladder and trestle to the bed that has been dragged from its customary place by the wall which had once housed a fireplace, long since gibbed over, out into the centre. No time nor need for fiddle, just kissing, unzipping, undoing and falling together onto this strange new bed, and fondling and sucking and her with him between her legs and he with her between his and the rhythm builds, harder, faster and the taste of salt on her lip where she has bitten down hard to stop the oh oh oh (mustn't waken Poppy in her room down the hall), and his face strange and inward above her and then the groan, the explosion of little lights behind her eyes, the release.

And later, parted now, each sinking on their own side of the bed to sleep, he murmurs, "Thank you." As if she has given him a present. It amuses her, these good manners after they've been writhing round one another, under and over, and here they are, all drying sweat and semen and general stickiness, yet from somewhere, deep in some past training of say "Please!" say "Excuse me!" say "May I get down from the table?" rises this muttered "Thank you."

"Thank you," he says, from a long way off, on his way down the steep slope into sleep. Snuffling at the pillow the way he does in the seconds before oblivion, its soft bulk clearly some primal substitute for the ample breast of his faintly terrifying mother, Ruth, who must once have sat and fed and fiercely loved, though now she exists as dotty doyenne of the Ambleside Retirement Complex on Edgeware Road. "Thank you," as he passes out.

What is he thanking her for? The writhing? When you have been doing something, anything, three times a week for fifteen years, you know how to rate the experience. There is Unsatisfactory. Not Achieved, for those times when they have been too tired, too distracted, too irritable from some earlier argument. There is Satisfactory. Achieved. A little predictable, but pleasant enough. And there is Excellence, for those occasions when everything feels exactly, intuitively right, and it has felt like flying, like lifting off.

And tonight? Achieved. Verging on Excellence.

Or is he thanking her for something more general? For their shared life, for the pregnancies, and the children and putting up with his mother, and listening to him moan about the council, for being his friend, his mate? Is he thanking her for being happy to spend Friday night painting a bedroom? Or is the source of gratitude a bit of all that?

"You're welcome," she says, as she rolls over, drifts out into oblivion. "And thank you to you, too."

For all that. The solid structure of their lives.

THE RIVER

Something happens.
She has stopped eating. She no longer snaps at smaller fish and errant ducklings, their tiny legs furiously paddling overhead.
Her guts have shrunk. Her body has become an empty cavity.
Something is about to happen.

THE FOUNTAIN

September 4, 2010

. . . was standing at the window, naked, looking out at the dark. Though it was not really dark. Not the darkness he recalled from childhood when he used to let himself out into the night time world while his parents slept, snoring mightily, in their bedroom in the house overlooking the bay and his sisters lay in twin beds either side of the scuffed rug that was their tightly policed frontier.

Now Rob is a man with a job and family of his own and he is standing at the window in his own home, but every cell of his body remembers wet grass underfoot and the sharp tips of gravel by the sheep yards and the cool watery lick of the wind on his skin, lit by the faint glitter of the river of stars that flows across the universe, and the air was rich with the smell of sheep dung and dry grass and the sea, and it echoed with the strange cries of night birds and the furtive rustling of creatures who belonged, like himself, to the dark, where he too was an animal, bareskinned, pyjamas cast aside, left folded under his pillow. Pyjamas had no place in the world of the animal, the hunter who finds his way about by smell and hearing and the faint light of galaxies.

He was remembering this as he stood by the open window, cool night air brushing his skin, while Janey slept on, curled on one side under their duvet. He is fully awake, alert, and not quite sure why. Disturbed perhaps by the blackbird that often sings at night from the walnut tree, deluded by the street lights into thinking it is dawn. The wind shimmies among leaves. His skin prickles.

And then the window gives a little preliminary rattle and something roars up, a rumbling rises beneath his feet, felt in every bone as much as heard, a deep visceral explosion that flings him up into the air, so that he loses balance and falls hard against the sill. Which is in motion as is the whole house. It sways and jolts as if gathered up by immense hands and brutally shaken and with the shaking the windows crack and there's the crash of things falling, dwang and soffit splitting asunder as the momentum gathers, stronger, harder and from long training he knows he must get under the doorway. That was the safest place. Beneath a lintel. So somehow as the floor bucks and jumps, he stumbles over trestles and ladders to its protective frame.

Janey has got there before him, flung abruptly from sleep face down on the floor, scrambling towards the door because above all the din there is a single, high pitched cry that pulls her like a wire to Poppy's room, to her daughter who is screaming in the jolting dark in her room along the hallway. And she would go to her, but it is like one of those dreams of fever where you cannot move, your legs are trapped though your children are howling as some dark force seizes them, threatens to carry them away. She tries to move, but there are things in the way: a mass of stuff that was not there before that she must clamber over as it shifts beneath her feet and it is all she can do to stay upright.

She hangs onto the doorframe, to Rob, as the roaring builds, then fades. It seems to pass on towards the east, leaving the house in its wake settling to an uneven rocking, and at last she is able to move out into the darkness that used to be the hallway but in less than a minute, has become a strange landscape of dust and stone and sharp slivers of glass and unexpected barriers over which, her feet cut and bleeding, she must clamber through the dark to her daughter who is sitting up on her bed, somewhere beyond the mountain range that is her wardrobe fallen aslant a bookshelf and a chest of drawers. And Rob is beside her, grunting as he tries to heave things aside and at last she can reach out, feel about for her daughter, for Poppy, her hair, her frantic little arms, the scream that is like an animal, like a rabbit when it has been hit and cries in the dark.

"The monster!" she cries. "The monster!" Reverting in an instant to the preschooler who had feared monsters beneath her bed, insisting they check before switching off the light, nighty-night. Janey holds her tight as Rob wraps his arms about them and they form a huddle on the bed. Shh . . . shhh . . . it's all right. It's an earthquake. Janey's shoulders quivering. The wet patch soaking Poppy's nightie.

Rob is all ears. Outside, the sirens are going off: car and house, and every dog in the city has burst into furious barking. The house creaks and groans and under all these noises, there's a strange whispering static he cannot identify. And Tom? Where is Tom? What's the name of his friend? VJ? VJ what?

"Phone," he says. "It's on the bench."

The house sways. They are in the belly of the beast, deep inside some living unpredictable thing. It heaves and moves and there's that breathing, that soft insistent sibilance. He feels his way through the creature's unfamiliar interior to the kitchen. No light to guide him: no comforting glow from the streets outside, no light within from all their various appliances waiting on standby, their computers and heaters and TV and stove. Beneath his feet, the kitchen floor is wet, a sodden morass that smells like vinegar, soy sauce. He feels around and there's his phone dangling from the bench on its charger, and the relief of the message on the tiny screen, "I OK. U OK?" His fingers are huge and clumsy on the pad but he manages "We OK. Where U?" The message wings off into the dark as he looks about by the phone's torch light. Every cupboard gapes open, contents spilled at random, the rangehood is detached from the ceiling, the walls split along jagged cracks, a layer of glass glitters on the floor like an unseasonable frost, and there's creamy stuff oozing up between the tiles.

Janey is standing beside him, Poppy glued against her neck. '"Tom?" she says. "He's OK," says Rob. The house jolts and there's a cracking overhead. "Outside!" she says, fumbling at the door. "Quick!" The door is jammed. But Rob is strong, stronger at this moment than he has ever been. He has the strength of several men. He could lift great weights, run great distances, leap meters into the air. He drags at the door with all this strength and the family steps outside into the safety of the open air.

Except it's not. The torch beam plays over the lawn and it is moving. It shimmers. It gleams and ripples and out here the whispering is louder and he is able at last to identify it. It is the sound of water. It bubbles up between paving stones, it oozes as white silt from tiny cones that have popped up like miniature volcanoes across the lawn, the lawn he mowed only last Sunday. Beside the clothesline a fountain erupts. It rises up meters into the air glittering, before pattering back to earth. It is weirdly beautiful, this fountain rising in their back yard into the night air.

His mind is racing, trying to catch up with his quick attentive body. Liquefied silt, he thinks. Quicksand. Of course. There could be nothing solid beneath us. They could sink into a bottomless morass.

Or drown. A flood. A wave. A massive tsunami like the one recalled from earliest childhood, a card from the Weetabix series of Great Catastrophes. A wave rearing up above tiny straw houses, tiny bending palms and tiny people running hopelessly at its foot. Ant people, like the ant people on the ship that was sliding down into the icy waters, ablaze with light. Like the ant people lying face down as the volcano's ash fell and buried them and the tiny dog straining hopelessly at its leash.

The wave. He looks out into the dark, listening for the tremor that will announce its arrival, looming above the plum tree, rolling through the dark from Pegasus Bay. The glittering wall surging up Savage Street gathering to itself all the houses, the cars, the tiny ant people. The torch beam plays feebly over the garage and his bike leaning against the wall and the row of wheelie bins, one fallen, the inorganic one, plastic wrapping floating on the grey ripples, a Styrofoam tray that had held last night's steak. Beneath their feet the ground quivers and in slow motion another bin topples. The lid falls open.

And all the time his mind is darting about, fixing on this detail, checking, correcting. If it is this bad here, what must it be like in Wellington, for surely this must be the offshoot of that other distant long-anticipated calamity. The Wairarapa Fault or the Ohariu or the Wellington Fault, take your pick, it could be any one of them, returning at their predictable intervals in this jumpy fractured country, Lambton Quay meters deep in fallen glass, towerblocks slumped, the sea rolling in as it rolled in back in that big quake in 1855, thirty-foot high waves, the harbour emptying, then filling, over and over. Only now it would scoop up Lyell Bay, Kilbirnie, Eastbourne, Petone. Motorway and railway and airport disappearing as the land sinks back below the sea leaving the ant people to scramble as best they can along the hilltops to safety.

Or maybe it's the Alpine Fault that has shifted. The most active fault line in the world and overdue for its next appearance. Vast avalanches of schist and granite may have fallen, chasms may have opened across the main divide, waves may have submerged Greymouth and Westport and the muddy green farms. The whole spine of the island may have been reshaped in a few seconds, and here they are, in steady reliable old Christchurch, experiencing the ricochet.

He has reeled off the figures to meetings and conferences, he has modelled the events: vertical movement on the Kekerengu Bank Fault, the Hikurangi Trench, the Wairau, Hope or Awatere Fault, near-field tsunami, waves of 5 meters, 7.5 meters, 14 meters, frequencies of 150 years, 300 years, 2000 years, 6000 years, shelf resonance on the Canterbury coastline, beach slope, permeability and viscosity, Synolakis's law and the mathematics of wave run up, and click another graphic for the screen. But now the graph is jumping beneath his feet. The deck is rocking. The lawn is inundated, and the wave, the wave. . . . And he is the ant person. His wife. His daughter. His son, wherever he might be at this precise moment. All ant people.

"Holy crap," says Janey, holding Poppy tight. Her voice is high and bright and strange.

Or maybe this is the symptom of some other event. Not seismic but volcanic. A break somewhere in this country's fragile crust. A cone rising out in the bay like that island off the coast of Iceland. Surtsey. The plume that rose, with no prior warning, no scientific prediction. A fishing boat found it, went to check expecting fire, a ship in trouble, men clinging to burning wreckage and found instead churning water about the tip of new land. Taking shape as new land has always taken shape at these opposite ends of the globe. Maybe somewhere out in Pegasus Bay at this very moment, steam is rising and a cloud of ash and this was the tremor that accompanied its arrival.

The water gurgles and licks at the step and he is thinking quickly. The car? Drive to safety? But what if the roads are impassable? And what if Tom returns and finds them gone? What then? He steps from the deck into the dark water, feeling cautiously for something solid under this feet as Janey says, "What the hell are you doing? Rob! There could be holes!" But the path is intact under that weird sucking mud so he wades to the shed where the kayaks are stored. He drags one then the other to the deck where he ties them to the railing. Should the water rise on a surge, above the steps, above the house, above the whole city, he will save his family. They will surf the great wave, they will paddle for the safety of the Port Hills while the rest of the city takes it chances.

Poppy whimpers. "Right" says Janey in the strange brisk voice. "We're getting chilled. We need a hot drink. We'll light up the barbecue. How about that, Popps? A late night barbecue. We'll make Milo. With sprinkles!"

There is, of course, no gas in the barbecue bottle, so no Milo. They should have made sure the bottle was full. They should have had a proper torch, with viable batteries, rather than the selection of dead torches among the rubberbands and birthday candles and general detritus in the kitchen drawer. They should have had a radio, one of those windup dynamo types, or something solar powered. But they don't.

Instead, while Rob tells Poppy a story about being a kid on the peninsula and how he used to go out at night all on his own while everyone was asleep and pretend to be an animal because he liked the dark, it was exciting, it was like an adventure just like the one they are having tonight, Janey fossicks in the wreckage of the kitchen and finds bananas and apple juice. She ventures further in, torch beam picking up the shadowy profiles of strange things: a table, a bookshelf, Rob's maps dangling askew on the hallway walls or fallen, smashed along with Ruth's ornate Victorian mirror. She clambers over the moraine that has materialized on the floor of the bedroom to snatch up warm clothes, shoes, another duvet. She makes her way cautiously to the bathroom at the end of the hall, obeying some long-distant injunction perhaps dating from her brief spell as a Girl Guide back in 1983, to fill the bath with drinking water. And all the time the house shudders, speaking its new language of creak and sigh, its strange foreign, unfamiliar tongue.

Then they sit together on the sofa on the deck wrapped in the duvets, adrift upon the waters, their yellow kayaks moored to the railing. They sit in the dark to conserve the torch batteries, waiting for dawn.

THE RIVER

Something is happening.

In the cavity that is now her body, the eggs which have hung there all along, tiny seeds in the dark, have begun to swell.

They are globules, twenty million glistening, strung like pearls on black velvet.

Something is about to happen. 📖

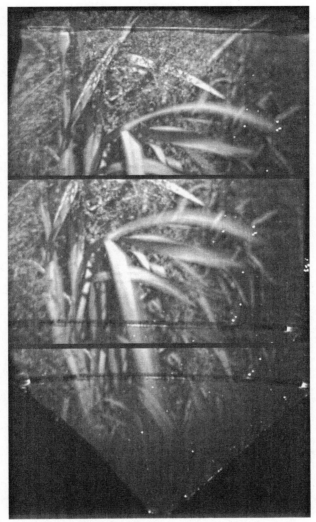

Harakeke, 2013, digital photograph by Bridget Reweti

Kotuku, 2013, digital photograph by Bridget Reweti

The Crimes of the Tolerant Left

Erik Kennedy

So much for the "tolerant left"! The tolerant left keeps
painting tunnel entrances on walls for fascists to run
into. The tolerant left is wearing a squirting flower on its
lapel to spritz in the faces of curious jackbooted scum.
The
tolerant left repeats back all the authoritarian talking
points but with a lungsful of helium. It's pretty
disrespectful. The tolerant left got shot in the stomach in
Seattle, but does it respond with its famous tolerance?
Does it fuck. No, the tolerant left is a headscarfed woman
holding aloft a cruelly mocking sign reading: "WE GAVE
YOU HUMMUS. HAVE SOME RESPECT." Has the
tolerant left gone too far? The tolerant left is imposing
a brutal occupation on the minds of the far right and its
apologists; they are unable to go anywhere in their heads
without seeing paid protesters chanting that the new
Fourteen Words is just "Punch Nazis" repeated seven
times in a row.

The Mustard Weed Poem

Erik Kennedy

If injured mustard weed releases chemicals to warn its
neighbours of a threat and not to save itself, as a recent
experiment suggests; and if a human audience to this story
of apparent selflessness coos about the morals of the
mustard weed and not about a chemical called ALMT1;
and if a writer from New York attacks the life-loving
credulity of this audience, which wants to see all around it
evidence of natural happiness, like turtles leaving shells to
other turtles in their wills—if all this pageantry of sacrifice
and resignation is only in the minds of goodness fanciers,
fond swains of optimism, ordinary folk who do to others
as they would have the world do unto itself, yet still by the
morning after the experiment the neighbour's roots had
grown distinctly longer and robuster.

The Overpopulation Poem

Erik Kennedy

There's always that one guy in the club who says it's not
climate change that's the problem, it's overpopulation.
This can mean a lot of things: that sub-Saharan farmers
can't grow enough corn, or that the coming water conflicts
will make recent wars look like chess matches, or that
in Buenos Aires there's a shoeboxful of green space per
resident, or that 1,638 credited actors have appeared in
Midsomer Murders, that teeming metropolis of warm-milk
telly. Seriously, that is too many actors, although if
everyone on earth was an actor we could just "act like"
there is no problem. Ha ha, that's just a sherbet-brained
jest. No, really, if everyone was an actor we could solve all
our problems in the way that art normally lets us: by
praising art's ineffectiveness but, for the first time, in an
entirely ineffective world.

I Am an Animal Benefiting from Climate Change

Erik Kennedy

Finally these flippers, so clumsy out on the city's
fissured, hummocky asphalt, will steer me gracefully.
This skeleton I've worn inside these many years,
which should have been supported from deep below by
   black,
dense, and creatureless water of the abyssal zone,
but which instead has weighted and hindered and limited
   me,
with my only compensation thin air and some sunshine—
this structure that was grown can now be useful.
My helmeted crest of bone will frustrate all the desperate,
fleeing predators who'd club me on the bonce
and eat me at the kerb. Not that the path from killing
to eventually eating me is clear (or possible).
My skin, which rejects all touch and which has always
   pained me
more than any other (though it hurt others, too),
is adamant, and neither now nor in the future
will it give or let pass.
                  Because my body did not change
or even adjust to change, the change adjusted to me.
I lost one niche (confusion) and found another waiting.
The only happy surprise is a sudden survival advantage.
I can hardly give up that! And I don't mean to. Bye.
The hot, wet climate suits my hot, wet brain.
I'll remember all of you, and what you meant to me,
when the fossils of inland seas return to the water again.

Memory #1, black/white photograph by David Rodríguez

Memory #2, black/white photograph by David Rodríguez

Ear to the Ground

Nic Low

Christchurch. I grew up in Christchurch. It was a quiet, peaceful place. At the age of twenty, I'd finish work round midnight, drop my skateboard to the cobbles and clatter home. My wheels were often the loudest sound. I'd roll down Colombo Street, past the straggle of hoodie kids awaiting the last bus, then cut through the bleak granite expanse of Cathedral Square. I could hear street-sweeper trucks, and the murmur of the last-drinks crowd at Warner's, and something else too, just on the edge of my hearing. From the eastern corner of the square rose a shrill electronic whine. It was like having a mosquito trapped inside your skull. It was maddening.

The sound was produced by a device attached to the offices of the local newspaper. People over the age of twenty-five couldn't hear it. Only young people could hear it. It was designed to stop us loitering and drive us away. And it wasn't just *The Press* broadcasting that needling drone. It felt like the whole city. The sound was the suburban status quo running smoothly in its tracks, and the tiny wheels of petty bureaucracies, and the antique machinery of monocultural privilege. Once you hit your late twenties and began thinking respectable thoughts, you'd gain immunity. But it was getting to everyone I grew up with. Change felt impossible. The rest of the country thought us stiff and stuck-up and white. The vibrant subcultures that grew in the cracks felt under permanent siege. No matter how we'd enjoyed childhood, no matter the family ties and lovers and landscapes, that sound drove us to leave.

I moved to France, then Australia. I remained proudly Kiwi, yet at odds with the city that formed me. Each time I returned to see family and friends, Christchurch felt a little more empty. There were flashes of colour, but the stern stone facades and endless one-way streets dominated. People and energy seemed to drain away like so much rain from the city's slate roofs. On one visit I published an overheated opinion piece in *The Press* about the city's out-of-sight, out-of-mind approach to youth and change. I was politely told to piss off back to Australia. It seems the feeling was mutual.

Then, early on a cold spring morning in September, 2010, I was holidaying with my parents in Tasmania. We stopped at a church fair. A man sold us a jar of honey. He asked where our accent was from.

Christchurch, he repeated, looking concerned. Is your house okay?

The question made no sense. Everything was always okay in Christchurch.

And so, a radical thing has happened to a conservative place. I have returned after each quake, full of love and trepidation, like visiting an estranged family member on their deathbed. I can no longer hear that whining sound coming from the square. Partly because I am a bit older, and I can see that plenty of the whining was my own restless impatience. But mostly because it has been drowned out by something much deeper, something much older. It is the sound of the earth, and the feelings the earth awakens in people. It is partly fear and it is partly strength. I am trying to understand the ruined city's new resonance.

* * * *

When the first quake struck, the heavy bronze bells in the cathedral swayed and rang a ghostly warning across the city. My younger brother woke to the jolt and his first thought was *Shit, that must have been Wellington, and it must have been catastrophic.*

Luckily, it was neither. The bricks and concrete and glass fell into empty streets. It was the first time in modern history a 7-plus quake had hit an urban centre with no deaths. The quake was an ocean swell, a great rolling wave that rose and fell but left things much as they were. It scared the hell out of people, and houses cracked and the ground flooded with a fine mud, but it did not truly destroy the city's sense of safety. We had building codes, by god. Building codes and insurance. We had our deeply ingrained sense of luck. Even our earthquakes fit the pattern.

When I visited in December, 2010, the main evidence of the quake was a rash of blue tarps over the city's roofs. Piles of fallen chimney bricks lined the streets like little altars. There were a few cleared sites and some older buildings were fenced off. Everyone I met was compelled to share their stories, and those of their neighbours, all of whom they now knew. It was as if the quake had been a synchronising of watches, a zeroing of disparate lives that gave everyone a common origin: *We survived the quake. We were scared shitless, and it's been a drag boiling the drinking water, but we all survived.* The gratitude was palpable. It felt like the city was a bit more willing to smile, even if its front teeth had been knocked out.

By the time I boarded a plane for Melbourne, the narrative was clear. You have a crisis, you respond, things get fixed up, and life returns to normal. *The Press* published a letter to the editor claiming damage to the red-light district was a warning from god. Those little wheels began to turn. Things were going to be okay.

* * * *

Somewhere down by the hospital, in the crook of the river, is the site of a disaster, perhaps the area's first. The place was called Puari Pā[5]. Our Waitaha and Ngāi Tahu ancestors lived here, moving through the landscape on foot, to the swamps and marshes, the grasslands and forests beside the river, hunting and gathering food, listening for the whoop of kererū. They used the long, hollow bones of bird wings as kōauau flutes, and made pūtōrino trumpets from hardwood. Visitors were welcomed with the high and lonely cry of the karanga,[4] and challenged with haka[1]. The language itself that filled the landscape is deep and round. To my ear, the word for "world" sums this up: ao.

European whalers came in the 1830s, and European interest in settlement grew throughout the 1840s. For the people at Puari and the other Ngāi Tahu settlements, here was the first great rupture, the break point between one society and the next. It was a slow-motion disaster; it was catastrophic, and it was not. It was the founding of the city—land for my first European ancestor, William Newnham, in 1850. It meant the ring of picks on rock as foundation stones went down, and the nasal stammering of Māori spoken with a common cold; the sound of corks worked out of bottles, fence posts hammered in, the sudden thunder of horses and guns. Demand for land was fierce. Kemp's Deed was inked in 1848 by the chiefs of Ngāi Tahu and the land passed over. Ten percent was to be held aside for the tribe, written into the deed of sale. The land was not held aside. The land was cleared and planted with oaks and willows. Christchurch would be an idyllic, pre-Industrial Revolution English town.

Ngāi Tahu were moved out to reserves. When visiting they camped near Puari at Little Hagley Park, squatters on their own land. The sound of their presence in the landscape was silenced, and this silence became the true marker of the disaster. Children were forbidden to speak Māori at school; the later Tohunga Suppression Act attempted to stop priests from practising their chants and prayers. Ngāi Tahu presence in the city was reduced to the cry of a produce seller in Market Square.

In Christchurch, perhaps more than any other sizeable New Zealand city, there has been almost no visible Māori presence. But even if a disaster is not named, or addressed, it doesn't go away. The damage of that forced displacement was felt through the whole of society. The tribe did not stop fighting for redress for one day. And the geography of the ancestors—the pā and kāinga sites, the trails, the swamps, rivers, and marshes—was still there, just beneath the surface.

* * * *

The sound arrived first. John Dodgson is an organist. To his trained ear it was the blast of a low *C*, the deepest note on the scale, coming from everywhere at once. He knew instantly what it was. My father, a jazz musician, knew it too. The sound came, and the fear came, and it surged up from a sound and a feeling into a mighty weight that roared through the house like an invisible freight train, twisting and popping the joists and beams, bursting open walls and floors. The ground tore itself up by the roots, and with sudden and extreme violence shrugged the people off.

The roar is louder than anything we can imagine. It's the sound of a tectonic plate moving, and buildings collapsing and books and furniture going over, and it rises up through the scale to the wild crash of every fork and glass and plate hurled from every cupboard in your house, in every house, in every street. It's the sound of *the ground beneath your feet*, and *bedrock* and *safe as houses* being torn down. It's the death of the city's narrative. Imagine the noise of it. Imagine the fear.

If the September earthquake was a wave, the February one was a sledgehammer. It was only 6.3 in magnitude but the g-force, the sudden ground acceleration, was among the highest ever recorded. From the quake's heart in Banks Peninsula the ground jolted violently towards the city then, as the crust of the earth rose, then fell, a second massive shock rose up to meet it. The two shockwaves collided. This time the impact was catastrophic.

The cathedral spire and its enormous bells were thrown into the square. All across the city old brick buildings exploded. The central city's Victorian facades were tossed directly onto people and cars below. Buildings corkscrewed on their foundations and buckled and fell, and great halos of dust rose in their place. The Pyne Gould Guinness office tower came down one floor at a time. Those on the top rode it down like a great concrete wave. Those beneath were crushed. In the Durham Street Methodist Church three people were killed while dismantling the huge pipe organ. I can only imagine the noise when the roof caved in.

As the buildings came down, the swamps and marshes and ancient, buried waterways rose up. From the sewers, from the drains, from garden beds and the cracks in roads, a thick, suffocating grey-black mud spilled out. It pooled in gutters, then spread across roads and up over the footpaths and into houses. It flooded through kitchens and living rooms and in some cases flowed up through the floor itself. It came out of the toilets, mixed with sewage. It swallowed gardens and cars and whole suburbs, turning them into toxic, feature-less moonscapes.

People knew what it was, technically. The super-fast vibrations of the quake turned the fine topsoil to liquid, and as the heavier soil and rocks churned and sank, the liquid was forced up and out. It's called liquefaction, but it felt like a nightmare. It felt mythical. It was as if the city's fear had been made physically real, and come spilling out of the ground.

After the noise, silence. A frantic kind of silence punc-tuated by car alarms, the rolling boom of aftershocks, the sharp, vicious clatter of masonry coming down on rescuers. Strangers first, then police, then urban search and rescue teams moved through the city grid, shouting to one another, building-to-building, rubble-to-rubble. The city was declared a no-fly zone so that the search teams' audio equipment could pick up the slightest sound—scratching, tapping, a voice, a breath. It was an incongruous picture: workers poised, almost on tiptoe, listening to the rubble; and at their backs, lines of huge steel diggers, claws upraised, listening too.

The strongest instinct was to get home to family. The city emptied out, but it was a slow and stressful process. The bridges across the Avon were all damaged, and the roads a buckled mess of debris, of mud, of people wandering in shock. I met a woman who ran home to find her children. She had been in the Family Court signing her divorce papers when the quake struck. She and the court clerk flung themselves under the table. *Fuck it*, she thought. I don't want to die married to that bastard. She reached back up, grabbed the papers and signed them anyway. When the immediate shocks subsided she ran. She finally got home, seven kilometres on foot through the mud, and her youngest daughter said, "What took you so long?"

Many had no homes to go to. Their houses had either collapsed, been thrown off their foundations, were buried in sewage and mud or lacked water, power and shelter from the weather. Hagley Park, where Ngāi Tahu had camped after being removed from their land in the 1850s, once again became a refuge for the displaced.

* * * *

I was in the Australian bush when I got the news. My friend Malcolm said, "Six point four, in Christchurch. Fatalities, they—" and I was gone, sprinting up the hill to get phone reception. I blundered into a thick spider's web that clung to my face, gummed my eyes and mouth shut. Christchurch was my family, my parents, my brother, grandfather, uncle, cousins, old friends and old flames. It was my memory and my history. I stood in perfect sunshine, and called and called and called. I've never felt so sick.

I went back a month later. The porcelain veneer of Christchurch politeness had cracked with the sewage pipes. As people worked to clear the rubble, they talked. There was a sense of disbelief that could only be whittled away through talking. Underneath each individual story the conversations were the same: people telling each other, over and over, *this is shared*, and *this is real*.

I sat up late one night with Mum in the dining room talking about family, about our own crisis that ran parallel to the earthquakes. She said, "I don't know what to say," and the earth said it for her. Thunder rose beneath us, and the shockwave slammed through, a sickening drag in the guts. It lifted and rolled the floor under our feet and set the house shuddering and moaning in protest. Every object reached a rattling crescendo then the shock passed on and was gone. I was terrified. Mum laughed, not unkindly. "Four point three, four point four," she said. "You'll be okay." She bounded upstairs to check the GeoNet website. She came back down triumphant. "Four point four."

It was a daily game, this filing of earthquakes under precise, knowable numbers, and a small attempt to assert human control. But the aftershocks were so relentless that citizens began displaying the symptoms of extreme stress usually seen in war zones. Grief for people, land and place was setting in. My friend Eric posted on Facebook: "Um . . . what do we do now?"

I went walking. The city did feel like a war zone. The streets were silent. Once private homes were visible in intimate cross-section, where a fallen wall or chimney had torn open the side of the building. Soldiers in tanks and troop carriers stood guard among the willows and oaks. An older woman with a lip ring asked what the tanks were for. "We're a tank unit," insisted the soldier. "That's just our ride."

Heading down to Armagh Street and the river, I felt like I had lost the power of speech. So much was gone, and something about the remaining buildings was wrong. They were dreamlike, somehow slumped or bulging, seen through distorted glass. On Armagh Street the Provincial Chambers were as if bombed. My experience and vocabulary were so inadequate that all I could write in my notebook was "like a large-scale public art installation."

I came to the Worcester Boulevard bridge, at the centre of a colonial vista running east to the cathedral and west to the museum. This was the apex of the city's conservative heritage, its visual link with the past. It was, as they say, munted.

At one end the city founder William Rolleston lay with his head buried in the brickwork. At the other end, colonial leader John Robert Godley had toppled like a stiff-legged old drunk. All along this vista and throughout the city, beautiful old heritage buildings had borne the brunt of the damage. They were from the era of colonial arch-conservatism, of tradition and entitlement. The old city's symbol, the Anglican cathedral, had been beheaded.

Beyond the ghosts of an archaic British culture, the streets also contained the personal ghosts of our earlier selves. Looking along Kilmore Street into the cordoned-off Red Zone, I could just see Victoria Square where I spent years as a skater. I imagined myself jumping up onto the bricks, gliding past my mum aged twenty, reading T. S. Eliot on her lunchbreak. From the Caledonian I hear the liquid-glass sounds of free jazz from my dad's band. My grandfather is up by the bridge, a crowd gathered round his open-topped 1936 Opel, the same model that ferried Hitler through the streets of Berlin.

I imagine myself hitting the amphitheatre at speed now. My great-grandmother Emerald Anne, a singer and a gambler, croons an old waiata to herself, waiting outside the courthouse where she translated for Māori prisoners. My wheels blur over the bricks, and as I crouch and launch myself off the stairs, the earthquake hits my imaginings.

Up ahead, the great wide face of the Park Royal Hotel, where I ate my graduation dinner of bloody lamb, and wondered at the weight of my great-great-grandfather's mortar cap: it ripples and bulges forward, and its windows shear down into the amphitheatre. Our Tūāhuriri ancestors are there below in the old Market Square, blankets about their shoulders, running. I imagine horses screaming in the streets, and my great-great-grandmother watching as the river, Te Ōtākaro, devours its banks and the willows, and its English name. The European city going under. Stones falling, the earth opening, a phantom geography of swamp and marshland welling up. Waitaha ancestors calling through the rushes. All those memories, all the way back, unearthed.

Standing there looking towards Victoria Square, it seemed to me that the memories bound up in the city were not erased, but unearthed. They had floated free from the wreckage like the haze of dust that hung over the city when it all came down. We were thinking and talking about our own stories, and the city's histories, as never before. Some would be retained and re-anchored in the new city. Some, like that thin, high drone of complacency, had already blown away.

* * * *

Down by Puari Pā, along the line of the river Avon and in the flooded suburbs, the ancestral geography of waterways and marshes was suddenly and terribly visible.

This is a disaster; it is catastrophic, and it is not. Like colonisation, the earthquake means the destruction of the old and the creation of the new. It marks a symbolic rupture to match the arrival of Europeans, the break point between one society and the next. And with the downtown to be rebuilt from the ground up, there is an opportunity for Ngāi Tahu to re-enter the city, and a bicultural identity to enter with them.

Ngāi Tahu are, to use an Australian term, the traditional owners of Christchurch. But they are modern capitalist owners as well. Following the iwi's[2] 1997 Treaty settlement the tribe has grown its assets to, at time of writing, $650 million,[3] and is now a heavy hitter in the city's residential and commercial development. Even before the quakes, Ngāi Tahu had bought the central police station, courts, old army barracks, and a 50 percent stake in the council buildings. The tribal leadership has an eye for reliable tenants, and a healthy sense of historic irony. The tribe will be one of the key partners and financial engines of the city's regrowth.

Beyond this economic role is the desire to give voice to iwi values and culture. Key Ngāi Tahu priorities are the enhancement of waterways, indigenous ecosystems, and sacred places, and a focus on sustainability and good urban design. The heart of the new city is likely to be a huge bicultural riverfront park, built in partnership with Ngāi Tahu. This is the land where our ancestors gathered, hunted, and sang, and may include the old site of Puari Pā. It would be fitting if the response to the current disaster helped break the silence surrounding a much older one.

* * * *

What does Christchurch sound like now? It shifts between the steady murmur of merely surviving the quake—filling buckets with water, rustling through insurance policies—and a healthy cacophony. Much is grief and fear, as people make sense of their loss by sharing it aloud. There is enormous anger too, ultimately caused by the earth, but being vented on those in charge of the clean-up. Civil Defence bulldozers are finishing off unsafe buildings and owners must stand by while their possessions inside are destroyed. In the working-class east, where a cold easterly whips in off the sea, whole suburbs are being written off. This is where most of the city's Māori and Polynesian communities live, and it is a part of Christchurch that has never bought into, or been included in, the city's Englishness. There is a slower, more subtle sense of tragedy unfolding out there, as each street is abandoned house by house.

The cacophony also contains a clear note of determination, and a healthy fuck-you to those who would downplay the city's value or the disaster's scale. Remarkable projects like Gap Filler are bringing music, film, and creativity back to the city's ruined spaces. Humour is present, too. In response to those who claimed that the first quake's damage to the red-light district proved God hates prostitutes, others have pointed out that the February quake destroyed most of the city's churches. Social connections formed through coping are moving from side effect to centre-stage. Whole streets have become more than just neighbours.

Another aspect of the city's new sound is intimate family conversation, prompted by the act of survival. Christchurch has been a stoic place in the past. Silence has been one of its strongest instincts. At my great-aunt and great-uncle's funeral, a theme was *they were so humble*, and *they never made a fuss*. If there is one thing Christchurch taught its sons and daughters, it was never to make a fuss. But at their funeral I began to learn about the full, difficult, human richness of their lives. The same has happened since the earthquake in February, when people, faced with loss of life and history, have given voice to more family stories.

I have learned about my great-grandfather, who survived World War I, lost everything in the Depression, and was forced to work on his brother's raspberry farm. His bullying at times drove his wife to an asylum. He spent his days shovelling strawberries and raspberries and a swift, sour anger into the vats of jam. His daughter, my great-aunt, made that same jam, but rendered it generous and sweet. I have heard about the Panzer tank that picked off my great-uncle in an Italian field. Shrapnel emerged from his skull decades later. He and his paralysed left arm helped build huts throughout the Southern Alps. I have heard the whisper of melancholia, that most subtle and destructive of tremors, starting with my great-great-great-grandfather who was a guest in the Lyttelton Jail. The superintendent treated him with books and conversation. Each of these stories tell of disaster; catastrophic, and not. In all of this, I've come to think about resilience and rebuilding.

These myriad conversations have come together in the City Council's Draft City Plan. The cynical, nineteen-year-old in me assumed the conservative old city would simply propose a conservative new city—statues, willow trees, and all. But, given the chance, Christchurch has collectively proposed something radically different from its old elitist robes. The plan details a green, people-friendly, low-rise, largely car-free space. Ngāi Tahu are front and centre, and the river, Te Ōtākaro, will form a bicultural corridor through the heart of the city.

It is easy to be optimistic from thousands of miles away. The proposal is part design plan, part PR exercise, written while the city is still in collapse. But if even half of the new plan could be achieved, Christchurch would become one of the great little cities in the world. I've never cried over a city council document before. Reading this one, I felt a surge of love and pride.

When the city is finally rebuilt, there will be a memorial at its heart. I have a suggestion. It is based on the resonance of the city. I think about the ghostly ringing of the cathedral bells in the first quake. I think about how church bells have rung in times of distress or celebration, and how the wave form of a seismograph resembles the wave form of a piece of music. After all, music and earthquakes are both a type of vibration.

I propose a set of earthquake bells, one for each of the 181 people killed in the February, 2011 quake. The bells would be made from the materials of the old city—the bells and organ pipes, the copper roofs and domes. There would be bells of greenstone, and of wood, the materials of the even older settlements. They would range in size from tiny, high and clear all the way down to that biblical, thunderous low C. They would hang in a glistening galaxy beside the ruined cathedral for people to walk among.

Most importantly, the bells would translate the Richter scale into a musical scale. The bells would be played by earthquakes. They would turn the surges of the earth into a strange, exquisite music. The tiny, high-pitched bells would ring almost continuously, a faint flickering sound just on the edge of hearing, a constant reminder not of complacency, but of the living earth. At memorial services, the bells would replay the actual 2010 and 2011 earthquakes, tremor for tremor like a vast symphony. As the vibrations increased, the larger, deeper bells would begin to ring, with great volume and intensity, all the way up to the strikes of the great 6.3 and 7.1 bells. They would transform the power of the earth into a musical, cathartic act of remembrance. 📖

1. *Haka*: an athletic war dance accompanied by rhythmical shouted chants, given as a challenge, a welcome or in support depending on context.

2. *Iwi*: the largest social unit in New Zealand Māori society. The Māori language word iwi means "people" or "nation."

3. The tribe's assets have grown to 1.4 billion in 2017.

4. *Karanga*: a high call and response sung between arriving visitors and their hosts, whereby senior women exchange information about who seeks to enter, and why.

5. *Puari Pā*: a pā is a fortified village.

Memory #3, black/white photograph by David Rodríguez

Memory #4, black/white photograph by David Rodríguez

When Gorillas Sleep

Frankie McMillan

I never touched the gorilla, I say. I got better things to do. Then the park ranger plonks his canvas bag on the table and pulls out a tranquiliser gun and we all stare at the gun and I know it will have my fingerprints all over it and then he's saying, funny how you target the adolescent males, none of the silverbacks are shot and I just about blurt out that's just chance, that is, but I hold my tongue and I'm thinking of fingerprints and even nose prints because each Ugandan gorilla has got its own, nobody else like it. Listen up! The park ranger bangs the table with his fist. A drop of sweat runs down his forehead. You think we're going to sit here, twiddle our thumbs while Rome burns? He leans forward, tells me the whole conservation programme is under threat, the government can pull its funding just like that and he's not going to see his job go down the tubes. Listen up!

I never touched the gorilla, I say. And then he tells me to think back to Lake Bunyonyi Reserve yesterday afternoon and what was I doing there? He knows I was there, he has proof. Didn't I know there were cameras in the trees?

All the candelebra trees? I ask. I'm just stalling for time. I'm just stalling. I'm just. I stare out the window. The red Burning Bush is shaped like a heart.

You ever laid your hand on a gorilla's chest? You ever felt the warmth of wiry hair, the roughness under your palm? Ever lain down with your brother, your ear listening to his heart beat? 📖

Keeping Evie Lu quiet

Frankie McMillan

While my father argues with the motel owner, Evie Lu and me play the quietest game I can think of, "Where is your nose, Evie Lu, point to your nose," and she swings her hairy arm up to her face, points her finger at her nose, her flat, chimp nose that always feels like putty under my fingers. I have my back to the car window and I have a leash around my sister's neck so even if she lunged past to unwind the window I can haul her back. Through the closed window I can hear my father's loud voice, not shouting, but raised like he's on stage giving a lecture to his psych students and he's telling the motel owner that Evie Lu is not a pet, she's a child, a family member, and he will pay if the carpet is stained or if there's any breakages, that is standard policy wherever you go in the world, and the motel owner in his blue shirt is almost levitating, he raises his feet, is on the balls of his toes in his eagerness to explain the motel regulations and later my father will point this out to me.

"Body language," he will say, "did you notice that body language?" But that is later, a hundred kilometres later when we sneak into the Waterfront Motel, Evie Lu curled over my shoulders and my father thrusting the key, like a gift, into the motel door. It is not now, in a stiflingly hot car where boredom sets in, where my sister suddenly scurries over to the passenger window, the leash slipping, slipping from my sweaty hand, the sky opening up to her outraged scream. 📖

he reads the welcome of swans

Frankie McMillan

the ferryman knows his own life
is rich with incident

his paper boat, creased and folded
and he at the helm

cockeyed from staring at lovers
their haul of picnic baskets

his own palms worn thin
with the exchange of coins

his oar all dip and pull, the sweet
drag of water and always

returning, the bare-footed ones
who miss nothing

who no longer expect
the arrival of others

the ferryman rubs his eyes
a penny for each of them

the swan unfolds
the huge breathing of water

1855 **Grinding the wind**

Frankie McMillan

and after chapel
         where every man bellows Amen with such
force it blows the hair from the temples

         it's back to the tread-wheel
the great barrel turning, each man in his dumb stall

grasps the hand rail, lifts his feet and lifts

    slow as horses in a ploughed field
but never gaining purchase

and it's here
         in the silent reek of sweat and dust
I hear a lark empty his heart. I have seen

       men laugh with their feet; rows
of shuffling shoes at some misfortune—

     a turnkey spilling hot coffee
a warden falling asleep in his chair—

but for a moment the tread-wheel spins
the great blades of the fan
          with purpose

   our industry turns cloud
          our industry mills the sky

My father, the oceanographer

Frankie McMillan

My father, the oceanographer
knew the language of whales
yet tripped over the sound
of his own name

They say the cure for death
is drowning and for a lisp
a bucket of salt water

*

In white gumboots he entered
the stomach of a whale
sat brooding under the great arched bones
of a church

invoking the mantra of LFA sonar
whale fall
and echolation

stripped to his underwear
so great was the heat, and
blubber he said

now there was a word to make you weep

Memory #5, black/white photograph by David Rodríguez

Lost Bearings

Heather McQuillan

All had seemed normal until the godwits amassed on the open spit, faced north-northwest, and failed, day by day, to fly. They hunkered down, shuddering as if they'd flown headfirst into a window; slender beaks tucked in grey-washed breasts. The mass of them shuddering echoed the shifting of sand.

The Council fenced them off with orange cones and plastic tape. We offered stale bread but the godwits were well-conditioned for the long haul to Alaska via Yalu Jiang; their bellies full of our estuary's worms, fat-cells loaded, flight feathers trim and strong; yet they stayed on the ground, stranded.

We considered our own culpability—you know the roll call, the proliferation of cellphone towers, fracking, heated air, and melting ice. If so, what were we to do? Should we lift them, one by one, and toss them into the sky? Tell them they have a place but not here, not any more? Perhaps they lacked the leader who would tell them, *now, this is the time.* Maybe they'd collectively decided it was no longer worth their effort. Some fault in their genes?

We heard that their shuddering ebbed away. The ones at the edges went first, the ones who bore the brunt of the easterly wind and driving rains. Workers in hazard suits grasped their bent wing bones and tossed the carcasses onto the back of a truck. If only, we said, if only they hadn't chosen here. 📖

The Damaged Ones

Heather McQuillan

I grew up thinking caterpillars were super smart because Nan said they were. She showed me the kawakawa leaves nibbled into lacework hearts, told me the damaged ones were the most potent. I picked the leaves for Nan's coughing tea and while it stewed I scrubbed the bench with Jiff. Nan said, "Quit it Baby-girl, you need some germs to build immunity." She said crazy shit sometimes. There was this yellow stain on Nan's mattress from when her bladder went west. "No school today. I need your help," she said. "You'll have to ring school," I told her. Nan left a message, said I had diarrhea, which was a lie. "If you want a day off tell them you've got the runs. They're not going to ask for proof!" "But it's still a lie!" Nan slammed the phone on the bench so I knew not to be a cheeky buggar and say it a third time. We lurched that mattress along the hall to the porch. "Dreamed I was having a nice warm bath!" said Nan, smooching her lips to make everything okay again. There wasn't room in the porch, what with the mattress, so Nan had her smokes in the kitchen. "Just this once. And you'd better bloody well not say anything because I've had a shitty enough day."

I said I was the one supposed to be having the shitty day, which made Nan laugh and cough. She said I'd better quit being a cheeky buggar or she'd piss her pants and make more washing. Nan said buggar isn't a rude word anymore. She reckoned you should hear all the bad words when you're little because that way they lose their shock value. My teacher, she mustn't of learned any rude words when she was a kid because she flapped like a hen if you said "bum" or "shit" and they're just everyday words. Nan smoked with her eyes closed as if there was a dream in the nicotine that she wanted to grasp on to. She used a pāua shell for an ashtray. When I tipped the butts and ash out and held it under the outside tap, the shell came back shiny except for a few burn marks where Nan had pressed down, grinding out the butts. On my thigh I have three tiny round scars, like craters, that appeared after the blisters burst. Mum gave me the first burn because I answered back, and the next because I cried. I'm a fast learner and swallowed up my tears but she still gave me the third burn anyhow, to make sure I had the lesson. "Don't tell your Dad."

I was sorry Nan's cigarettes had scarred the pāua's colours. I told her that she should use something else for an ashtray, like a cracked saucer, but she told me the shell's got sentimental value and she'll leave it to me in her will. I told her I'm never going to smoke and she shouldn't smoke either. She flashed her yellow fingernails at me. "Been at it far too long, Baby-girl."

You never touched Dad's stuff. That was the golden rule. His mug. His stash. Don't touch it. His girl. He told her, "If you hurt her again I'll fuckin' kill you." Mum's smudged eyes looked at me like I was her biggest mistake ever. But Mum was blasé about doing things she shouldn't. Me too. Next time she smacked me, I told Dad. You know that word blasé? It's French for you don't give a fuck. Sometimes, when Nan was watching telly, I'd sit in her chair on the porch and pretend I was smoking. I'd blow empty smoke out and whisper, "Who gives a fuck!" Before they closed the lid on Nan's casket, I put her pāua shell in so she can smoke in heaven and dream. Someone had painted over her nails and made them pearly. Nan didn't know everything. I looked on the Internet and it's the leaves that are the smart ones. When the caterpillars come munching, the leaves react by producing chemicals. It's the leaves make themselves potent. Smart leaves! Now that's some crazy shit right there. 📖

Memory #6, black/white photograph by David Rodríguez

As Seen Live on Fox News

Heather McQuillan

When Thor tested both his hypothesis and his thunder hammer, the people deposited their money into the accounts of the televangelists. No one stepped forward to explain the rapid expansion of air within the lightning strike so the deities knew for certain that Science was dead and came strutting back to the world.

Tāwhirimātea mobilised his armies of cloud children to throw icy thorns from the heavens. In response they built pyres of books and tractor tyres. In an attempt at appeasement the people flung a thin-boned calf onto the flames. Its leather creaked.

Neptune's jubilant belly-flop displaced the waters, which rose to meet the land that mankind had claimed, and reclaimed, and he set his barnacles to attach to the municipal buildings, and to the beachfront houses of the 1%, and to the sea shanty towns of the dispossessed. He was a trickle down sort of god.

The meek inherited both the groaning earth and the seabirds that washed ashore with bellies full of plastic. Gaia heaved deep sighs.

And still the bogus seers called on the people to see the wonders of their own prophecies they had made absolute. *Behold the end times.* They reached their childish arms to the Christ, calling him father and lord and friend.

"Depart from me, I never knew you."

They should have read the books.

It was Eris who claimed them, plucked them from their television studios back to her milky nipples. When they screamed in horror at her myriad arms, she devoured them. 📖

On A Thread, Archival pigment print by Megan Magill

VII

FEATURED THEME:

BALANCING ACTS

Duwamish Waterway, Seattle, 2017, photograph by Anna Bálint

When The Tide Is Out

Kathleen Alcalá

I knew I could find some people who remembered working in the berry fields, the last of those big fir trees, and the lifeways that marked the transition from forest to farmland. I convinced Doreen and Dan Rapada to come over to my house and tell me their stories one afternoon. Doreen Almazan Rapada grew up on Lovgren Road. She was born on August 3, 1943. Both she and her husband, Daniel Rapada, who is the same age, are the children of Filipino fathers and First Nations mothers from Canada who met on Bainbridge Island.

Doreen's father, Felix Almazan, came from the Philippines in the 1920s to work in the Alaskan canneries. Like other Filipino men, Felix spent winters living in boardinghouses in Seattle's Chinatown. There, he discovered that the Japanese farmers on Bainbridge needed year-round help, and he went to the island to work for them. In the 1940s, he purchased twenty acres, a few acres at a time, on Lovgren from the Pope and Talbot lumber company for fifty dollars an acre. With help from his brothers and some dynamite, Felix cleared the land of stumps, scrub, and second growth, and put in strawberries. Doreen and her brothers and sisters were raised on the original five acres and in the house on the hill.

The family, says Doreen, grew all of their food on those five acres, supplemented with seafood, and, in the winter, rice from Chinatown in Seattle. They grew strawberries, corn, Blue Lake string beans, cucumbers, and tomatoes. Doreen's father also had a raspberry patch that the University of Washington monitored for productivity. The families, Dan reminded her, also grew big cabbages.

Most of the Almazan acres are now owned by the Sears family and used as equestrian fields. Highway 305 took three acres, and the Morales farm, a public trust, occupies the rest, just to the east of the highway. Dan and Doreen's son still owns and lives on the original five acres.

After the Japanese families on Bainbridge were sent to internment camps in 1942, the Filipino farmers became caretakers for much of the farm property owned by the Japanese. The original immigrants, like Felix Almazan, were too old to be drafted to serve in World War II. Both Doreen and Dan's fathers worked instead as welders for the Hall Brothers shipyards during the war.

Felix and four other Filipinos—Felix Narte, Daniel Bucsit, Anacleto Corpus, and Toby Memberi—founded the Filipino American Hall in 1941. They all spoke Ilocano, the dominant language of the southern Philippines. The five purchased property on Strawberry Hill for the hall with their own money ("It was strawberry money!") as the Filipino Farmers of Bainbridge Island. It cost five dollars a year to become a member, and the other Filipino farmers on the island soon joined.

Shortly thereafter, the Army requisitioned most of the property, paying each of the original purchasers for it. The five founders took the money and invested it in Town & Country Market, the eventual successor to Eagle Harbor Market. In the late 1960s, when the federal government reclassified as surplus much of the land it had requisitioned for use during World War II, the Strawberry Hill property was sold to the Parks and Recreation District for one dollar, without offering it back to the Filipino community. In more recent years, the Parks District returned two and a half acres to the Filipino community, on which it built a new community hall next to the original shed used for shipping and receiving strawberries.

Felix Almazan and the other farmers supplemented what they grew by fishing off the piers at Point White and the ferry dock. They caught perch, red snapper, big cod of several varieties, octopus, and sea urchins.

"There used to be lots before," said Doreen. Sometimes her father would let the children go with him to the beach at

Fay Bainbridge Park at night to catch Dungeness crab. There also used to be lots of shrimp in Eagle Harbor by the ferry terminal—but no one eats fish out of Eagle Harbor now that it is a Superfund waste site due to heavy concentrations of the creosote once used in the shipbuilding industry.

Today, the mouth of the harbor is taken up by the ferry slip and a repair yard maintained by the Washington State Ferry system. Visitors can gaze across the harbor and see what looks like construction in and close to the water on Bill Point. But the cheerful orange buoys and markers instead delineate the Superfund site, and the seemingly endless efforts to mitigate the seeping creosote as it bubbles up from the harbor bottom.

The Indipino families also foraged for wild food, although it wasn't called that at the time. When Doreen's mother went to work in the packing shed, her grandmother came from Canada to watch the children. She took them out to gather berries as they came into season. Doreen recalled that they ate huckleberries, salmonberries, dingleberries, thimbleberries, and salal berries, which she pronounced the old way, "slahal." Where logging had occurred, they found the small, dark, indigenous blackberries that her grandmother, or "Ta'a," preferred. They ate them raw and made pies or pudding cakes out of them—placing the berries on the bottom of the pan and covering them with batter. "The children would go outside and eat berries, or peel fern shoots and eat them as snacks," Doreen said. The young sprouts were called saskis, and they look like asparagus when small. "There used to be three kinds of salmonberries," said Doreen. "We'd stop for dessert."

Ta'a was a member of the Squamish tribe. Stanley Park in Vancouver, British Columbia, used to belong to them, and the Queen leased it from the tribe. Now, a ceremonial gun is discharged daily at the spot where Doreen's grandfather, Ta'a's husband, once maintained a salmon-drying shed. He was born in Capalano, a district of North Vancouver, on Mission Inlet. Doreen's mother was born in Chilliwack, BC.

Ta'a showed the children which plants were poisonous—on Bainbridge this included tansy ragwort, poison hemlock, and certain fungi—and which were medicinal, such as lichens, red cedar, and Oregon grape. Once, when Doreen fell and skinned her leg, Ta'a took a frog leaf (plantain), washed it, put it on her leg and wrapped it. "Nice bandage," her friends said. Ta'a told her it would "pull off" the infection.

"Was the food you ate healthier then?" I asked Doreen.

"Well, it was all organic!" she responded with a laugh. I suspect that in those days quantity of food was the driving factor, rather than whether or not the source was uncontaminated. But then, they fixed all their meals themselves. When fishing and wild harvesting were not enough, Felix Almazan got his family through the winter by keeping credit at the small store located on Rolling Bay.

Like Felix Almazan, Dan Rapada's father, Anacleto Rapada, came to the Northwest to work in the canneries. Dan's mother, Mary Louise (George) Rapada, came from a family of fishermen in Chilliwack, Canada. Other members of the Rapada family married into the Nooksack Nation, located north of Seattle. Fifty of those descendants live on Bainbridge today.

"My dad did a lot of hunting," said Dan. They used to drive out to Forks to hunt deer and elk. In summer, Dan still goes to the Fraser River in British Columbia to fish. As a Native, he can bring as much salmon as he wants back across the border.

Anacleto Rapada would share his bounty with the Japanese American Takamoto and Suyematsu families. Then, like Felix Almazan, he would go to Chinatown and buy two sacks of rice, and they were set for the winter.

Dan's grandmother was probably born in Squamish Valley. In 1948, the Fraser River flooded, and all of the Squamish were displaced. Now, eighty percent of the tribe lives off-nation, even though there is a thirty-mile radius from the original village that is considered "on" the nation. Dan holds a hereditary position as an off-nation councillor.

Dan, who grew up near Island Center on Bainbridge Island, said that his father, Anacleto, worked in the shipyards, where he was known as "Papa Joe." "All the Natives had nicknames," Dan said, because the owners could not pronounce their real names, so they went by "James, Joe, Harry."

Neither Dan nor Doreen learned Ilocano, the Filipino dialect of their fathers, or Squamish, the language of their mothers, because their parents "wanted us to do well in school." Doreen's mother attended St. Paul's Residential Boarding School in Vancouver, where her best subject was English.

Their property still contains some of the small log cabins built for the Squamish pickers who stayed with them during harvest. First Nations people often followed the crops for half of the year. In the winter, the men worked as loggers or longshoremen, and then they brought their families and picked in the summer. Dan called them "crop chasers." Many had no other homes to return to, so they stayed year-round in exchange for doing farm chores.

I asked about the associations that existed between Filipino families and Japanese families. Doreen recalled that Felix Narte, one of the other founders of the Filipino American Hall, worked for the Kitamoto family. When the Kitamotos were sent to the camps, he took care of their farm, and drove to Minidoka in Idaho regularly to take them money and other things. Later, they gave him five acres near the water. Thor Madayag, another Filipino, worked for the Kouras, Doreen recalled. There is now a map showing many of these mutually beneficial associations, pieced together by volunteers at the Bainbridge Island Historical Museum.

By the late 1800s, First Nations people of Canada, including the Squamish, were growing potatoes to eat along with their fish. This makes me think that yes, perhaps there was a hole in their diets that could be filled by potatoes. Or perhaps this was the beginning of their decline in health, as fewer and fewer fishing and gardening spots were available to them. "The Suquamish used to live on the coast of Bainbridge Island to fish, until they were kicked off. That's why it's called Arrowpoint Drive," Doreen said. Indigenous women from Canada were able to form and feed their families by marrying Filipino men who eventually became landowners. However, knowledge of the land skipped the generation of Doreen and Dan's parents, who were sent to boarding schools—it was transmitted to them instead by their grandmothers.

At the Big House in Squamish, Dan remembered, his grandmother had a big garden that she worked with two Clydesdale horses. "All the food that was left at the end of each summer was canned, since there was not much fresh produce at the grocery stores in the winter." She taught her husband how to hard-smoke fish. "To eat it, you boiled it with water and ate it with rice or potatoes."

The joining of these two cultures has resulted in an amazing cuisine. The Filipino way of cooking is more flavorful, since it uses more spices, such as ginger and garlic. Adobo, a spicy red sauce, includes soy sauce, vinegar, pickling spices, and paprika. For adobo, "the second day is best," Dan told me.

The First Nations women, for their part, knew how to find and prepare clams, salmon, and wild game. "Our moms taught our dads how to cook that," Doreen said. The meals were prepared in big woks. "All the Indipino men are good cooks," Doreen said. "Our moms made the desserts. Now, our sons are the cooks."

This is an intensely social culture, springing from two family-centered cultures with a complex web of family relations among them. Weddings, births, and funerals all demand the group preparation and consumption of food. "You don't have to ask people to bring food," said Dan, "they just volunteer."

"Indipinos just like to get together and share," Doreen said.

"We just had a softball game at Battlepoint Park," Dan added. "Everybody brought food for a potluck afterwards—about fifty or sixty people. People brought salads and leftover roast pig from last Saturday. It was roasted in a big pit. That's pretty much the culture."

People have specialties. Dan is good at barbeque salmon. One of the younger men has asked to learn from him. All this cooking knowledge is "word of mouth" and hasn't been written down.

Doreen, thinking about her childhood, grew wistful. "I took my dad's garden for granted. During the war, one of the servicemen's wives was struggling to feed her children, so my father took her food." She remembers "planting parties," when people would go from one farm to the other, with the Filipino cooks preparing food at each homestead—a pig on a spit, goat meat. It was a combination progressive dinner and flash-harvesting.

How do they harvest now? I asked.

"Before, there were no jobs, so our dads had big families, and even the grandkids picked berries," Doreen said. "They would call families to come and help, and the pickers would come from BC."

"The kids don't care now," Dan said. "There is only one big farm left on the island, Karen Selvar's at Day Road, that grows strawberries and raspberries, and it's mostly U-Pick."

"You can't get even kids to pick, because it is hard work. Once, the Nartes had a pick order for the next day," Doreen said. Dan offered to help. "I'll pick berries, but I won't carry the flats," he told them. "'That's okay,' they said. 'The kids will carry the flats.' They have seven kids."

This was once the norm for all agricultural families. The more children, the more hands to bring in the harvest, although it means more mouths to feed.

When I asked them, neither Doreen nor Dan thought the people of Bainbridge could live off food grown solely on the island. The soil is played out, they said—Doreen's father had told them that Bainbridge Island could no longer support strawberries. We could not grow rice, either. People used to live on seafood, but the waters are too polluted now, and much of the sea life is gone. Plus, "deer get into everything," Doreen said. "Growing up, the farm dogs lived outside and chased off the deer," she added. I pointed out that we could eat the deer if we needed to.

Another reason the island could not sustain itself now is because of the larger population. Before, each family had about five acres. When the berry prices dropped and taxes increased, most Filipinos sold their farmland. The problem of this ratio of land to people is something that other farmers echoed, but didn't necessarily agree on, as I continued my interviews. 📖

you will not have this lesson
if you don't hunt

Luther Allen

i heard a deer snort in the little canyon. he knew i was there.
i studied the oaks and their leaves for a long time but found
nothing and moved to the rim. rifle halfway up, safety off.
sure of everything. i expected the buck to be across the
canyon, perhaps moving away, perhaps a frozen ghost behind
a tangle of limbs. but he had come to my side of the canyon.
perfectly still, 20 yards away. a clean, easy neck shot. a gift.
i was 19 and he would be the biggest buck i had ever killed.

his eyes to mine, mine to his. i never raised my rifle.
the buck knew i wouldn't shoot. he was not there to be shot.

the rifle a chunk of wood, a strangeness of metal.
i was no longer hunter, he was no longer prey.

his death and my life. between us
a single wildness and nothing at all.

i went inside his being, he came into mine.
i began to understand that nothing dies.

i am not sure what he saw but he saw me
naked. more naked than i'd ever been.

something moved from one dimension to another.

two minutes—enough time to be reborn and die
a thousand times. he slowly bounced off. disappeared.

i called it sacred, holy.
i told no one.

Ghost Trees, Metolius River Canyon, Central Oregon, 2015,
photograph by Andrew Wesner

mid-september at sumas mountain redoubt

Luther Allen

Drinking cold snow-water from a tin cup
Looking down for miles
Through high still air.
—Gary Snyder

those tin cup times
are in me forever, nothing
but frigid water, wild
everywhere.

but snyder, here's the deal: the structural drawings
for the new house are three days late to the engineer &
the addition design has finalized and i need to get it
to the drafter & the commercial job downtown i started
in march is now due and i haven't worked on it for months
& the nice couple from puerto rico will be back here
in a week and i haven't even opened their file.

the leaves are turning in the high country.
huckleberries will ripen and fall
without me this year. again.

let's be naked here.
i can't remember things i once read.
my body seems to be losing the sense of itself.

outside
through the window

everything still as an old photograph.
between breaths, suspended.

    except one frail
             alder leaf

still tethered, but fluttering as if possessed

beckoning
and waving goodbye.

Water, Cleaving

Janée J. Baugher

I remember once catching you cutting yourself," my little brother, Shawn, said. While I have no recollection of that scene, it pains me to think of what my suicide would do to Shawn, a man who can fix anything electrical or mechanical but cannot fix me. While it's useless to surmise the effect that my death would have on my only sibling's life, I sometimes wonder if it'd make much of a difference.

Driving to Leavenworth that summer, my Honda was low on gas but I thought there should be enough to get me to our family's river house. On the descent after Stevens Pass, the road was dangerously graded and winding. Although there was ample fuel to deliver me the twenty miles into town, the way the gas would slosh to the left in the tank as I veered right, and would slosh right when I veered left, I'd lose the ability to accelerate. Only when equilibrium was restored and the gas leveled out in the tank and the line, was I able to proceed. My losing acceleration every few minutes no doubt frustrated the cars that stacked up behind me on that two-lane, no-passing highway.

Leavenworth is an Eastern Washington town on the Wenatchee River. After some economic lows, the town settled on a gimmick. It could have modeled itself after Leavenworth, Kansas, home to one of the largest maximum security federal prisons in the U.S. Instead, it transformed itself into a mock Bavarian village, which boasts the Kris Kringl store, a Nut-cracker Museum, and an annual Oktoberfest.

I pulled over at the only rest stop on route, thirteen miles outside town. After I let the dog out to pee, I opened the hood, stood there for a minute, and soon made conversation with a married couple. It was they who suggested the theory about the gas in the tank sloshing away from the tubing that fueled the acceleration pedal. Since we were all headed to Leavenworth, we agreed to caravan. They drove ahead, and any time I slowed down they slowed. After twenty seconds of no pedal pressure, I'd get fuel again, and then would rev easily to 60 mph. Driving beside the Wenatchee River, I considered how it cuts land. It's not just the water which razors through, it's the sum of all that river carries: sediment, soil, rock. Water rushing brazenly over boulders so sure of their solidness, and their immobility, are merely weathered to sand by water. Earthly formations yet are the results of water's insistence. The Wenatchee is a composite of tributaries such as Icicle Creek and Chiwawa River, collective waters mapping a singular course. That Wenatchee could not be tamed.

As we age, we assume new roles in the family. Not so long ago my brother and I were something to look after. Now, my brother is our trusted jack-of-all-trades. At the river house, originally a joint real estate adventure between Shawn, our uncle, and Mom, he climbs ladders to saw off dead branches from ponderosa pines, stoops in the cellar to replace clamps, and crawls about the attic to thread electrical wires. Recently, our mom was certain that her entire oven range needed replacing, but Shawn suspected a loose switch. Ten dollars later, the appliance cooks to perfection Mom's incomparable macaroni and cheese.

When I finally arrived at the house and relayed the story of my trip, Shawn, who has never allowed his tank to dip past half-full, and was probably incredulous at my having taken an unnecessary risk, just shook his head.

Not long after Shawn was born, he began to reveal an unsubstantiated mechanical talent that none of us could relate to. By the time he turned three years old, his fascination for the knobs and sliders on the stereo had turned into an obsession. Typical children's toys languished in a corner of his room while he focused on functional things with magical moving parts. He'd sneak Dad's tools and start in with a light switch or portable radio. He'd pull apart anything with a removable panel to see, I suppose, if he could determine the inner workings of the thing. Yet there were no experts he could ask for guidance. Unconcerned, he would dive into a project, communing with an inanimate object, which meant patient hours of trial-and-error. He wanted to know something; his curiosity was so fierce that he was willing to break a thing open in order to get to the heart of its mechanisms.

Over the years friends and family would gift him with small appliances (hair dryers, toasters) that worked intermittently or had stopped altogether. After he'd fix the thing, he'd return it without ceremony to the astonished owner. We started handing over more complex items like computers and cars, and he would miraculously repair or somehow enhance the thing and we'd be amazed, and in this he found his voice.

When my brother was twenty-one, he acquired an electronic radio kit and a friend's FM transmitter, extended his CB antenna, and made separate amplifier boards from a busted VHF marine radio. Shawn's own pirate radio station, which broadcasted 1980s music from our parents' basement, often transmitted over four counties. The first warning by the Federal Communications Commission arrived by post. Months later, a knock at the door: "We can see your antenna. What you're doing is a federal offense." The legal wattage for a hobbyist transmitting on the airwaves was 0.01. Shawn's wattage was 30. After the home visit he dropped his transmission to 0.5 watts.

More months elapsed and one day Shawn got the notion to crank the wattage up to 30 again. "I don't know what possessed me," he later admitted. Within hours a Chevrolet Caprice Classic and two police cars pulled up in front of the house. Two FCC agents in suits and sunglasses, accompanied by three cops, stepped inside and followed Shawn down the stairs. The punishment could have been a fine of up to $100,000 and a year in prison. After Shawn had disabled the entire system, the authorities left. His response was, "I got caught, that's just the way it works."

Years earlier, in preparation for leaving home for college, I spent hours one summer day recording favorite albums onto cassette tapes. While I was upstairs dubbing The Police album, *Reggatta de Blanc*, thirteen year old Shawn and his friend Jason were in the basement playing with their new swap meet-bought CB radios. During my first uncertain months in Boston, my depression had resurfaced. My dormitory was a fourth-floor brownstone which overlooked the Charles River. I'd play Cat Steven's song, "Trouble," and look out over the Charles, crying for nothing and all things. It never occurred to me that jumping into the river could end my misery. One day, though, for the first time since my arrival, I cued The Police tape. In the first song, "Message in a Bottle," Sting sings, "I'll send an S.O.S. to the world, I'll hope that someone gets my message in a bottle." In the final eighty seconds of the song, Sting repeats the chorus, "Sending out an S.O.S." All of the sudden there was static interference on the tape, and I heard Jason's voice, "Breaker, breaker. Can you read me? Shawn, are you out there." Sting sang the chorus a few more times, and then my brother's voice, "Roger. I can read you."

For the taciturn, there's a comfortable distance that comes with transmitting one's voice over airwaves. My brother's intention, I believe, was not to build interpersonal relationships; one motivation perhaps was to establish confirmation about the distance and strength of the signal. Hearing from the receiver was validation of a mechanical and electronic feat.

Finally some high-pitched feedback, Sting's voice faded, the song ended, and the rest of the cassette played without interruption. Hearing my brother's voice unexpectedly through the speakers of my dorm room felt like a beacon from home, reminding me that the answer I sought could be out there. Yes, I had packed up my Seattle life for a new chapter in Boston, but my only sibling was still a force in my life; exactly where I needed him, closer than I had thought.

At the river house, Uncle Brad and Mom donned swim suits, plucked inner tubes from the garage, and plodded down the flagstone steps to the riverbank. They strapped on life vests, connected his grab rope to her tube, threw her rope to Shawn on shore, set their bottoms down into the mesh seats, and dropped their hands and feet into the Wenatchee. A breeze ricocheted off the river, momentarily relieving us all from the high desert heat. Shawn and I remained on the sandy shore, where he minded the rope and I watched Sadie dig a dog-sized hole for burying and excavating four tennis balls. I couldn't appreciate the objective: To outsmart the balls? To search for cooler ground? Sadie continued in that manner for an hour, seemingly without completing the task to her satisfaction.

Moving water caused a depression through that land. The river's sound was a signaling, as water ran downstream, past our uncle's house. The riverbed was exposed in places that summer, for the mountain snow runoff was minimal and the valley had little to capture. The river was a force of nature between where we were and where we weren't. As long as the Tumwater Canyon Dam just outside town stayed open, the river would proceed without hesitation.

After sunset the stars seemed to flicker on. Stepping out onto the back deck which overlooked the river, I attempted to identify some constellations for Shawn. That night the river sounded like a chorus of slapping, crashing, beating water against and over stone. Water roared over boulders which hampered an otherwise pedestrian journey through the valley. What a person says and what's heard is not often a perfect translation. We were forced to speak up near the river, for its guttural timbre was louder than our own voices. When I asked Shawn if he'd ever thought about my suiciding, he shook his head and responded, "It'd be a lonely life."

Next day our uncle suggested that Shawn and I ride inner tubes down the Wenatchee. Although we were greenhorns, we agreed. Uncle Brad drove us four miles to where Icicle Road crossed the river. We slipped on life vests and flopped down on the mesh seats of the inner tubes. A long nylon rope was attached by an overhand knot to Shawn's inner tube, the free end of which he tossed to me. I held onto the rope at the bight and allowed the standing part to be heaped in a pile beside me on the seat. The only control we had over our tubes was our arms and legs. No paddles, no plan. We could always clutch the handles, but I could not foresee what good that would do. I reckoned we would simply coast along, beholden to the river's course, and carried by its current.

We said goodbye and floated off. Initially, there was a subtle breeze off the flat water, shallow enough to see the smooth, silty riverbed below. No foliage, root systems, no rocks. Uniform bank, bed, and channel leads to slow waters— easily ridden, but without the excitement that whitewater rafting brings. Riding calm waters brought few challenges and little momentum. During those times, we had to push ourselves along with our hands, sometimes out to the side, sometimes leaning forward and between legs to reach the water. Occasionally I just leaned back, faced the sky, and relished being hauled along by my brother's tether. He didn't seem to mind, until we'd hit an opposing current, that is, and he'd implore me, "C'mon, Sis." So I'd begin to hand paddle until we gained speed, and then, almost as soon as I would, I'd regard my pruning fingers, feel an ache in my shoulders, and I'd lean back again to catch rays on my sky-turned face. Besides, what was the hurry?

Quaking aspen, bigleaf maples, and fir trees lined the riverbank, and we glided past the exclusive Leavenworth golf club, where men in tidy white outfits attempted to send balls into holes cut out of grass. Then, because we'd never been down the Wenatchee, we took an unforeseen detour. By veering left we entered Enchantment Park, slid quietly past the kids' trout pond and along the downtown riverbank of Blackbird Island. Summer guests flung themselves into the cool water as Shawn and I clumsily navigated through water riddled with gleaming wet bodies.

Along the journey, minor rapids happened seemingly randomly, but not randomly at all: at places where the channel was uneven and the bed irregular, punctuated with boulders and vegetation. Before we reached those fierce waters, we heard it first, the hazard of the river pronouncing itself. The violent sound of white water plowing over impediments. Some sections of the riverbed were lined with fist-sized rocks: grey, taupe, red-rust, and like an artisan's grand mosaic creation—beautifully seismic and covered by green-tinged water.

In that river water I was not afraid, as I could see clearly what lay beneath me. Worst case scenario, I would get bucked from the inner tube, but I'd definitely land on my feet. Before that trip, I expected to gaze down and regard only a void, the hint of perils so palpable it would ignite my panic, and I was a child again, so sure that drowning would claim my life that I imagined hurling myself into the water just to be done with it. That day I wanted to live in the joy of meandering down the Wenatchee River with my only sibling.

The weight of our inner tubes turned the quiet surface of water into crosshatches and small white caps which captured glints of reflected sun. I studied the way water swirls over a boulder and then seemingly gets sucked up under it, and considered how any river's journey is dependent on the interferences it experiences.

One group of tubers we encountered on the river had a designated inner tube just for their cooler, and as we bobbed by, we watched them distribute cans of beer to each other. The dramatic rock face and the peaks of the Northern Cascade Mountain Range loomed behind us. The mountain line of the eastern slope hadn't exceeded the tree line, so everywhere I looked was shades of green. Conifers and deciduous trees sprang right up at the shoreline—dogwood, spruce, and pine. When the river turned us around, I named the blue heron on the lee shore, and Shawn spotted red-haired ducks. I cautioned him about pilings up ahead, and he warned me to arch my back to hold my behind out of water when we were headed toward a shallow, rocky stretch.

Stately cliffs of earth towered over us in that valley. Centuries of earth shifting while water phased solid, phased liquid. That day, Shawn and I floated down the canyon, the two of us carried by water tenacious enough to shape land, fixed on our task, how we needed to manage the rope and mind the river in order to stay connected. Sister and brother cruising down the Wenatchee River, taking all afternoon to get nowhere.

We came around a bend and plunged through our first major rapids. We continued to meander along, with Shawn face-forward, though the river had turned me around. Frantically, I attempted to correct my direction, to face the violent river, as a strategy to face my fear of water. Before plummeting over each rapids thereafter, I wrestled to situate myself for a visual advantage. Yet I had no control over how the river would take me down. Fighting was futile. I did my best to correct the inner tube, but when I was being pitched backwards, I'd just grip the handles, arch my back like Shawn suggested, and try to trust that everything would be alright.

After riding what we thought were the last rapids, we came around the bend and I heard someone calling my name, "J.J., J.J.!" Our uncle Brad later admitted that he had felt guilty about having dumped us off two hours earlier. He had shuttled us to the river, left us empty-handed, and drove back home where the TV program *Mad Money* and

Rain on Glass IV, Shenandoah Valley, Virginia, 2014, photo by Sarah E.N. Kohrs

a margarita awaited him. He later told us that at home he began to think about recent news stories of rafters drowning in the Wenatchee, so when his nerves got the best of him, he left the house after announcing to our mother, "I'm going to find them."

We hand paddled over to our uncle on shore, where he reported that giant steelhead trout had been launching themselves seemingly gleefully out of the water. Since fishing was not permitted on the Wenatchee, I could envision trout taunting our fisherman uncle. Brad offered to drive us home, but since we had come along nicely and the house was close by, just under Highway 2, we decided to continue. We proceeded downriver, with me fraternally tied. If I'd known then what was in store for us, we would have quit that river then and there.

After we said goodbye to Brad, we rafted on, under Highway 2, and down past the River Bend neighborhood. I told Shawn that I loved when, after we had successfully ridden the river's rapids, he'd exclaim, "We really hauled ass." It tickled me to hear him say we "hauled ass" because in our daily lives we never spent any time together, so, for me, affixing a phrase to the action was hope for another sibling adventure. My little brother and me riding inner tubes down the Wenatchee, conquering anything in our path.

We drifted along for a while, and then braced ourselves for the next rapids. Suddenly, fast moving water sent Shawn's tube ahead of me, with the grab rope still tied to the front of his tube and with the other half of the rope heaped next to me on the seat. As soon as his tube rushed forward, mine ran aground. The rope started to uncoil and stupidly I reached for it, the nexus to my brother, and somehow the rope entangled my finger. After nearly three hours in the water, my hands were practically lifeless and with the oceanic power of my brother's inner tube downriver, I panicked. The river intended to separate me from my brother, and my finger from my hand. How many pounds per pressure must be exerted to break a human digit, disarticulate it from tissue? "Shawn, Shawn," I screamed but sending an S.O.S. over the roar of that river was useless.

At the beginning of our trip, so cavalierly did we attach the grab rope to Shawn's tube, tossing the standing end to me. We should have used a highwayman's hitch or another type of quick-release knot. We should have evaluated the knot's security and strength. An unsecure knot will break, and a weak knot will slip. It's imperative to know when to quick-release a knot and when to let it ride. During most of our trip, I didn't need to secure the rope in my hand in order to stay near to Shawn, as the river sent us down at roughly the same pace. But, when the standing part of the rope began to unravel, I thought that I could strong-arm the separation, undo what was about to be inextricably done. If Shawn had known that I had grounded my inner tube as he proceeded helplessly on, he could have assessed the rope's tether and released it. By instinctively reaching for the cord to Shawn, I unwittingly introduced my tissue and bone between the rope's bight and standing part. The nylon kinked and snarled around that finger in a confused arrangement of gravity's force and river's strength. My intention was to pull Shawn to me, stop the cleaving. As the elder sibling, it was within my power to protest the parting that neither of us had submitted to, wasn't it?

There was still no sign of Shawn. I somehow had the good sense to create slack in the rope by pulling on it with my other hand, and after great effort I freed the finger and released the rope. I watched it as it snaked down the river and vanished. Getting back on course now meant standing on the slick flat riverbed, which looked as though someone had taken an auger to it, and struggling with proper footing while I searched for water deep enough in which to launch my tube. Fording the river was a simple solution but for one thing: I had lost a lot of sensation from the waist down. That morning's long run and the frigid river had rendered my legs cramped and my feet virtually lame.

As for Shawn, I did not know how he reacted to that moment where I was stopped cold and he was allowed to float merrily on. At what point had he realized we were drawing farther apart? At which point, if at all, could he sense the panic that had washed over me? In that moment of pain and fear, despite being minutes and mere feet from help, I had little control over my body and thus was incapable of delivering a distress signal; I lost all faith that I would be saved.

Earlier, as Shawn and I barreled through the Wenatchee River rapids, I felt closer to him than I had ever felt. Even though I had to cast the rope out and watch Shawn go on, it would not be my defeat. Ultimately, I managed to stretch the legs and relieve the cramps. Unsteady, I stood, flung the inner tube over my head, and I looked up: Shawn! He had stationed himself behind a boulder just a few feet away and was waiting for me, worried.

Next day, driving back to Seattle, I popped in a cassette and followed the course of the swift Wenatchee. On that clear summer day, I admired the river's surrender, as it traveled over anything in its path, untied and free. Uproarious water carving a place for itself here on Earth. 🕮

Origin of the Apple

Kyce Bello

The center of origin is where the greatest diversity occurs.
—Nikolai Vavilov

1.

Every family is a mountain
nooked with hollows.

Variations of trunks, twisted and rising on the long slope.

      Bud and bloom, pip
and slowly ripened fruit.

Deep in crested ridges,
                the first two become the rest.

2.

If I could trace this body a long way back,
      through teasel beds and clear cut meadows,

I would be home.

Familiar to the people who look up in surprise
      at the stranger who wears their face,

who carried a bucket
      —it must be milk—

across the fields to their table.

3.

I am sometimes religious,
but I do not know if it is god I believe in, or apples,

or if there is any difference.

I look at this forest, even in its falling,
and am brought to my knees.

Where god created the apple,
the apple can be anything.

It is what color it chooses,
what flavor it wants,

wife to whichever wandering bee
with dusty feet it pleases.

Every star-seeded apple ever set on your plate
was born from this place.

4.

Every thread
you unravel
from your dress

splits in its threshing,

each ancestor whose name you learn
is undone before you reach
her face.

You will never know the feast
from which you were born.

A Coral Polyp Considers the Nature of Its Identity

Eleanor Berry

I am connected by a thin sheet of tissue
to other polyps identical to me. I am
one member of a dynamic collectivity of clones.
Together, we form a bulwark, sheltering
the edge of the land from the battering sea.

Although as fixed in place as any rock formation
or rooted plant, I am a predatory animal.
I am a stomach, a mouth, and tentacles.
Coiled within my skin are spring-
loaded stingers that shoot poison darts into my prey.

I host a crowd of minuscule creatures, some dwelling
in my mucus coat, some inside my endodermal cells.
All pay their rent in kind: The food they manufacture
they share with me. Defending themselves,
they save me from disease.

They are my farmers and my armies. I depend upon them.
If their crops fail, if their troops fall to invading throngs,
I die. So it is for all of us polyp clones—
if our microbes cease to nourish and protect us, we succumb.
This living reef, built of our bodies, begins to crumble away.

What am I? Am I an *I*? . . . If not an *I*,
then what? . . . I'm not myself alone—I'm nothing
apart from my neighbors and my tenants.
We, all of us together, compose a *holobiont:*
a great chorus where none can sing solo.

And you, smug reader, supposing yourself
sole and entire—you are no such thing. You, too,
live by what lives around and within you.

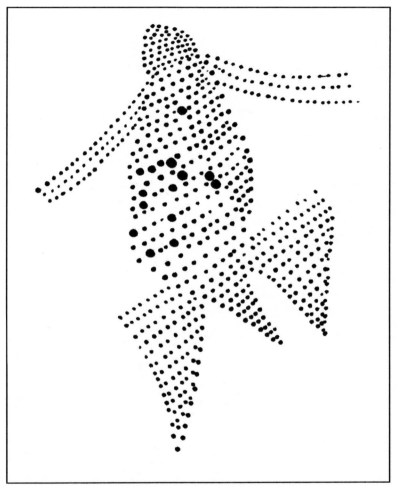

Amptification 5, a dotty drawing by Daniel Ableev

Asteraceae

Danielle D. Billing

Wild sunflower from cracked
interstate. Bright yellow petals
against browned summer
grass. A cheap metaphor
snubbing its mythic
namesake as offshoots blossom
unregimented. A heart
needs more rain and richer soil.
I didn't belong here.
Weedy pioneers colonize disturbed
ground. Complete life in
season. Make way for hardy
plants. Rabbitbrush is the West's answer
to green. Life cycling in muted sage.
Things grow slower here,
homeness rooted fitfully.
There is no rabbitbrush along interstate;
on slower roads, less trafficked, it quietly reclaims
home. Edging towards the scars I've carved
in search of open sky.

Sealed for Your Protection

Michelle Brooks

If I were a locksmith, I'd call
my company Open Sesame
and I'd list my services in free
circulars, and I'd be able to open
anything except myself and this
would be the price I paid for my
gifts. While you breathe a sigh
of relief as you walk into your
life, I would wait for someone
to break my windows, as if I
were the one thing that mattered,
struggling to hide the inevitable
surprise finding nothing inside.

Saved

Thomas Brush

The same wind moves
Everything: shells, brass
Casings, the thin lace of ice at the edge
Of the pond, colorful scarves
That litter the desert floor, spiders weaving
Their intricate webs through the glister
Of morning, rising from the safe shadow
Of sleep, or the flight of a model airplane
When age was a number I could count on
One hand. And there's more: tonight the melting colors
Of twilight aren't the only sorrow. Sparrows
Light the orange trees, kids play
Stick ball in a vacant lot, the remains of a corduroy road
Lead past a beaver dam nearly hidden
Beneath the soaring flanks
Of ponderosa pines, that could be
Steeples for the only church
That has any meaning.

Allium, Deschutes River Canyon, Central Oregon, 2016,
photograph by Andrew Wesner

Cold Calling

Sarah Capdeville

Twenty-six below and only the old bay Arabian is shivering in his stall, frost tracing the ridge of his jawline. The other horses and sheep greet me with eyes soft in the dim morning. I pitch green flakes of hay to them, sweet fuel to flare warm in their bellies. Pins of stars fade to a pale sky above, plowed west by the smear of sunrise. I stand by the hay loft, motionless for the first time that morning. A week into this job taking care of a former professor's animals, my body has settled into the rhythms of morning and afternoon feedings, this Montana cold always company. Snow muffles the city across the Helena Valley. Responsibilities only extend as far as the hay loft, burdens as uncomplicated as fifty pounds of alfalfa.

I return to the house, and, watched by two restless collies, pull off layers in the mudroom. Stiff winter boots skirted in snow. Insulated leather gloves worn thin on the pad of the middle finger. Knit hat, headscarf damp with my breath. Outer shell, down jacket, Carhartt coveralls, flannel shirt. Face flushing hot, I go into the kitchen and crunch on handfuls of multigrain cereal while sunlight pours across the countertops and poinsettia in the windowsill. I could boil a pot of water for tea, tuck myself into the La-Z-Boy beside the fireplace. I could fill a mug with leftover hot water, pull back the sliding glass door, and cast it into the smarting air. Watch it burst from liquid to a plume of rising steam.

Outside the kitchen window, past the poinsettia, the sky has set a hard blue. Not quite twenty-six below now, I think, but no warmer than twenty below. And what's the point of twenty-six, twenty-two, twenty below if all I'm going to do is sink drowsy into an armchair reading Stegner? The cold is calling again, no longer tied to the animals' well-being, no longer tied to expectations. The animals are nuzzling into wreaths of hay, sun-lifted steam trailing from their hindquarters, and I am back in sixty-five degrees of normalcy. I'm not finding much relaxation here, only news, and a smoldering anxiety, and memories I have no space to sort through. Outside, hollow azure sky opens over the valley. The snow radiates sunlight, crystals too tight to sparkle.

The La-Z-Boy can wait, I decide. As can Stegner. I'm expected to spare my lungs from frostbite, read twenty below as something to fear. I know no name for this desire, only the nudge of its persistence. I tug on a long sleeve pullover, then another. Sweatpants, wool socks, treaded running shoes. Down vest, headscarf, hat, mittens. Back in the mudroom, the dogs watch me with bottled excitement. "Too cold for dog paws," I tell them. Too cold for bare faces, they seem to say, yet there you go.

My eyes sting again, breath condensing with a lurch in my chest. Lips split, cheekbones and chin go numb as I run past the breakfasting horses, past the railroad crossing, snow squeaking like styrofoam beneath my feet. With windchill, it's more like forty below, but my mind isn't sensing the weight in that number anymore. My thumbs have cracked along their creases, and like those calluses I feel the dry air stripping significance from digits. My breath blooms into my eyelashes, sticking there in blades of ice, a furry white haze cutting my vision short. And maybe I should be afraid. Maybe I am afraid, but this is a danger I can charge into. A risk edging on madness that freezes over the lukewarm spill of worry.

If not for my cheeks set numb, if not for the ice fringing every bare throb of skin, I would feel a grin pulling across my face. Or maybe I'm not smiling at all; maybe that expression is frozen too, hard-set as the gibbous moon glinting above Scratchgravel Peak. What I feel is that comfort as wide as the powder blue sky above, that deep wholeness in my belly, nudged against my open lungs. Stirring there, like good green alfalfa. Here is a cold stripped of numerals, of doubts, of reason. Here is the joy of sprinting bare-bodied into a river, except all currents are banks of snow, except all bareness is wrapped in folds of sunlight. 📖

Instructions for Balance

Nancy Christopherson

You need a balance in life
a friend says
while we are standing in
the middle of my west side-yard looking
at all the dead and dying weeds.

She's right of course. Who
can go around on
one foot hopping forever.
Yesterday while giving the horses carrots
and grass and they deliriously

chomping, my neighbors
sailed past one by
one smiling, waving. Diamond
stole grass from Tommy's mouth—just
reached over, grabbed and pulled.

Two cats screaming at each other
for space on the front
porch. Laying claim. I guess
that's what happens. Put the stake here
and say mine. Hunger

does that. Let down the other
leg for support.
Lean on a stick. Reach over
pull the food straight out from another's
mouth. Put that aside.

Be quick about it so no one falls
over. Try not to dig
the claws in. Try to forget about
publication—it will never happen to you.
Anyway, steal some letters from

your own mouth, take out
bread from your
pocket. Leave crumbs. Leave
some crumbs for the birds. Try not to
worry too much about it.

Out at Sea

Ng Yu Ci

lay down light, dear gone-as-always,
lay down lilies by my bedside when you
come and wake me up,
bleary-eyed with hair like matted hay and
tell me I look beautiful—
tell me lies, tell me stories
of the things you've seen out
at sea when you come back,
sweet murmurings of forever
smoothed over pebbles and
the tongue of your skin,
cheek on cheek, meeting fingertips and
a lead weight in my heart like an anchor.

when you go again take the lilies with you;
leave the light.

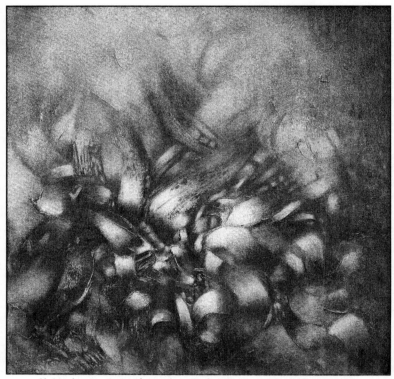

Al Atardecer, painting/mixed media by Vivian Calderón Bogoslavsky

Eating the Earth

Deborrah Corr

I did it with a spoon I stole
quietly from the kitchen,
away from my mother's eyes:
a serious endeavor.

There was a special spot
out back behind the house
where the dirt was soft,
a powdery dust.

It coated the roof of my mouth,
got gritty on my teeth,
mixed with the wet of my tongue
and crusted on my lips.

Deep satisfaction,
I remember it still:
ingesting the body
of the beloved—
my first communion.

Logjam

Mary Eliza Crane

The logjam broke, washed downstream
and reassembled at the mouth of the river.
The main channel shifted north
and cut away the bank to a sharp curve.
Gravel deposits on the opposite side
dropped riffles where ouzel bobble in the surf.

I contemplate the tangle of riverine dynamics,
anticipate the changes with every coming
turbulence and flood. If I can stay ahead
I won't be swept away when the water rises.

Nothing stays the same.
Your age, or the hue of my hair.
Growing old together was supposed to be a figure of speech.
We order our lives to the wheel of the seasons,
swell and fall of the river, and phase of the moon.
We believe in next year's corn.
The run of the salmon renews the earth,
but leaves a rotting carcass on the shore.

Even trees grow old and die
and fall to rest in the bed of the earth.
I have grown, procreated, will decompose,
and reconfigure into future forms of being.
I can embrace this as a spiritual thing,
but being alive in this moment
is more linear than I care to concede.

Let's rest a while by the mouth of the river
and commune with a dead tree.
Let water rise over our feet.

The Other Virgin

Sharon Cumberland

Yes, an angel came to me, walking over the dirt
and rocks we try to raise grain in. No,
he had no wings, nor lilies in his hands,
just that look all men have when they want
a woman to do something for them.
It had not rained for months, we scavenged
for anything to stay alive. I was glad
when he said God sent him. I thought
Rain at last! Or perhaps he brings manna.
But all he wanted was the same old thing—
get married, have a son. Do your duty.
They all think a boy will save everything,
when it's the girl who does the hard work:
the washing, cooking, hauling water from the well,
the spinning, the weaving cloth, the scraping
grains from dust. I was sick to death of saying yes,
and so I said No, go away. Yes, I felt a twinge,
but it didn't last. Just this once, I said to myself,
Just this once, let some other girl pay.

The Great Snake Hunt

Chris Espenshade

The Great Snake Hunt occurred when we were eighth- or ninth-graders. It was prompted by a long-standing argument about the geographical range of the water moccasin. My friend Billy had volunteered for a few months at a local nature center. One of their main attractions among the school groups was a display of North Carolina snakes, which included a water moccasin. Billy told the director of the center that we had all seen water moccasins in our neighborhood, outside of Winston-Salem. The director allowed that, no, water moccasins were not found this far west. It was the classic clash of book learning and practical knowledge.

While out fishing, trapping, hunting, frog-gigging, and generally stomping around, many of us had seen water moccasins. Their distinctive, thick body shape and diamond-shaped head were not easily confused with the common water snake, nor with any of the other poisonous snakes in our area. In an early attempt to prove the director wrong, Billy caught a small catfish, maybe three inches long. He put the catfish on a larger hook, and cast it among the large rocks, where we frequently saw snakes. The rocks were right next to Mill Creek, just below the dam that formed the fishing lake. The fish only thrashed for a few seconds before the water moccasin struck. Billy had a good fight for maybe thirty seconds, until the line was rubbed through on the edge of the rocks. The catfish had fallen off during the struggle, and when Billy retrieved it with the longest stick he could find, there were clear fang marks and poisoned flesh. And, yet, the director remained a disbeliever.

Thus, the Great Snake Hunt was clearly required. Armed with snake sticks—a three foot long section of one by one inch lumber with a retractable wire loop stapled to it—burlap bags, and a four by four inch stop sign post salvaged downstream, four or five of us (all the usual suspects) returned to the large rocks. We began prying and moving and rocking the rocks, catching up any serpents to slither forth. The action was fast and furious, and we barely had time to throw one snake in the sack before having to snare another. In five minutes, we had captured seventeen snakes. Nobody had seen an obvious water moccasin during the melee, but things had been going pretty fast. Now, having seventeen snakes in three sacks, the question became how do we check them all without any escaping?

As a little aside, Billy and I had disturbed a green heron nest one summer. We were so fascinated that we could easily capture the chicks, we didn't really think too clearly. As a result, we both had adopted a heron for the summer, and we both were fishing a lot to keep the herons healthy and growing. I was out one morning catching some bream (sunfish, to the non-Southerners), when I spied a snake in a lake-side bush. I quickly snagged it, and eventually captured it. I figured herons eat snakes, and it was probably one or two meals. I did not know then that certain water snakes bear their young live, and I did not know that this particular mother snake was about ready to burst. When I got home, I slit the belly to gut the snake. Mordecai, my heron, was standing by as probably twenty baby snakes slithered forth. He needed no training and no coaxing to dispose of the meal. By the way, at the end of the summer, I turned Mordecai loose. He flew across the back end of the lake, attempted to land in a bush, and promptly fell in the water, suffering only bruised pride. From then on, any time any green heron called on the lake, my mom was sure it was Mordecai saying hello.

Meanwhile, scanning the three sacks, Billy, the de facto Master of the Hunt, decided it best that we haul our catch to the sand bar at the other end of the twelve acre lake. The sand bar was devoid of vegetation or any hiding places.

What's more, if a snake did make it to the water, we could catch it again as it swam. Once we arrived at the sand bar, we tried to pour out the snakes one at a time. The best analogy is probably the quintessential Southern waitress trying to give you a little more ice from the iced tea (sweetened, of course, Honey) pitcher, without spilling all of the ice. As the snakes hit the ground in ones, twos, or threes, we would again snare them and pry open their mouths. Billy was desperate to find fangs. Alas, despite a huge haul by any measure, and despite targeting the known hangout of a poisonous snake, we struck out. In the end, we turned them all loose on the sand bar at the same time, and watched the befuddled snakes head for home.

I told my family about the hunt over dinner that evening. Rather than showing any concern that we had purposefully gone looking for a poisonous snake, my parents were only worried that the snakes had not been abused. This provides a little window into my childhood, and how good it was.

It was probably several years later when I read John Steinbeck's episode about the Great Frog Hunt. I remember wondering if the other students in the class had any possible means of relating to the story, having never fought an epic battle themselves.

In the end, Billy never convinced the director. A new director arrived a year later (according to Billy, the old director had probably been bitten by a water moccasin, dying in denial: "You can't be a water moccasin. Those can't be fangs.") and the new director completely agreed with Billy that water moccasins were present in the area. 📖

Degrade, painting/mixed media by Vivian Calderón Bogoslavsky

Balancing Solitude and Loneliness

Anne Frantilla

I've always craved time alone. In fourth grade, it was a stack of books from the library and the luxury of my own bedroom. In my twenties, it was a day I could stay home all day, not leave the apartment, not talk to anyone. I somehow knew time alone helped me survive in this world, stay centered, stay afloat.

For awhile in my early twenties, I had a Latin American boyfriend who was always around people, usually his family and their friends. There was always an event, a party, a picnic, dancing, music, food, something that meant large groups of people. I tried it out. I tried to pretend I was having fun. But, I never smiled enough, I didn't want to drink as much alcohol as everyone else, and I ended up exhausted long before whatever event it was ended. I got tired of being alone in the middle of a party. And eventually, I figured out the relationship wasn't a good one for me.

By the time I was in my thirties, I'd figured out that moving—whether walking, hiking, running, biking or swimming—made me work better as a person, just be a better person all around. Part of that, I can see now, is that while doing any of those moving things I was usually alone. I'd started doing the little triathlons, sprint triathlons they're called, because it forced me to move three different ways. It kept me busy and gave me an excuse to be alone. I trained by myself, and loved my time alone. Maybe it was a counterbalance to being in the workplace forty hours a week, around other people all day.

Once I had kids, time alone was more difficult. But, I also didn't find myself craving it so much. My baby girl was born, then a baby boy. They were so different; they smelled so wonderful. I fell in love with each of them, so wonderfully themselves. So easy to love. I loved time alone together as a family. Raking piles of Michigan leaves to jump and roll in, we all moved together. Splashing in the water at Friends Lake, we floated through the summer. Sledding down the hill at Hunt Park, we didn't mind pink cheeks in the January cold. Moving together was better than moving alone.

Years later, in my forties, navigating my teenage daughter's foray into a never-ending midnight of drugs and alcohol, I had to come face to face with myself. I tried books. I tried counselors. I tried support groups. I tried everything I could think of to escape the loneliness, to find someone to stand in the darkness with me. I still ran, but knew I was running in order not to sit still with myself. In the end, the decisions were mine. The decision to ask the court to help parent her, the decision to transport her to a wilderness program, the decision to keep her sober until she was eighteen, even if it meant she was far from us. This was loneliness, not solitude. Lonely, in part, because I didn't like the person making these decisions. Alone, I was the person who didn't feel like a good mom, the mom who felt helpless and unsure, the mom who lost her temper, the mom who said things she wished she hadn't and couldn't take back, and, worst of all, the mom who was losing the family she loved, the family she moved with.

Chasing my daughter's childhood into a dark cave of self-destructive adolescence, I realized I couldn't run away anymore. The not "good enough" feeling had to change. I couldn't depend on anyone else for my strength or my clarity. In order to be good enough, I had to learn to like the person I was. I had to like the person who picked up her daughter at 2 AM from the police car with the blue lights flashing or the person who attended the high school open house knowing her daughter was failing over half her classes. As I started to find myself "good enough," I slowly felt stronger. I found a way to run with myself instead of away from myself. It was easier to say no when I wanted to say yes, easier to talk with my son about the craziness in our family, easier to ask my neighbor about the parent support group she attended. By the time I came out of the cave, I found myself at my own door, as the poet Derek Wolcott says, and I was good enough. Loneliness was being with the person I didn't like; solitude was satisfying the craving to be alone with a person I loved, someone who was good enough.

I can see now that my mom struggled with solitude and loneliness, although I resisted seeing that while she was alive. She incorporated tools into her life that I use now, like yoga and meditation—ways of being with yourself that help you find ways to like yourself. She seemed to isolate herself, though, without meaning to; my sister and I never knew if we'd be met by sarcasm or kindness when we came down the stairs to the kitchen in the morning. We protected ourselves by staying out of her way. In the house we were together, but each alone. She wanted the family to go to church but she went to the early 8 AM service, alone, while my dad took my sister and I to the 10 AM family service. On backpacking trips in the North Cascades, she hiked ahead, alone, so she could hike faster, get more intense exercise. Our dad stayed back to hike with us, playing "I Spy" or letting us look for a rock or log to sit on at the end of the next bend so we could stop for water and trail mix. She thought she could control how much her grown-up daughters loved her by offering "this" in exchange for "that." We knew she loved us but her love didn't speak in a way we could hear. We saw her as not good enough and she must have felt it.

I don't know if she struggled with being good enough. She must have known she needed time alone and maybe she found it at the early morning service or ahead of us on the trail. Maybe she didn't mean that she didn't want to be with us, maybe she just took that time alone where she could find it, as self-protection. Now that she's gone, I wonder some-times if I would be able to speak to her in a way she could hear, or listen for loneliness in her words, now that I know a little more about the stabbing pain of loneliness.

In my fifties, it's easier to find the kind of solitude I crave. Being forced into a corner as my daughter's mother helped me escape the loneliness my mother must have experienced. I still crave time alone. I still move a lot. But my favorite part of the day is an early summer morning where I can sit outside in the back, possibly in the very same spot my mom sat in the afternoons to drink her tea, and drink my coffee. I take my first sip, listening to the quiet sounds of the morning waking up: the neighbors on one side stirring, getting ready for work, my neighbor on the other side getting back from her early morning walk. I sit, still and alone, relishing the solitude, and my own company. I savor being with myself in my own lucky life. 📖

Ode to the Waitress

CMarie Fuhrman

who doesn't mind
when she is called
waitress. Who knows
serving is a euphemism
for time spent locked
in the prison next door
where the sons of the mothers,
husbands of wives serve
ten to life or twenty while
their warned children wait
for refills of cherry Coke
and the waitress, waits
until the women unlock
their clutched faces, return
smiles before giving
them a check that never
includes the coffee,
the refills, the extra
bacon on the BLT
that the cook, who looks
out from behind the ticket
window adds to the toast
before ringing the bell, free
as he is from the said same
prison where a visit
was the extra meat
the inmate rarely got. So ode
to the cook, too, then, who confesses
in bacon, who checks

his principles while he watches
the waitress talking, stealing
glances only at the tips
the guards give
such as how other jobs, other
engagements may give her more
chances to escape this prison
town and beat-down
look on the faces of the just
released stopping only for directions
and sweet potato fries
before blowing by this big house
town, so owed
by its inhabitants whose
dues are paid by
the state or the fed, who
clock out and walk out
from behind concrete walls
into mortgaged walls, who,
god love them,
spend the better part
of their lives as servers
and who, like the waitress,
like the cook, like
the sons and husbands, do their time
penned up in uniforms, in support
soles, in dirty white aprons
dishing out compassion
with paper napkins one free
slice of meat at a time.

Unloading

David D. Horowitz

I stuff more meetings into calendar and cram
Responsibilities; soon leisure cannot breathe.
I sprint through morning schedule, brake through traffic jam,
Text "I'll b L8. Jam. C u soon." I smile and seethe,
Imagine weeping myself calm. And then I rush
Once traffic clears and pray I don't cause accidents.
But now . . . No, please. Please, nothing. Just a tranquil hush.
Please. Nothing. Let me sit here. Please don't make me tense.
Just nothing. Clear the underbrush. No meetings. Time's
A room where I can play. Tell jokes to jonquils. Laugh
At dust. I needn't guide a novice, lead five teams,
And run for city council. Now I need to loaf
And not be told I owe. I love this scarlet rose,
Vase, lamplit valley view. I love how twilight glows.

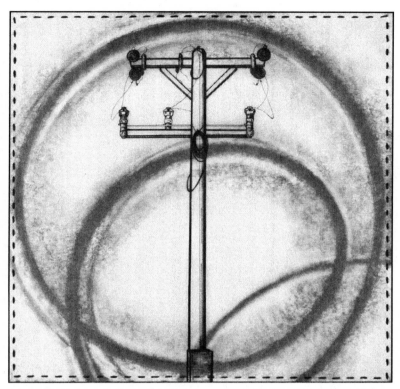

Edit–High Tension, ink, charcoal & thread on paper / glassine, 2005, by Paul Flippen

Consejo para el Equinoccio Otoñal

Rafael Jesús González

Andar en equilibrio no es fácil—
    pisar tan ligeramente
    que la hierba no se doble,
    pisar tan firmemente
    que nuestra huella señale
    el camino por la maleza.

En verdad nuestra naturaleza parece
ser sin balance,
    un pie pisando tan ligeramente
    el otro tan firme
        que perdidos en el desierto
        siempre caminamos en círculo.

Hay peores destinos; entonces
aprendamos a caminar el círculo en gozo.
Las estaciones voltean y vuelven
y no hay a donde ir;
    la Tierra es hogar suficiente;
    el camino, demasiado breve,
    a nada nos lleva.

    Para aprender a andar en balance
        practica el baile.

Advice For the Fall Equinox

Rafael Jesús González

Walking in balance is not easy—
  to step so lightly
  the grasses are not bent,
  to step so firmly
  one's track points
  a way through the thicket.

Indeed it seems our nature to be
off balance,
  one foot stepping so lightly
  one so firmly
    that lost in the desert
    we always walk in a circle.

There are worse fates; let us then
learn to walk the circle in joy.
The seasons turn & return
one upon the other
& there is nowhere to go;
  the Earth is Home enough;
  the walk, all too brief,
  leads Nowhere.

  To learn to walk in balance
    practice the dance.

Side by Side

Alicia Hokanson

*In forms of life other than human, there is a vitality that
isn't trapped in the sorrow.*
—Brenda Hillman

all around the clearing
summer's gold fuse firing the alders

the click and sway of juncos
gliding to grass-light
under apple trees

first heat from the wood
stove kindled to flame;
coffee in the blue cup

while the radio reports
police have shot
another child armed
only with his blackness,

and refugees spilling
from flimsy boats
mass at ragged borders . . .

hummingbirds buzz
the closed blooms of honeysuckle
twining the porch rail

on the trail to the beach:
kingfisher poised on his low branch
chatters before the dive

walking barefoot along the low tide's
selvage, where creamy foam
wreathes our ankles

the only footprints on the beach
the ones we are making,
that the sea dissolves
as if we had never been

Raptor

Jill McCabe Johnson

Today in a flutter of leaves
a sharp-shinned hawk balanced
with one leg tucked under
his freckle-feathered chest
on a fence post
at the edge of our garden.

To get a closer look
I crawled through the living
room and onto the porch
crept to the ledge
and quietly lifted my head.

The hawk turned
razor eyes toward mine
with a gaze that sliced
open wonder
and startled that other
wild bird flapping
against the fenced cage
of my chest.

On the Banks of the Teanaway River

Susan Johnson

Mountain bluebird lightens the pines,
snowfields let go their winter hold,
churn brown in roiled crests,
bear blackened branches of
charred trees to a final rest.

You have lifted beyond our bond,
summon our sorrow to rise with you.
Your song drifts down to us
from green of needled branches
in trembling throats of birds.

The Khan Rules

Eugenia Kim

A man peers into the stroller and says, is that a Mongolian?

It may have been late fall or early winter in 1989, since I rarely took Van outdoors his first months home. He was a June-born premie measured in grams until at a five pounds he was released from the hospital in August. His medical monitor was hidden under a blanket in the bottom rack of the reclined stroller. On this day, we were at the National Gallery of Art, in what was probably his second public outing.

His first was to see the inaugural display of The NAMES Project AIDS Memorial Quilt on the Washington, D.C. Mall—Van in a front body sling I'd sewn myself sitting by his Isolette incubator. Jeff and I walked the yellow fabric paths between the panels and found our friends' quilts. The bionic baby's electrode wires trailed around to the monitors in my backpack, and I thought his little breathing noises were cute until I understood he was gasping for breath in this position against my chest. I was an unsure new mother, especially unsure for a baby this fragile.

The National Gallery had broad beige walls and smelled of cold stone and regulated humidity. Clusters of people jockeyed to view the artwork around obstructing heads and shoulders—too crowded for a stroller.

Neonatal specialists had charted Van's almond-shaped eyes, measured the distance between them, commented on his flat nose bridge, his pear-shaped nose. I said, couldn't that be from me? Jeff is Norwegian plus other Caucasian races; I am all Asian of Korean descent.

The man who asks is eager, earnest. We are near a blank wall, waiting for an opening to ease out of the crowd. He is

Should've Never, digital art by Henry Hu

ignorant of the inappropriateness in his question; one that is inappropriate on so many levels that I'm not sure which inappropriate observation he has addressed.

We knew little to nothing. We'd been told he might not walk. His muscles were soft—they said, *a floppy baby*. I thought of marionettes, seals, rag dolls, Silly Putty. But none of that really mattered; he was breathing, eating—a tweak of a smile now and then.

When Van is one year old, and I take him to the park down the street, I sense other mothers staring at him. At us. Now monitored only when sleeping, they cannot see the sticky terminals stuck to his chest nor the flowing wires tucked into his trousers, but they see his feet encased in strange orthotics, his limp legs and arms, those wide-apart almond eyes across a flat bridge. All of his facial differences shift seamlessly into my differences, and after a few failed attempts at friendly (and one what's-wrong-with-him response), I cease making overtures as a way to avoid the comparisons, the measuring up without a scale for Van. Or me.

Home from the gallery exhibition, Jeff and I laugh, incredulous, and wish we'd been quick-witted enough for rejoinders.

In 1989, the People First movement was still a novelty—the literal positioning of "people" before the disability: people with disabilities instead of disabled people, or the handicapped, the mentally challenged, retarded citizens. Mongoloids.

I wish I'd said, do you mean like Genghis Khan? Do you mean the New Ashmolean Marching Society and Student Conservatory Band?

Two years at Easterseals, a child development center, then age three and newly taking steps on his own, Van is in physical therapy in a public school setting mandated for early intervention. I attend his therapies, sitting in a little kid's wooden chair across from Van and the therapist, who are in a diorama of red and blue mats and big inflated stability balls. She straps yellow plastic Playskool roller skates on top of his orthotics. Each skate has sturdy Velcro bands and six plastic wheels wide enough to keep a toddler steady. She helps him stand and take a step. The wheels spin and he falls. And again. Isn't it a little early for roller skates, I ask. She says he needs to learn how to fall.

The man by the stroller is sincere and unaware. Curious? Well-intentioned? Needy? Is he a father, too? Nearby but standing apart is a woman who appears to be attached to him. I visualize her as arms crossed, tapping a foot, but that's probably projecting.

We enroll Van in a special education school where he learns how to talk, run, button his shirt, read and write, and he graduates from post-high school at age twenty-two. After an internship, he will work at the National Institutes of Health to collect and clean wheelchairs, deliver hospital equipment, and pick up lab specimens in twice-daily rounds. Alone, he will take the subway and a shuttle to and from the hospital. He will thrive in his job, his route peppered with waves and guy-half-hugs from people he's befriended.

Gripping the stroller handle, astonished by the man's question, I say no, he's half Korean.

Much much later, after genetic testing gets sophisticated enough to identify his disability, I could've said he has 17q21.3 microdeletion syndrome, meaning a seizure disorder, weak muscles, droopy larynx, two years of vomiting, going blind in six weeks with cataracts at age eleven (and its surgical correction), thick lips, a round-tipped nose, vitiligo, congenital happiness, and good-old fashioned mental retardation. Even later there's an official name and a website with a support group. And still the geneticist can't say for sure if what prompted you to say *Mongolian* results from the missing shard of genome or the mother's genes.

He will become a painter in his teens, and his work will sell for hundreds. In his twenties he will play the shekere, tamborine, and caxixi with a Ghanaian drumming group. His short-short stories will be funny and his poems will surprise. He will text frequently and send out rows and rows of happy faces, thumbs up, heart and kiss emoji. I will frame and hang in my kitchen entryway the notebook paper on which he scrawled his rules for living:

1. Be nice to people
2. Do good work
3. Make art
4. Be healthy

At the park down the street, I spread a cotton duvet cover on a corner of grass down from the playground by the hedgerow near a squirrel run, and tickle one-year-old baby Van beside me. His calm features are chubby now, with merry eyes and whole-mouth smiles. I lift him against the sky and he laughs and laughs, the blue behind him intense and wide, a clear hue of immeasurable depth. He claps to hold the crisp sweet summer in his hands, and I grasp the folds of his soft orange t-shirt as he soars in his flight, taking me with him. 📖

Ode To A Dog

Barbara Johnstone

I hope the dog was named—I praise his name.
I praise his early life that I don't know

but still I'll write what maybe was: praise
the brown-spotted pup that ran erratic

zigzags past rocks, in and out of waves;
rested in shade of the uprooted fir

and snapped at sea foam. Praise to his humans—
he must have had humans—who threw sticks

for him on the waves those good years the mill
was hiring. I'll guess—the man sorted green lumber

'til the mill closed. He bought dog food first
when his government check arrived;

by the end of the month he dumpster-dived.
But he got booze-sick; his wife got sick too

and they were evicted. Praise them who played
with the dog 'til they couldn't and bless

them who ditched him—now I'm telling truth—
to scavenge the beach past six-pack rings, cracked

chunks of Styrofoam, tires and broken shells
for some bologna sandwich a kid dropped.

Praise fleas that scavenged his blood, left scabs;
squirming maggots that ate dying flesh,

left holes; mange that took fur off his back,
right rump. Praise the gull eaten out by crows;

praise its stench that dragged the dog by his nose
near a triangle of logs and thank you,

thank you to the dog that bedded down
in those logs, laid his sticking-out ribs

against the ribs of the sleeping girl
and gave her his dead-animal-smell warmth.

Praise him and his humans. He remembered
them, leaned on her leg, leaned more when she

shoved him away and—I'm telling you truth
so I'll say this—kicked him once as they walked

down the beach, past crows congregated
on a broken fence line, past gulls gathered

with yelping cries, to the rip tide that would
take her out past the breakers to sink. Bless him,

he herded her away from the water
again and again. Yes, Dog, you did this.

You stayed with her all day without food, kind
words or touch. Forty-some-odd years later,

I say—no, I shout—wherever you are
I shout, Dog, thank you, and Dog, I'm sorry.

Then A Glint

Sarah E.N. Kohrs

there are
>no birds' black silhouettes rising into a cloud

there is
>only the sun's slant across the gray shadows

then a glint
>gleams like a tocsin up the still city-street.

on either side cement-white buildings & bridges
barricade as readily as thorny acacia branches
woven into its own tapestry, depicting only itself:

no ring of ripened quince trees, no solemn-mouth's
chanting, no purview of a river valley well-loved
by steeples & smoking chimneys, no delicate unicorn.

there are
>cars amassed moving in retrospect of traffic laws

there is
>no unstudied guide for anyone not living here

then a glint
>and I am driving toward incoming headlights.

Rain on Glass, Shenandoah Valley, Virginia, 2014,
photograph by Sarah E.N. Kohrs

Passing by an apartment building

Daniel Lee

A woman eats her
soup in the rain   she has found
the secret to more

Blue

David Lukas

The most important facts I know
I learned in bars or bedrooms
ignoring, of course
all those runs along the mountain
after a storm
when the sky exploded
and god spoke to me
about love this
and soul that

but what I know of people
of the ones reading this now
I learned sitting
on a barstool
watching lovers talk to strangers
and spill beer on each other

I learned lying
beneath a blanket
listening to you sleep
dreaming of me
I hope
but maybe
dreaming of someone else.

A Yellowish November in Bellingham

Jamie McGillen

Through a small square window in the upper loft of the Woods Coffeehouse, I see blue ocean rippling under the weight of the sky. A kayak skims through my framed piece of the Pacific, then only water. I smell roasted coffee beans and white chocolate raspberry scones baking. Not the hard kind; these are moist, like muffins with chunks of white chocolate melted, covered with powdered sugar.

On the streets leaves turn gold, drift to the ground, leaving trees half-naked. They carpet grass, sidewalks, parked cars. The season has changed slowly this year. Leaves cling to their branches—many are still shades of green. It's a yellowish November, with few reds and browns. Streets are lined with yellow trees afraid to change, to be so naked.

Buses blur by as I walk and strangers pass me on the left, heads down, headphone wires dripping from ears into pockets. Bumper stickers from parked cars: *Pacifism Kicks Ass, Namaste, Question the answers, The government should be afraid of its people, not the other way around.*

Here is what you need to do to blend in on the streets of Bellingham: Walk briskly—you have somewhere to go, you're getting exercise, and you're taking care of the environment by not driving. For all anybody knows, you are walking from your front door to your destination. Don't carry an umbrella—even if the wind is blowing at such an angle the rain goes up your nose. Wear a hood and deal with your soaked clothes like everyone else. Do not lock eyes with people as you pass them on the street. If you accidently do, either look down at the street quickly, or nonchalantly look past the person and move your eyes to an object somewhere behind the stranger—the eye contact was purely coincidental as you scanned the horizon.

I see a pink rose, thorny and clustered. It's nearly dead, blooming to excess with its outermost petals browning and pushing away. Delicately peeling off the dying petals, I breathe the unexpected scent that comes from a rose blooming through frost. In my enthusiasm to get my nose even closer, I yank the thorny stem to my face, smacking my upper lip and splashing dew on my glasses.

Leaves raked into uniform piles on yards blow rebelliously around, onto the streets, in heaps in between cars, high up into the air. Wind and leaves spin around me, making whirling tornadoes. My mind tries to anticipate the direction it will blow next, but instead I let myself enjoy the unknown, the beauty of surprise. A short man with dark hair strides down the street, a trail of leaves chasing him, blowing him forward.

I sit down next to the statue-man sitting leisurely on the bench in Fairhaven; he watches over my shoulder as I write. The bench is cold, but the sun is shining through stubborn leaves still clinging to trees. I consider striking the same pose as my relaxed friend: leaning way back, both arms resting softly on the back of the bench. His coat is lying gently beside him—politely close enough to him as to leave enough room for me. His left ankle rests on his right knee. I recreate his position and it feels fine.

I hear the hum of construction truck engines—the clang and pound of a jackhammer around the corner. Cobblestone restoration that requires drilling through destroyed brick first. A boy has tied his dog to a bench while he shops at Village Books. The dog is black and white; he looks like a little cow, tongue hanging out. There is a man sitting on a neighboring bench. He's wearing tiny glasses that make his eyes look enormous, like a fly. His face shows strain from the

Leaves of Autumn, Shoreline, Washington, 2017, photograph by Phoebe Bosché

walk he just completed and his body melts into the bench. I see myself through the enormous eyes of this man. He is a mirror. We share silence.

The smell and sight of the ocean can't reach me here, but I know it's only a few blocks away. Three teenage girls with overflowing ice cream cones pass me without a glance in my direction. They sit down on brick steps near the grass in the last light of the setting sun.

Now, walking through Bellingham nightlife, lamp posts shine on Railroad Avenue, while people swarm from bar to bar, enjoying Saturday night in a college town. Lines of people wait to get hands stamped. A homeless man has a kitten on a leash and some drunk girls have stopped to play with it. The man watches them with distrust.

Dark evergreen trees reach the night sky while the moon rises through their branches. The town rests as the tide laps loyally on the rocky shore. As I drift off to sleep I am warmed by the thought that I have been both seen and ignored in perfect measure by all the strangers in Bellingham. 📖

Leaning Into the Grip

Jayne Marek

Placing the oyster knife against the vee
at the longer end of the bottom shell,
I press the blunt tip in, as I've been told,
and wiggle and twist—inelegantly,
spraying white bits, liquor, grit—a messy
end for this fighter's fist of a bivalve
knuckled like conglomerate in my palm.
This knife means business, though, and so with me—
it's time to learn how we eat what we eat,
how to kill, even to this simple end,
so that I understand my appetites
and take responsibility, open
my guilt as I open this oyster, grasp
the balance between pity and ruthlessness.

To Eat

Gigi Marks

Buds on the small branches
that you can reach, head lifted up,
small branch tips and twigs
that brush the grazing face,
bark that can pull away in plates
or strips or one piece against
the insistence of mouth and teeth,
dried berries, too, on limbs
that shake in the wind, that hold on
into February when little else
decorates the river birch or alder
or whatever else that might feed you.
Grass under snow, flattened and
only barely green, scraped clear
and free, the impatient shoots
that break dormancy for early warmth,
they seem to wave a hand to you,
call to you, and you will find them,
bend down to them and eat.

April 1

Gigi Marks

You do not need to melt the snow
and swell the roots below with all its sudden surging
and you do not need to pull each
green leaf from the still closed bud or
shake the frost off icy branches, and you do
not need to bring the spring geese back, the robins,
and fill each blade of grass with green
and lift the early chick from its broken shell.
You do not need to bring the flying bee
out into the sun one by one
or find the place for it to be fed:
the first purple crocus—bright yellow stamened—
that you did not need to bring to flower with your
breath or with your hands or fingers
but flower it has, anyway, and feeds the bee.

Endless Dread, digital art by Henry Hu

Emerald Mound, Looking Glass Prairie, Illinois

Ruby Hansen Murray

The bus crosses the Mississippi and drives toward gentle bluffs beyond the hard-up city of East St. Louis. I'm on a tour with the Osage Nation Historic Preservation Department. We're staying in St. Louis, following the route commuters take from the city. We travel roads our Osage ancestors walked between Cahokia and the Big Mound that gave St. Louis its nickname. It's threatening rain when we pull up beside a small shopping center that anchors a new subdivision. We're meeting a husband and wife archeology team from the University of Illinois who are coordinating summer digs at nearby Emerald Mound, an older and more sacred site than Cahokia. The modern subdivision overlooks the soft green of the bottomland. The one paved street is called Wakanda Drive, and I wonder if Osages live here.

We're in an area that was once filled with villages associated with the agrarian civilization of Cahokia. They radiate out from the Great Mound where the high priest lived, called Monks Mound today, because of Belgian Trappist monks who arrived centuries after Cahokia peaked around 1200 CE. The Trappists stayed long enough to plant an orchard before they went home.

We're visiting an older group of temples near Looking Glass Prairie. Mounds line the routes that connect these sites with those in Illinois and Missouri. We walk uphill from the shopping center and Wakanda Drive to the modern highway that overlies the Vincennes Trace. The suburbs here are bedroom communities for St. Louis; workers hopscotch all over East St. Louis to work at corporations like Express Scripts, Monsanto, Arch Coal, Pfizer, and Edward Jones.

St. Louis Gateway Arch, seen from Monks Mound at Cahokia, 2015,
photograph by Ruby Hansen Murray

A developer named Tommy Bow has built a subdivision over and among the rolling mounds. Some were likely dwellings, some were funerary, and each has a story to tell about the people who lived here. Modern houses with big lawns line the road. A white Southern-mansion style building has benches and a flagpole set on a mound.

It feels strange to contemplate the distance between what is underfoot and the life around us. Some homeowners allow their property to be surveyed and some don't. I think of a Chippewa friend whose town built a playground on known burial mounds in Wisconsin. "No, we don't go there," he said.

A golf tee stands on top of one of the larger mounds in the Trees Golf Club.

Developer Tommy Bow was fined $144,000 by the Illinois Historical Protection Agency for bulldozing a road that the agency said destroyed a significant portion of the site. Bow named streets for himself, such as Bow Drive, and named Wakanda Drive after our Creator.

Before lunch, we're back on the bus, nosing up a narrow driveway between newly plowed fields toward a tree-covered hill. Emerald Mound is fifty feet tall, a landmark on this rolling river bottom. There is evidence of five Cahokian mounds and a village close by. A blonde woman comes from a modern-looking house to direct us to park near a barn and a silo. Covered with tarps, the archeological site faces west. Beyond the dig, fields of mocha soil, and in the distance trees curl like hair along a creek. We meet archeologists, both graduate students and faculty, working on the project. Young men and women bend over open squares with sieves and buckets. There's a tent, a buffet table with lunch and gift bags, coolers of lemonade, and folding chairs set in a horseshoe.

The American Bottom is Mississippi River flood plain, formed of loess like the Palouse country in eastern Washington State where the soil can be 246 feet thick. Winds blew silt from mud exposed when glaciers melted, depositing the finest particles into bluffs. The long, gentle swells of this land, the few green stands of trees, cottonwoods maybe, along the creeks, with the soil open to the sky, make me feel I'm standing on an ocean bed.

Archeologist Susan Alt explains the survey that has identified temples across the site. I wonder how it would feel to sit out here when the team has gone home. Some of the research staff is barefoot and some wear sandals. Their calves are smeared with mud. I picture them cleaning up after a hot day and heading to Collinsville or St. Louis for drinks. The farmer's girlfriend comes to talk. She tells me she comes from a nearby town—Summerfield, maybe.

"I make sure to come out whenever the moon is full." She sounds like a person who feels the vibrations in crystals.

"I'd like to be here at night, too," I say. The land has a softness in daylight; I imagine the palpable darkness of a warm night.

"When I walk at sunset or sunrise I can feel those early people." She has ashy-blonde hair and is in her late thirties.

"That's when I find them just sitting on the ground." She means shards of pottery, pieces of stone.

"I don't dig for them, but if they're here, I think they're a gift." Like so many white women I've worked with, she seems to have a comfortable New Age religion. She waits for me to say something.

Osages seldom answer an outsider's questions and rarely explain to people how offensive they are. I remember how long it took for James to tell one of the California Osages, whose campaign speeches were like other American stump speeches, full of things he and his family had accomplished, *don't say that, you sound like you're bragging.* I remember Mogri Lookout talking about the questions he receives from mixed-blood Osages about bringing their sons into the I'n-Lon-Schka. *They ask me if they can bring 'em in. They ask me, but I can't tell 'em.*

I catch up with the group walking up the north side of the mound beside a field with corn taller than any of us. Our elder is in Susan Alt's SUV, while we walk the path some of the project people cleared. We take a picture on top of the mound, surrounded by brushy maples and ash. We are a clump of people in jeans and summer clothes. Osages with brown or black hair, the light brown hair of French-Osages, a blonde non-Osage nurse who grew up in Pawhuska and our red-haired Osage archeologist Andrea Hunter and her staff. We all look pleased.

We sit under the white tent for lunch, in the kind of reflected light a photographer could make use of. Timothy Pauketat explains his theories that these temples may have been part of the cause of Cahokia blossoming so quickly. He says Emerald Mound is oriented to a lunar eclipse that occurs only once every eighteen and a half years, a process that was known to Cahokians long before Europeans understood it. There's the large mound, but there are also many temples that line avenues to Cahokia. I love the idea that you made sacrifices and maybe celebrated your way to the city. I'm also curious that this white man is considering how the Cahokians' values grew, and I wonder how Osage elders sync this with our oral history.

We're here with the Nation's archeologist, an Osage herself, but there's a tenuous relationship between Native people and anthropologists and archeologists. The Native American Graves Repatriation Protection Act was finally passed in 1990. Until then, highway contractors in Iowa, for example, reburied Caucasians, but sent Native remains to museums for study. There's tribal conflict about where to put the people (the remains) if you bring them home. Elders want to know if words were spoken over them in the past and who will do that now.

After lunch Susan Alt shows us hearths in the temple houses. I love the absolute symmetry of the rectangular pits. The dirt doesn't break off in chunks or fall in upon itself, but is stiff enough to be sliced into precise squares in each corner and spooned carefully from a circle where a fire was built 1,000 years ago. Small indentations, tiny dents and scratches in the tan-brown soil show where the archeologists have worked. Susan Alt describes the bags of seeds the people brought to the temple so clearly—tracing the shape of the bags with her hands—that I can feel the size and weight. I imagine the ribbon that might have held them closed.

The Cahokians painted the floor of the temple with yellow plaster. She shows us one man's footprint. Just one large, clear print in the yellow ground. It's as if the golden footprints reminded the people who came to celebrate their life events that they carried the sacred back into the world with them.

Seven hundred years later, we Osages still remember the sacred on the soles of our feet. After we've been to the graveyard, done that sacred duty of starting someone on their journey, we go to the community center to re-enter the world by having a meal together. When we walk up the sidewalk toward the old metal building in Hominy, an elder—last time

Sacred Eagle, Washington State Park, St. Louis, Missouri, 2015,
photograph by Ruby Hansen Murray

it was John Maker—stands with a brazier at his feet and fans
us off with cedar, our face and body, the soles of our feet.

The farmer's girlfriend leads me to the house. It's a
functional space where you can walk inside in muddy boots
without ruining a carpet. There are aerial photographs of
a pioneer's house built higher on the mound. The settler's
house has since burned; there's a picket fence down a grassy
slope. The land is littered with artifacts from those living here.

"We've found these around the place," she says, showing me a basket on the counter holding varied stones, as
well as glass and ceramic fragments. "Would you like one?"
She says. I assume I haven't heard her, and she says it again.
When I travel, I bring home round rocks for paperweights,
but I won't take anything from this place.

Years ago farmers crated up potsherds and sold them by
the roadside. Johnny Morris, the founder of Bass Pro Shops, is
a collector who found many of the artifacts and thousands of

arrowheads displayed in the Ancient Ozarks Natural History Museum at the Top of the Rock. He jokes, "My wife says she's going to put me in AA—Arrowheads Anonymous." They lost a collection when a building burned, so he built the new museum underground. He also peruses the Missouri State Museum of Natural History and has borrowed pieces from the collection. Unfortunately, curators say the items are not stored properly, and they'd like them back.

Before we leave, the girlfriend comes to the tent holding a cardboard box while people stand around saying goodbye. She puts rocks and shards in a line on the table. I can't identify them all; there's a part of a weathered conch shell, like one I have from a hurricane-strewn beach in Galveston. "Take one if you like," she says to Art. She steps closer to me, and says, "I'd like you to have something." I manage a noncommittal face. Art looks at the table and back at her. Dr. Hunter stands under the tent, staring like a peregrine falcon. She looks like she might give a lecture, but after a moment she turns away, still frowning. 📖

To Time in Late August

Jed Myers

Don't tell me. I know. It's you,
catching up from behind,
sound of your steps disguised

in the mix of whispers, wind
through the leaves and the freeway
not far beyond the trees.

Glorious, isn't it, this
late summer mid-afternoon?
You don't have to warn me.

I've been opening drawers,
lifting the old moments out
to hold them up in your light,

each till I see its interior
flame, more than reflection. So
like its own species of small bird,

same as no other, in its turn
it takes flight from my palm. I know,
I'll follow, into your blue body.

There's Only One Dance

Michael O'Brien

There's only one dance and
you're just a dancer.
There's only one question and
there is no answer.
You are your only
choreographer.
The lonely autobiographer.
So keep spinning, turning and
gyrating.
And keep grinning, and learning
and waiting.
Some will convene on a
consensus.
On a style, and we come
to the routine the rest of us
will follow.
The mighty sword of knowledge
thrusts, only in
glancing.
Near the edge is faith and trust
and yet
no one knows why
we are dancing.
The indifference of the universe.
That just is.
Circumstance has spent all
It could never give.
All the varied pirouettes around

Girl On Top, Archival pigment print by Megan Magill

the same point.
Carried by what we can't forget
and what will always
disappoint.
Search for new costumes
and the perfect dress.
Unearth and exhume only to find.
No.
Gilgamesh.
All headed for the same dance hall.
It's the only one we're seeing.
In this web
That is all
a human being.

The Fun In Funambulism

John Olson

I take balance very seriously. The last time I lost my balance, I dislocated a shoulder. My wife took me to the emergency room, for which I was later billed $1,800 (not including the X-rays, which were $100) and, a few weeks later—very much to our shock and surprise—we were billed again, this time by the doctor who attended me in the emergency room. That one came to $800. The doctor palpated my shoulder, looked at my X-rays, and the entire visit took less than fifteen minutes. That doesn't sound like balance to me. That sounds like racketeering. Fortunately, our insurance covered most of the two bills, so a little balance was restored. The practice of being billed twice for the same service is called "balance billing," and although currently legal, Washington State Insurance Commissioner Mike Kreidler is proposing legislation to remedy this nefarious practice.

If the health of our country were examined, the diagnosis would not be good. Confusion, vertigo, lightheadedness, hallucinations, delusional thinking, historical amnesia, blurry vision, morbid obesity, sclerotic ideologies, dysfunctional institutions, willful ignorance, denial, free-floating rage and anxiety, temper tantrums, fits of violence, convulsions, cuts and bruises, bone decay, ulcers, open sores, the impairment of fundamental human needs, chronic diarrhea, and poor hormonal balance are all symptomatic of a system totally out of whack.

We live in a society grossly out of balance. Income inequality is grotesquely asymmetrical, and I'm not just referring to the ignominious one percent. There is also a twenty percent: this is a group of people, mostly professionals, who make more than $117,000 per year. One percenters get the

Liber ludicum (Judges), Kent, United Kingdom, 2017,
photograph by Alexander Chernavskiy

blame for the plummeting incomes of the working class and enslavement in minimum wage jobs while also saddled with debt from a college education or medical bills, which can be daunting even *with* insurance. But, in fact, it's the class distinctions of the twenty percenters that contribute significantly to the miseries of the "have-nots." Thomas Frank observed in a recent interview that tenured professors do little to nothing to help the plight of their colleagues working as adjunct professors. "The de-professionalization of the faculty is another long-running tragedy that gets a little sadder every year," he observes in "Academy Fight Song," an essay that appeared in *The Baffler* in August, 2013:

> . . . as teaching college students steadily becomes an occupation for people with no tenure, no benefits, and no job security. These lumpen-profs, who have spent many years earning advanced degrees but sometimes make less than minimum wage, now account for more than three-quarters of the teaching that is done at our insanely expensive, oh-so-excellent American universities.

Their numbers increase constantly as universities continue to produce far more PhDs than they do full-time, tenure-track job openings, and every time cutbacks are necessary—which is to say, all the time—it is those same full-time, tenure-track job openings that get pruned.

So why aren't the tenured professors stepping up to the plate to defend and protest the egregious mistreatment of their non-tenured colleagues?

Good question. Frank explains it as a matter of ego and meritocracy:

> There is zero solidarity in a meritocracy, even a fake one, as the anthropologist Sarah Kendzior demonstrates in a recent series of hard-hitting articles on the adjunct situation. Just about everyone in academia believes that they were the smartest kid in their class, the one with the good grades and the awesome test scores. They believe, by definition, that they are where they are because they deserve it. They're the best. So tenured faculty find it easy to dismiss the de-professionalization of their field as the whining of second-raters who can't make the grade.

If you shouted "Jesus, what douche bags!" just now, I forgive you.

It's not just academics. Tell a doctor, lawyer, IT worker, college administrator, controller, developer, or financial manager how you just got screwed by your healthcare provider or about your difficulties in making ends meet and their eyes will glaze over. At best, you'll get a shrug of the shoulders. But tell them you voted for Jill Stein in the last election and their head will explode. You will be blamed for Trump. You will be excoriated for not supporting Hillary Clinton. You will be branded as Cain and banished from the realm. You will find yourself living alone in a trailer near Moses Lake,

Washington, seeking solace in opioids and George Bernard Shaw.

What would a society in balance look like? Maybe it wouldn't even be a society. Author Derrick Jensen cites civilization itself as being the central factor in getting everything on our planet so far out of balance that the human species may be extinct by the next millennium. "To pretend that civilization can exist without destroying its own landbase and the landbases and cultures of others is to be entirely ignorant of history, biology, thermodynamics, morality, and self-preservation," writes Jensen in *Endgame: Vol. 1: The Problem of Civilization*.

That ship, it goes without saying, has sailed. We've had civilizations spreading like kudzu on this planet for thousands of years. As soon as people gather by the hundreds in a place and begin drawing on all the resources—water, dirt, minerals, animals, forests, labor—their community must begin colonizing and exploiting and enslaving the outlying resources, other countries, weaker communities. The equation becomes very simple: the civilization with the biggest meanest weapons, the greatest military power, gets it all, rakes it all in with their gargantuan claws. The leader is sometimes someone charismatic and charming who perpetuates all the right metaphors and narratives to make the population feel better about their abuses, but sometimes the leader is just a schmuck who either inherited giant wealth or was equipped with the right sociopathic skills to get what they want and bully other people. A slob, pretty much, on steroids. Godzilla with blonde hair and a fake tan.

Maintaining power is even simpler: just get one group of people to hate the other group of people and they'll be too busy fighting one another to notice how much they're being robbed, oppressed, and exploited.

Musician and poet Patti Smith was recently asked what advice she had for young people trying to make it in New York City. The long-time New Yorker's take? Get out. "New

York has closed itself off to the young and the struggling," she said. "New York City has been taken away from you."

The above paragraph is quoted from Sarah Kendzior's essay, "Expensive Cities Are Killing Creativity." "Creativity," she observes, "—as an expression of originality, experimentation, innovation—is not a viable product. It has been priced out into irrelevance—both by the professionalization of the industries that claim it, and the soaring cost of entry to those professions."

"Over the past decade," Kendzior continues:

. . . as digital media made it possible for anyone, anywhere, to share their ideas and works, barriers to professional entry tightened and geographical proximity became valued. Fields where advanced degrees were once a rarity—art, creative writing—now view them as a requirement. Unpaid internships and unpaid labour are rampant, blocking off industry access for those who cannot work without pay in the world's most expensive cities.

Failure, in an economy of extreme inequalities, is a source of fear. To fail in an expensive city is not to fall but to plummet. In expensive cities, the career ladder comes with a drop-off to hell, where the fiscal punishment for risk gone wrong is more than the average person can endure. As a result, innovation is stifled, conformity encouraged. The creative class becomes the leisure class—or they work to serve their needs, or they abandon their fields entirely.

But creative people should not fear failure. Creative people should fear the prescribed path to success—its narrowness, its specificity, its reliance on wealth and elite approval. When success is a stranglehold, true

Puyallup Ferry, Seattle, Washington, 2017, photograph by Emily Townsend

freedom is failure. The freedom to fail is the freedom
to innovate, to experiment, to challenge.

I recently turned seventy. This is relevant because at age
seventy I can reflect back on a time when it was easy to be a
creative person. After living for a decade in San José, California, I decided, circa 1975, to return to Seattle. San José was
just beginning to morph into Silicon Valley. I saw the early
signs—escalating real estate, aggressively commercialized
industrial parks—and fled. I thought of Seattle, where I'd
gone to high school and my father and brother continued
to live, as an attractive alternative. The gray, gloomy skies,
temperate marine climate, plentiful bookstores, convivial cof-
feehouses, and funky eccentricities would be the ideal place
to get a part time job and pursue a writing career that would
resemble that of Jack Kerouac or Washington State's Richard
Brautigan and Tom Robbins. These were guys that made a
livable income from their writing—not *Fifty Shades of Grey*
or *The Da Vinci Code* writing, crowd-pleasing, conventional

writing that caters to bourgeois tastes, but wildly creative, colorful, idiosyncratic writing. Writing for people who get drunk on language, who get high on novelty, who seek the equivalent of Philippe Petit on a high wire, writing that is exquisitely balanced between order and chaos, between adhering to some rules and circumventing others. You could do that in the 70s, especially in Seattle. Not only were rents eminently affordable (my first studio apartment which had a brick fireplace and spacious kitchen rented for $125 a month), but there was still an audience available, readers willing to spend money on a book of carnivalesque non-sequiturs and lunatic metaphors.

What happened, of course, was beyond ironic. It was a cruel joke. Within a decade of making a new life in Seattle, the counterpart to Apple that is Microsoft bloomed (Audrey II, the plant that needs human blood to survive in *Little Shop of Horrors* comes to mind), soon to be followed by Starbucks, Amazon, and a gazillion little start-up companies awash in IT money. Soon after, writers and artists began making their exodus from the city, forced out by escalating rents. Many found refuge in the fly-over states.

I'm still here. My wife and I are among the older set who established roots before the tsunami of affluence turned Seattle from a funky urban port to a glitzy techno-utopian dystopia of whiny rich people and nail salons. We abide. But the tightrope is wobbly, and there ain't no net. 📖

Heceta Lighthouse, Oregon, 2017, photograph by Emily Townsend

Single Handed

Heidi Seaborn

Hold steady
Ease into the wind
I remember my father's
directive to hold a firm tiller
in headwinds sails luffing.

Sail in, come up, catch the wind's
edge. I know to ride its strong thrust,
anger seething along a straining seam
blowing apart, when to fall
off, let the wind
rage on past. To need
no one, to sail solo.

There Was Always Something Wrong With Her

Anna Reaney

When her father died the crows began to watch Aleta. When she went out, there'd be a dozen or so, up on the wires. As she passed below them, they'd go on ahead and wait for her to catch up. One or two would swoop down to check out a spot about ten feet above her head, then return to the group to click castanets and caw in crow-talk to the others. Aleta had never thought much about the past, but when Father died, dreams came, and trepidation about images that hovered at the edge of thought.

She went to the mental health clinic nearby and interviewed to join a Sexual Abuse Survivor's group. The therapist had dark curly hair that framed her heart-shaped face: "People think I look like the cartoon character Betty Boop, and, since my real name is Betty, they call me Boop," she said, in her sweet Melanie Griffith voice.

Aleta nodded.

"Hmm . . ." Boop tilted her head to one side, "you're not like the others in the group. Frankly, you don't look like a Sexual Abuse Survivor. You look competent. If you join the group I will think of you as being like a Co-Therapist." This sounded wrong to Aleta, but she didn't know the rules.

"You can help me keep the others grounded. You know what they're like, it's a very disturbed cohort, there almost isn't anything to be done to heal that level of trauma . . . but we structure the group in such a way that disturbing things can be brought up safely." Here she demonstrated, holding her hands out flat as if covering a vessel. "Like a pot with a lid: when it threatens to boil over, you lift the lid slightly to

Modern Angel, 2017, drawing by Ndubueze Okonkwo

relieve the pressure." She lifted her hands a bit and looked an enquiry at Aleta to make sure she understood. Aleta didn't move her face at all, but Boop seemed satisfied. "At the first group meeting, bring a short autobiography, to get to know each other."

But at the first meeting, Boop stopped Aleta halfway through her life story, with a giggle. Aleta didn't blame her. She had lived twice as long as the others and knew she was boring to listen to: she spoke in a low voice and tried not to show any emotion. As the weeks went on, she sat and pretended to listen to the women sharing about their abuse. Though she had acute hearing, she didn't hear most of what was said in the group. At a certain point, her brain just seemed to turn off when they talked about that.

She heard one though, the skinny one whose hair was falling out: "I'm living with my abuser, I have no job, I'm losing my kids!" She cried like a baby, her mouth open, her face red. That girl's pot was boiling over. But Boop's face was set like a glazed candy heart. Her eyes, like chocolate kisses, didn't move. Aleta wanted to scream, Lift up the lid! Release the pressure. But her voice was caught in that place just below her throat.

Instead, she walked out. But the outside door to the clinic was locked since it was after 5 PM. Aleta sat there, arms over her head and head between her knees, for several minutes until the night janitor happened to see her and let her out.

Boop called several times, furious: "You know you're required to stay for the whole eight weeks. You signed the contract! At least come in and say goodbye to them. What about all those times I gave you a ride home?" Aleta quit answering the phone.

Then one day there was a story in the newspaper about a woman who had gone to a wooded area and shot herself. She could tell it was the woman from her group, even though the picture in the paper was from a better time, when she was smiling and holding her kids.

* * * *

Jackie was in the elevator, sitting on the bench that folded down from the wall to sit on, and up to let a wheelchair in.

Jackie was always in the elevator. She'd ride up and down all day until it got stuck and then ring the emergency buzzer for several long minutes with that ear-splitting clang. She wore those fuzzy bedroom slippers, her legs crossed in an X and feet splayed out to the sides, elbows resting on her thighs, head down in her hands. But now she angled her face up enough to catch Aleta's eye. She twinkled more than smiled. Aleta responded with a nod.

"What's wrong with you?" Jackie said.

Aleta raised her eyebrows, surprised.

"To live here, there has to be something wrong with you."

Jackie bopped her foot in time to a beat only she could hear, and looked up with a conspiratorial smile. "I'm schizophrenic," she said.

There had always been something wrong with Aleta. She never talked or smiled. It wasn't like she didn't know what was expected. They could see in her eyes that she knew, all right. She just couldn't be bothered. She'd sit there in haughty silence. She acted like she was being forced to sit there, her face tense but inoffensive, like a mask of inoffensiveness, like she knew she was being watched.

Aleta's knee felt like it was dislocated when she walked. Her doctor couldn't see any reason for it, but thought for a moment: "Oh yeah, I had pain like that after a soccer injury once." Physical therapy didn't stop the pain. Then a doctor of Physical Medicine, at the hospital, put her on a tricyclic antidepressant, for knee pain.

She had never slept well, waking after two or three hours, with pain and premonitions. The Celestial Waters and Salts, of the Archangel Michael, had arrived from the All-Spirits Catalog. They were supposed to give protection during sleep. She spread the salts around the bed and anointed her forehead and chest with the water, then meditated after reciting, out loud, the Invocation printed on the card. Then rings of fire circled her body. And there was a tiny angel, typical, golden-haired, with the wings and white robe. Aleta slept all night.

The second night she woke as usual after a few hours. There was a presence a few feet from the bed: like an outline of a man, with big boots and a Stetson hat, it seemed made of pieces of earth, sky, and water, mountains and reefs, forests and seas, like a geographical map, tall and faceless, with patches of dense blank spaces, dark vacuums, between the elemental places. It disappeared when she looked directly at it.

It was three o'clock. There was a heavy breathy sound like panting, she couldn't place: a garbage truck?

She switched on the radio to easy listening and was just going to close her eyes again, when she saw something shiny on the floor in the four-watt circle from the night light. She rose up on an elbow, sending a jab of pain to her neck. She sat all the way up to look at it. Gold, with a braided tail, it was raised up on its back feet, if it had feet, and its antennae twitched toward the light.

A sense of dread filled her. She should get the Glock. No. It was a cockroach. She grabbed a newspaper to bat the bug, knocked it all the way over to the hallway, and she turned on the light there and hit it again and got a can of Raid. It died turning in a circle making a wheel with its head almost touching its long tail. Too late, she realized cockroaches don't have tails. She recalled its antennae lifted to the four-watt bulb. It only wanted to live in the light.

The next day she went off the antidepressant. It wasn't helping her knee. She went back to the mental health clinic, but the group had been disbanded. She could do individual therapy. Boop had recently acquired a Geriatric Counseling Certification.

Boop seemed to accept her, but complained: "I'm not sure how to help you. With others, I can just hold their hand while they cry, but with you. . . ." She shrugged and scrunched her mouth to the side.

Other clients would scream with anger, complain, whine. Aleta was quiet, polite. Father taught her this. He watched her all the time to make sure she learned to zip it, to close down her face, to swallow her words.

To a therapist, that's the goal. So Boop saw her as a friend, saw she was competent and could get a good job and make a lot of money and travel and have a nice place. As Boop put it, "I mean, I have an M.S.W., and a mortgage and a failing marriage. If I can do it, you can."

She told Boop about the crows. "I used to think they were emissaries from my father, they came to me after he died."

Boop tilted her head to one side. "What do you think they want, what is their message?"

"I think they want me to ask him to forgive me."

"So you are saying that he sexually abused you but you need to be forgiven? For what?" "For hating him, for not understanding. He punished me for what his father did to him and I need him to forgive me so he will stop punishing me. I still carry his weight on my head and shoulders." She raised her arms high up as if holding a giant boulder.

Boop sighed. "It does seem your affect is more like someone who is guilty, the way you won't meet my eyes, you aren't emotionally open, you sort of skulk out the door."

"I can see his face looking at me, twisted in pain like a little kid about to cry. He was beaten by his father, and maybe raped. Seeing me at that age gave him so much pain. I caused his pain."

Boop frowned. "Your father abused you because he was abused, but that doesn't excuse him."

"Father and I were the closest to each other of anyone in the family. Now I am alone. Jackie says the crows are my friends, not from Father at all."

"Who is this Jackie?"

"She lives in my building. She hangs out in the elevator all day. I've been talking to her."

Boop frowned and made a note in a notebook she had open on her desk.

"Jackie says the adults want you to give up your true self. They beat it out of you, then replace it with a Play self and they get Play friends for you. But she doesn't accept the fakes, she holds out for the originals, but they are all either Dead or Co-opted.

"Jackie thinks I have a chance, that I can maybe see more than some, that I stopped the co-optation, I defied them, I am holding out. But she also warns that what I don't know is, part of me is Dead anyway. We're all in the same shit, they rip off our wings, then they turn us loose and say, go do whatever you want, kid. But me, I can see the crows, and they see me . . . all I have to do is learn to listen to them . . . to accept them . . . they will lead us to another place . . . this place is dead . . . it is fake, a Play world, the real world was destroyed long ago."

"Hmm . . ." Boop said, doodling in her notebook. She looked up, with a direct look at Aleta: "Look. These things happen. You had a terrible time back then, but now, you look good. It turned out okay."

She made a fist and set her chin on it. "So, what do you want to do now? What have you always wanted to do?"

Aleta shrugged.

Boop opened a file drawer. "I know, we have a women's social group that meets here. I can just see you, laughing and joking and gossiping." She put on a merry smile. "Come on, you do like to be with friends, don't you?"

"I don't have any friends." A thought occurred to her: "One reason I stay away from other people is because sometimes when I get to know them they invade my space and I can feel them watching me when I'm alone."

"Well," Boop laughed, "if you ever catch me watching you when you're alone, just tell me to get lost."

Aleta knew her reality of being watched and judged was the same as her father's: he felt watched and judged by everyone all the time. She supposed she loved him in a Stockholm Syndrome kind of way. She was his dirty little

Wave of Pain, Walks of Life, digital art by Henry Hu

secret that everyone knew about, but denied strenuously at a holiday meal: "Smile dear!" Mother called to her, and looked out from behind the camera to demonstrate, lifting up the sides of her mouth with two fingers. But Aleta just stared, knowing her mother wished she'd had a different little girl.

The extended family sitting around the Thanksgiving table saw his eyes ever pointed at her, with the look they could pretend was parental, paternal: as if he was afraid of what she might do or say, as if she might start a fire or leap from a high window. She sat there silent, staring, not eating. She'd sneak candy or sugar to her room later. She'd wet the bed for years.

They asked each other what on earth was wrong with her. What did she get up to, they had to wonder, to act so guilty: looking down and away, blushing, then raising her eyes to see if you were still looking. She was only ten years old. Her parents were regular folks, both working, kept a clean house. Clean car. Neat yard. It was just, you'd think she was expecting to be arrested and taken down to the station: like she had the murder weapon on her person that she was concealing by constantly smoothing down her skirt in the back. Her own father didn't seem to like her much, he was a good host, hearty and smiling, but when he looked at her, a darkness came over him.

One time she was in the basement watching him do some carpentry: she'd asked if she could help him and he glared at her: "You want to help me? YOU?" He gave a harsh laugh. "Why don't you go and help your mother." So she started to bang her heels against the trunk she was sitting on. He looked up annoyed, "Stop that banging," he said. She stopped for a moment, then started up again.

"If you don't stop that," he stood and wiped his forehead with a shop towel, shooting her a frown, "I'll stand you up naked in the convertible and drive you through town."

She stopped, but started again, curious to see what he'd actually do. He crinkled up his nose and sneered as he sniffed at her. "You stink," he said.

Then someone was coming down the stairs and he snapped to attention, "Darling," he said, with an ingratiating smile, as her mother came over. She watched her parents embrace. Her father watched her out of the corner of his eye as he put his arm around his wife, kissed her cheek and whispered something in her ear.

* * * *

She hated the malls and bought her clothes through mail order catalogs, but you never knew how it would turn out. Like this coat. It didn't look, on her, like it did on the model. It was supposed to make her look like "an adventuress on the Trans-Siberian Railway, in the velour cape lined with nylon and quilted with polyester, and the matching Cossack hat." But it was too much trouble to return. The next time Aleta got on the elevator, she asked Jackie what she thought.

Jackie sat up, and looked her over as she tried an awkward twirl. "Well," said Jackie, "that's nice. Real nice."

Aleta began to like that coat.

She exited the elevator on the ground floor. Two ladies sat on the plastic molded chairs across from the mailboxes; they stopped talking and watched as she made her way to the door. The large one, in a flowered rayon dress, had her tabby cat on her lap, even though pets were not allowed in the lobby. As Aleta passed by, the cat reared up to stare at a spot about ten feet above her head. It yowled and tried to jump down, but the large lady held it close. She glared at Aleta and yelled in a cracked voice, "You're scaring my cat!"

As Aleta moved toward the front door, fast, the lady went back to talking to her friend. "It's just terrible, she takes up all the room, no one can sit down, and some of us need to. I did complain, dear, but Bob says she isn't doing anything wrong."

Her friend was a tiny woman with a prominent hearing aid and thick lisle stockings. She made two syllables out of one word, raised her voice on the last, "Who-oo?"

"Bob, dear, the manager: I went to his office to complain, this morning."

A sign on the wall said, GOSSIP-FREE ZONE, put up because of the way people complained all the time about Jackie, who didn't fit, even in public housing.

"It's just terrible!"

Aleta limped to the supermarket across the street, hoping not to set off the right knee. With her left hand, she pushed down on the cane that had a splint to allay pressure and flexion on the wrist. She used to work in the supermarket sometimes. As a night stocker, she'd wheel pallets of packaged food from the storeroom and stock the shelves. The Temp Agency had sent her out to different jobs, always at night, by her choice. Sometimes she worked as a cleaner in the big office buildings. Or she'd sit in some office all night and run reams of paper through the shredder.

Boop was skeptical when told that Aleta had always done minimum-wage temp jobs: "You don't look like someone who would do that type of work." Temp work didn't pay well, but she preferred not to stay in one workplace too long, to avoid the inevitable intrigues, or someone who might start trying to talk to her. That kind of work was okay until the arthritis started up in her hands, arms, and back after Father died.

Her building was on a mixed residential street lined with elms and maples, so old their roots buckled the sidewalks. Crossing the street, she looked up at the wires: only one crow. He swooped across the street after she stepped up on the far curb.

* * * *

Boop was solicitous as she came in next time: "What's with the cape?"

She didn't answer, just sat down. "I took a free computer class at the library."

"Good for you."

"I googled: 'Children Who Don't Speak.'"

Boop rolled her eyes: "Why are you bringing this up?"

"I still have uneasy questions about the past, about why I became an outcast back in the fifth grade."

Boop sighed. "Go on."

"I lost all my friends. I stood alone on the playground. No one talked to me. But this explains why: I had changed, not them; I stopped talking, I shut down."

"What age are kids in the fifth grade?"

"Ten."

"Hmmm . . . You have a very good memory."

"My teacher hated me for being too smart."

Boop's head snapped up: "How did she know you were so smart?"

"I was mostly silent, but would sometimes show her up with words she'd never heard of. They have a name for it now: Selective Mutism."

Boop grabbed a book and searched the index, then looked up in triumph. "It's not in here. Not in the DSM." She held the book over her stomach.

Later, on Google, Aleta looked up the DSM number for Selective Mutism: 313.23. She called and left it on Boop's office answering machine.

The next morning, she woke to someone screaming words she couldn't make out. Her heart thudding, she sat up, looked around. Silence. She was alone. It was seven o'clock. Boop once said she always arrived at the office just before seven o'clock.

Next session, Boop acted like nothing had happened. That's when Aleta knew she had to get away, fast.

"You know," Boop said when Aleta told her she was leaving, "a lot of times I complain to my therapist when he makes mistakes. I mean, how many years have I been seeing him? But the point is that you can't expect your therapist to be perfect: they're only human! I mean that's part of it, and I've learned to be honest with him and tell him when I'm upset about something."

But Aleta set the Cossack hat on her head, and limped toward the door.

"Okay, I'm going to put in your chart: Borderline, with Schizoid Aspects."

Aleta turned back. With a finger on the spot in the DSM, Boop scowled up at her, reading glasses crooked, one side cocked up to her forehead.

Later, on Google, she found Boop's maiden name, and it was a big deal back in Ohio where she came from, as well as her address and a picture of her and her husband's house. Great, now she was a stalker. But after all, Boop knew every-thing about her.

* * * *

Back in the apartment house elevator, Jackie was worried. Her body swayed in a tense rhythm, arms crossed tight. She scowled at Aleta. "Not gonna be no more checks. Saw it on TV. Gov'ment closed down." She swung her crossed leg with force, and almost tipped off the bench due to the insecure way she was slumped.

Aleta humored her. "Sure there will be."

"Nope, no more checks. They closed." She pointed at Aleta. "You can't pay your rent, you get kicked out. But not me, I got a place."

"No way." Aleta sat down next to her on the bench, but Jackie turned on her so harshly that she got up again.

"Ha, you don't know. I know where I'm goin'. You be out on the street. But I got a place."

"No." Aleta looked into her eyes. "Don't worry. It's just a game."

But Jackie stood and leaned toward her, a fist raised. "You don't know nothin'. You just like those Christmas ladies who come with packages for us poor worthless people. And they look at you like you're dirt."

The doors opened at Aleta's floor.

When she next rode the elevator, Jackie wasn't there. Her seat was taken up by boxes containing organic shampoo and soap. A sign said not to touch them: they had been brought for the residents by volunteers, and would be distributed soon.

The ladies in the lobby were in their chairs across from the mailboxes: "Jackie's gone, they took her away."

"Why-y?"

"She hit Bob! She screamed at him, then she hit him."

"Who-oo?"

"Jackie, dear, she's gone."

Though Bob, the onsite Housing Authority Manager, had a hot temper at times, he was always helpful when she needed something repaired in her apartment. But now she could imagine him: arms folded, watching with a smirk as Jackie was dragged off into a van headed to Western State Mental Hospital.

* * * *

Outside, only one crow: up on the wire, waiting for her. When he saw her he strutted and clicked, then lifted his head back and cawed in triumph. She dropped her cane to the ground, pulled the Glock from the pocket of her cape, took a shooting stance, aimed at his throat. But he cocked his left eye at her, flapped his glossy wings, lifted off. She stood down and gazed after him. She knew he wouldn't be back. 📖

Dragonfly

Dave Seter

Faceless we wander these trails
until we see another like us,

or not like us another
living thing with fractal eyes.

Face to face on the trail,
another human face

quietly interrupts the day
so full of mechanical thinking.

Face to face with another hiker,
my world opens on a hinge.

A dragonfly in her palm barely
flickers light from its iridescent wings.

Is hospice possible
for a too slow dragonfly in winter?

She goes on, I go on, we all
go on living as long as we can.

Beauty in death,
death in beauty,

with light touch we carry
the faceless, the weightless.

In this season of the urgent
dragonfly seeking a meal:

whatever can be found on acorn,
mid-air, or on skin,

the lucky in all this world
are those handed gently into the next.

Open Range

Dave Seter

This otherwise calm basin ringed with hills
was once a caldera, inactive now, but capable of fire
that could melt the fakery of this car, bold
in appearance but with a weak heart that whines.

At altitude, it can't handle this hundred degree heat.
On the way out of Boise the sound of my approach
scares a few sage grouse into sight and I watch
their low flight with the longing of a city kid uncaged.

Driving across the Snake River to heal scars and meet
with tribal councils, I hope wild horses mean it's not
too late. Reflexively I wonder about the meaning of home,
what it would be like after territorial wars to be told

where to go to live, having grown up myself roaming,
my own heritage fading into each move. I slow
for a steer—he stares me down—meets me in the middle—
of this ribbon of roadway. The car seethes standing still

so I pull to the shoulder, switch off the ignition, admire
the steer so comfortable in its hide. Who will win
the day, this open range? If I say he smiles, call me crazy,
but do no harm and certainly don't sing of electric fences.

Learning More

Luisa Kay Reyes

He was at it again. Jumping up and down and yelling at the top of his thunderous voice. He was really riled up this time. With the hue of his face rapidly changing from a light pinkish red to a deep strawberry red, leaving me to wonder if he might not need some hospitalization soon. After all, he appeared to be in the age bracket where health becomes a concern. Yet he seemed to defy the laws of health and gravity. And he adamantly continued his jumping up and down routine, all without the need of an ambulance.

I couldn't believe it. Here I was. My first semester of law school. Trying to figure out why my simple comment in favor of helping out the individual over the demands of the almighty corporation was eliciting such a strong reaction on the part of my contracts professor. Oh dear. Bewildered as I was, he was getting ready to go in for the kill this time. Progressing from merely jumping up and down and rattling the walls of the cinder block classroom with his thunderous voice, to calling me and anybody else who might harbor ideas in favor of the individual over those of private industry a *Communist Russian*. This being my first exposure to the notion of the focus of law being the protection of property against the mob, I had no idea why we had transitioned from discussing entry level contract cases to Communist Russia. Completely ignoring the confusion written all over my face, my professor continued his jumping up and down routine. Adding the detail of bellowing "*Communist Russian!*" with every breath that he took.

I tried to think. Was I really a *Communist Russian*? I had heard of Russia, before. It was a big country somewhere on the other side of the world. When I was little, I even had a pen pal from the Ukraine. We had been connected via a world peace initiative with the caveat that those of us in the Western Hemisphere not try to address the envelopes to our new pen pals on our own. We were forewarned that there might be symbols that would appear meaningless to us but would be significant to the Russian mail service. It was best, we were told, that we photocopy the addresses and then cut and secure them on the front of the envelope with glue or scotch tape to ensure their safe arrival. As we began our letter writing routine, I was relieved that my pen pal could write well in English for I knew not a word of Ukrainian or Russian.

However, one day, the youthful side of me decided to rebel. I was going to write my Ukrainian pen pal and address the envelope with my very own hand. Determined to succeed in my rebellion, I studied the photocopies of her address that I kept handy and noticed that there was a random dot. I squinted my eyes to be sure, but I was fairly certain this dot was merely the result of it being a photocopy of a photocopy of a photocopy. Nonetheless, I decided to err on the side of caution. Making sure to include that dot as I addressed the letter to my Ukrainian pen pal, all in my very own hand. When I received a reply a few weeks later, I felt a thrill that my little rebellion had been successful. And sitting in my contracts class that day, while enduring the unyielding harangue of my contracts professor, I figured out that the closest I ever got to being a *Communist Russian* was that dot.

When the class came to a close, thankfully bringing with it a reprieve from my professor's jumping bean routine, I went up and spoke to him. He was calmer one on one. But with his eyes gleaming he told me that he had had students come in with ideas like mine before. Unconcerned, he said I needn't worry. Informing me with much pride that he had successfully brought every one of those doubting students of his around to his supply-side economics way of thinking. He felt sure that when we spoke again at the end of the semester, I would be one of his biggest converts. It would be a rough road for me, he said. I just needed to give it a while and soon I would forgo my "Sunday School lessons" by coming around to his more enlightened economic analysis.

I was doubtful. And with this being my initiation into the free market and economic analysis of the law mindset, I starting reading what I could find on the matter. I learned from my textbooks that it was a way of thinking that had developed primarily out of the Yale Law School, with Yale heavily promoting it to the point where it was pretty much ingrained into our legal framework. In my torts textbook, I soon learned that my reservations regarding this school of thought were not unique to me, for I came across a passage where it stated that there was heavy concern on the part of the American people when this economic analysis of the law first became widely known.

The concern being that it was not in line with the teachings of Christ. While the basic elements of American law were derived from British common law, there had been changes made to it early on to reflect a more congenial, people friendly, and democratic nature. However, now this economic analysis of the law was being institutionalized into our legal system using such mild and benign sounding words as the "balancing" of interests. And when we discussed our assigned cases in torts the next day, I asked my torts professor about the passage that I had just read, where it stated that there was concern the economic legal point of view was inherently not in line with the teachings of Christ. Since my law school was affiliated with a Christian university, I anticipated that this would be a matter of deep discussion. But to my surprise, the simple answer that my professor provided to my question was, "There is some debate on that."

Stunned that there wasn't more concern reflected over my question, I recalled a time when I went to Morelia, Michoacán, Mexico, to visit some of my friends and family. I took a college friend along with me and we were excited about getting to do some exploring of the Spanish colonial era architecture that is one of the hallmarks of the beauty of Morelia. Of course, we were also excited about getting to eat real Mexican food that wasn't Taco Bell. As Sunday approached, we went to the First Baptist Church in Morelia, the church I always attend when I'm in town. The pastor was very happy to see us walk in and we proceeded to introduce ourselves, even meeting some of my long-time friends that I had in the Church.

When the hour arrived to begin our Sunday School lesson, the teacher opened by reading a passage from the book of John. My friend, who had been leafing through the pages of her Bible, was astonished and stopped short. "They sure do use John a lot" she said, leaving me at a loss for words. John is usually considered one of the main evangelistic books of the Bible, so I couldn't fathom why my friend would be so surprised that it was being used in our Sunday School lesson.

Then I recalled my senior year in my ultra-conservative Presbyterian high school. The big send-off for us as we entered the world beyond was to memorize the entire chapter of Romans 8. It wasn't really that difficult of a chapter to memorize. However, while we were standing in line for graduation, the Bible teacher came and stood in front of the boy who hadn't been able to commit it to memory throughout the course of the school year. He listened to the boy skip verses and rather faultily recite the passage with its heavy emphasis on predestination. Yet despite the boy's obviously half-hearted attempt at memorizing the passage, the Bible teacher yielded to the late hour and stated that he had met the requirement—allowing the boy to walk in the graduation ceremony.

It was something I noticed frequently as I actively participated in college church groups and continued attending Christian educational institutions. It seemed that in U.S. churches the writings of Paul were mentioned often and with the utmost import while everything else was placed on

Star, 2017, photograph by Michelle Brooks

the back burner. Other than the basic John 3:16 passage, the teachings of Jesus were almost an inconvenience compared to the writings of Paul. Now I comprehended my friend's astonishment at opening up the Sunday School lesson with the book of John. Perhaps this was one reason why my torts professor so easily slighted my question.

Sitting once more in my contracts class, this time my professor began extolling the virtues of Judge Posner while also making periodic references to Ayn Rand. According to his lecture anybody—and he made sure to look at me in a manner that made it clear of whom he was speaking—who didn't subscribe to the Ayn Rand worldview was blatantly un-American. Again, I found myself pondering his accusations for a moment.

Granted, my early childhood years were spent in Mexico City. However, since my mother had minored in history in her undergraduate days, she made sure we learned our American heritage. We read biographies of George Washington, admittedly not the full James Thomas Flexner ones that my mother had read as an adult, but the smaller children's biographies that focused on how important it was that George Washington had chosen not to be King. My mother also taught us about the Fourth of July and the Declaration of Independence. And when we proceeded to learn about Abraham Lincoln and the Gettysburg Address, my mother even went so far as to explain to us that a score, as in "Four score and seven years ago," meant a span of twenty years. Somehow, Ayn Rand, who expressed a desire to be known as the *Antichrist*, didn't make it into our early childhood American history lessons.

Undaunted, my contracts professor continued his daily display of his hopping prowess, even going so far as to say with much disdain that poor people just wanted a "piece of the economic pie." Rather than trying to "create wealth" and expand the economic pie, according to his lecture, they were just lazy and wanted "a free lunch." Once again, I found myself wondering about this generalization of his. After all, we were now about midway through the semester and I wasn't coming around to his economics-above-all point of view. He had assured me at the beginning of the semester that by the end I'd be seeing things from his more intellectually approved economic analysis of the law. And so far, I was not relenting.

Finally, I started trying to ignore my professor's added detail of playing an imaginary violin in the air with his arms while criticizing the concepts of "life, liberty, and the pursuit of happiness." My mind went back to the time I went on a medical mission trip to Nicaragua. A friend of my brother's organized it, and since I was fluent in Spanish I joined the team as one of the translators. Arriving in Nicaragua, those of us who spoke Spanish laughed at some of the local colloquialisms we were encountering that differed from our Spanish. Toalla, we learned—while it means towel in Mexico—in Nicaragua referred to a feminine hygiene product that comes in handy every thirty days or so.

Going from village to village while providing basic health screenings and services, I sat by the doctor and translated from Spanish to English and vice versa. In one particular village we encountered, nearly every patient we saw had vision problems. Looking out at the people sitting and standing in line, the busy doctor took the time to ask me, "How many people do you see out there with glasses?"

"None" was my reply.

He then pointed out to me that no one around us, except for the doctor himself, had eyeglasses. When one laborer came and sat down for his appointment, the doctor took his vital signs. Then, in all seriousness, he put down his pen and paused for a moment, deliberating in silence while I began fearing for what catastrophic news I might have to translate next. Then he looked right at me, saying, "These are numbers one usually only sees in Olympic athletes. The people here aren't poor for lack of work and physical labor. They are simply the fallout from the cash society." So much for the poor being lazy, I thought to myself.

This trip to Nicaragua wasn't the first time I had been exposed to poverty. The disparity of wealth in society was something I became aware of at an early age. As a little girl, I was the pitiful scholarship student at the prestigious German school in Mexico City. Yet, in my neighborhood, the neighbors all looked up to us as the well-to-do crowd of our enclave. We received U.S. dollars in the mail from our maternal grandparents. They even felt that, since we were so well off with all that American money, they were entitled to secretly get our mail before we did.

In sharp contrast to the attitude of my neighbors, when my mother hosted a birthday party for me one time, the activities she planned pleased my classmates very much. There was lots of laughter to be heard throughout the day. But, as my classmates made sure to let me know, to them my house looked like a peasant's shack.

One time, while sitting outside of the Southern Annex of the German School, after classes had been let out, one of the older students began talking to me. She, too, was waiting for her parents to come pick her up. To while away the hours, she began venting her frustrations about how difficult it was to find good servants nowadays. Presaging the words of my contracts professor many years later in law school, she told me that the maids were just so "lazy" these days. And one had to be "firm with them to get them to work." "It was just so rough having to find new maids, all the time," she sighed.

I tried to sympathize with her as much as I could, but I couldn't help thinking about the beggar lady who frequently sat a few blocks down the street from my home. She was elderly and blind and dressed in the faded and worn traditional native garb of her people. Trying to make sense of the world around me, I asked my mother one day why God had made some people poor and some people rich. "Why," I reasoned, "didn't God just make everybody rich?"

As parents often do when their children ask profound questions, my mother gave me the best answer that she could think of. "Well, we're put here on this earth to learn. And one learns more when they are poor than when they are rich."

Displaying his athletic stamina the rest of the semester, my contracts professor continued jumping up and down and espousing anything but absolute unrestricted and uninhibited free market economics. He sometimes started in on his condemnation of the poor even before I had a chance to startle him with my questions. When the semester finally came to a close, he didn't have to ask. His arguments hadn't persuaded me one iota. Thinking I would be able to relax after that, I discovered that as fate would have it, I was condemned to have him for contracts my second semester as well.

In our second semester of contracts, he still argued against Communist Russia with every other breath that he took, but he was quite receptive towards Communist China. He reasoned that China was no longer Communist since they had opened up to trade. The fact that they still had a variation of the one child policy seemed to matter not one whit to him. And when the second semester of contracts finally came to a close, he realized he had failed to convince me. He had failed to get me to join the ranks of his reverence for the economic analysis of the law. And he could no longer boast that he had successfully convinced all of his students of the virtues of his money-above-all-else school of thought. For I had held out. Nonetheless, he expressed unyielding faith that his economic views would take root in me, sooner rather than later.

Then one day, during my third year of law school, I was walking out of the school building. On my way out, I noticed with much dismay that my first year contracts professor was tormenting an innocent-looking first-year law student with his diatribes on supply-side economics. Echoing my feelings that first semester in law school, the student was looking traumatized and miserable—resulting in me feeling sick to my stomach. The shock and incredulity displayed on the face and in the demeanor of this student were sentiments I could still recall very well.

I gingerly walked past them hoping to remain unnoticed. Rolling my eyes while overhearing this determined professor trying to convince the doubtful student of the finesse of "balancing" the interests. And, then, just as I was going up the steps to leave the building, my first year contracts professor took note of my presence, much to my chagrin.

Turning to the boy, he said "Just ask her, she can tell you what she thinks of the economic analysis of the law!" More than a little peeved that I was being forced to speak to this professor again, I looked at him and told him the people who subscribed to his point of view were "all going to Hell!"

This time, he didn't jump up and down and start playing his imaginary violin. He actually laughed. Giving me the impression that he was quite pleased. After all, the teachings of Yale pale in comparison to the teachings of childhood . . . for one does learn more when one is poor. 📖

Miniature Dachshund

T.J. Smith

Nature could never make me.
I spit at God, I shriek shrill hymns

To myself— am I not beautiful?
My too-short legs, my too-long

Body like a snake, eyes always oozing
Greatness. I am my own majesty,

Sleeping twenty hours a day
Without waking to admire sunsets

Lighting up the sky with infinite color.
I have no need for any color, eating

Shit bathed in beautiful light to feed
Fleas who gorge themselves on me.

I am my own color. Divine, I am
Father to none. There is nothing

After or before me. I enrich
The cardboard world on which I piss.

Taking the food from your plate,
Rending your favorite shoes to nothing

Belly dragging on the floor and wheezing
Wet nose that nature did not make.

You made me. Watch me go.

Restraint

Judith Skillman

Not Pandora's box, that old trouble
opened yet again for the sake of a script
memorized in childhood. Nor the abominations
of a misogynist father who never understood
the pleasures of girlhood. Who raged against
his daughters' fancies. Again, not a genie
in a bottle, nor an apostle of whimsy and delight.
Not even the tiniest portion of a bear claw
slathered with almonds and icing. What
the body holds back comes only in the form
of a rope. A rope and a trapeze. A rope
and a trapeze and a circus artist whose curls
thicken with light. Her arms extended,
she climbs above the audience, drapes herself
in a shawl of beautiful poses, pouts, falls
deliberately into the trap of hanging upside-down.
When the muses and nymphs fly out
of the box, jar, circus tent, what a ruckus
can be heard for miles as all the birds
and distant relatives of silk monkeys begin
to wake from their century of slumber
in the baobab.

Saved

Mary Lou Sanelli

In my last book, I mentioned that when my mother was dying, writing saved me.

I think it was the use of the word "saved" that prompted a reader named Kristen to write to me to say that writing is the only thing saving her, too, hiding nothing about her despair in a funny email that took some of the fear out of her situation both for herself and for me.

Kristen, thank you. Because I think in times like this, when we wonder if we can get through it, we need to laugh. It lifts the misery right out. I know because I'm the same way.

But, to be honest, writing wasn't the only thing that saved me.

Now, I would have sworn when I first visited the island of Oahu where my mother lived, I would never have wound up swimming in the ocean to save myself. I hugged the shoreline, afraid to venture out.

My world had grown very small by then, the way it does when someone you love is dying. My mother's bedside, to the beach and back, that was it. With houses and trees out the window and blankets between us, sitting with my mother was more physically challenging than any work I've ever done. There wasn't much I could do for her other than be there. I longed to talk to her, but she couldn't talk. I longed even for the sound of her constant complaining, but she couldn't wake. I stared at her face and relied on my memory. Oh, the expressions it once made. When we are young we take so much about our parents for granted. I know I did.

Helplessness, I found, is exhausting.

Pacific Northwest Nostalgia, 2017, photograph by Emily Townsend

Spent from sadness, I wanted to leave my mother behind and be part of life again and do things that made sense to me. I'd ride my bike from the hospice home, past the ridges of continuous Honolulu, to Kaimana Beach, a mile east of Waikiki. It was there I first watched a man the locals lovingly call "Big Brian" swim out to the horizon.

You wouldn't know Big Brian was a distance swimmer to look at him: he is the paunchiest athlete I've ever met. He reminds me of Roland Martin: no neck. Before he swims, he likes to stand with his ankle-less feet in the water and talk with other swimmers before diving in. Listening to him, *studying* him, was the beginning of my swimming education. For instance: I learned to call the fluttering cone mounted on a mast at the end of the swimming channel a windsock, not a flag, and to never get in a swimmer's way once they hit the water or I'd have to endure a look that is weary of tourists and totally indistinguishable from a chide. I never knew how nuanced a smile could be until I swam alongside Polynesians.

The first time I struck up a conversation with Big Brian, he told me that if I stopped swimming "like a chicken," I'd eventually "be lucky enough" to swim over a reef shark. I didn't feel it was my place to say, "Please don't tell me that."

And then one day a woman named Deb swam up beside me and said she'd swim to the windsock if I did. That worked. From then on I knew that swimming toward the horizon offered something so unlike "chicken" swimming, so much *more*. "So that's how we're gonna roll from here on in," Deb said, soon as we reached the shore, "because that's how it's *done* in Hawaii."

Big Brian mentioned other creatures I'd see, too, and he was right. A few days later, I bumped into a turtle, something I never thought even remotely possible. The sea was so churned up, we just didn't *see* each other. It might not sound like a big deal, but the experience changed the way I thought about the ocean, and myself within it, for good. As if, upon impact, I shed the life that was behind me.

Or part of it, anyway.

Or maybe what really happened was that I'd begun to rely on the ocean for emotional support, and for something else, too. I wanted, *needed*, the fluidness to fill in for my missing mother, mad as that sounds. I have a clearer sense of this now.

The Green Sea Turtle, known as "Honu," symbolizes good luck to the Hawaiian people, and, according to one of my mother's nurses, "will show up as your guardian spirit." I took her words to heart. I'd wanted a guardian spirt to help me ever since I'd arrived at the airport. I followed the grace of the turtle's movement, feeling I'd received what I'd hoped for, out of nowhere a soul had risen strong, a basic survival mechanism, that's how I experienced it, how I *chose* to experience it, and I thought, *you are my guardian.* It took no effort to convince myself of that.

This same feeling came over me when I was surprised by the heft of a monk seal.

And startled by a moray eel.

I personally don't care as much for moray eels. But I imagined its guidance anyway. Even though I had wanted to bolt, I swam closer to it. Instantly, it pulled back inside its hole. I pictured it down there saying to another eel, "just another crazy *haole*."

And I was crazy. A little. It's another downside of helplessness.

But still, no shark.

Until my return to the island a month later to face that awful, gut-wrenching week of cleaning-out-your-mom's-belongings, when more than once I went a little ballistic. "I can't do this!" I screamed.

And when it was over, I came undone. Swimming felt like the only effort that could stitch me back together. I gathered my courage and swam *the* brag-able swim of Kaimana Beach, from the windsock to the pink landmark of the Royal Hawaiian Hotel. Except I swam from the hotel to the windsock, *against* the current. I remember thinking the struggle felt like a good metaphor for the rest of my life.

I'm not exactly sure what I did when the shark first came into view, sort of lodged between two shelves of coral, as if resting. What I am sure of is that it felt as if I'd been holding my breath for all the swims before. I swam away faster than I've ever swam, boy, did I, resisting an almost unbearable urge to stand on the reef and yell, "shark!"

That sighting united my respect for sharks and my overwhelming fear I had conquered to see one. And in the process, I felt like I *got* what it really means to call oneself an ocean swimmer. It made me feel like I was living in a world only swimmers and divers are privy to, where a creature that can kill you in one pounce never looks quite as bad as it does above the surface.

"Hey, Brian! I saw a shark!"

His take? "How big?"

"Too big!" I said.

"Whitetip!" he said, as if they knew each other, which changed the neutral look in his eyes, used to suppressing most visible emotion, to full excitement. Not that he'd say so. "Four feet, yah? The little guy, *Uuku.*"

Little did I understand that it was Brian's way of telling me that there would always be bigger challenges ahead if I kept swimming.

Another metaphor? Absolutely.

Later, years later, writing this, I realize that the older I get, the more I want to be up to them. 📖

Crow Balance Scale Seesaw, still life vintage photograph, 2017, by Marilyn Stablein

At Laugh Out Loud Café

Scott T. Starbuck

At Laugh Out Loud Café

it's so quiet it makes the history museum
seem like a carnival ride.

"What's up with the name?" I ask.
"Previous owner," I'm told,

and think of bad storms
that change coastlines,

Titanic lifeboats
leaving half full.

Come to Stay

Joannie Stangeland

The water is rising
in the house, the water
follows the full moon's invitation
over the threshold, the bodies
of water running, the water
with salt on its tongue
licks the carpet's edge,

splays out, old cat
in a patch of sunlight,
the water climbs
on arthritic limbs,
a spray of seaweed in its hair.
A seed of mutiny, kernel
of catastrophe, the water swells

in water, a time-lapse school movie,
sets down its roots,
sprouts along the walls,
seeps up the drapes to swallow
the last third of the world.
The water is taking
over the lease

and has it in writing.
Remember the hall of only
air and color, wall and shadow,
door agape to blue wave
instead of these wooden steps,
the dirt path we're walking
as the water's moving in?

The ocean our avenue,
our new address. By water
we will miss the grass,
miss the snowdrops and the snow.

Earth Science

Willie Smith

In seventh grade we took earth science. Miss G was the teacher. I had her Fourth Period right after lunch. She was scrawny. On the tall side. Skin leathery from having been a tour guide at the Grand Canyon after graduating with a B.S. in geology. Five years before returning for her Masters in Teaching. Then moving back East to land this job cramming the names of rocks into the hormonally-electrified skulls of thirty-five adolescents at a pop; five classes per day, five days a week.

She affected slacks, western shirts, string ties with turquoise clasps, Tony Lama boots. Wore a silly little five-gallon Stetson to and from school.

She exhibited a fondness for stones. Disliked indoor work. Hated kids—especially twelve to fourteen year olds obsessed with mating rituals and the rudiments of human sexual behavior. She was somewhere between thirty and fifty. Flat-chested, narrow-butted, no-hipped and had nothing to fear from menopause because her meno did not seem ever to have started.

As for me—I was that snotty, gawky, word-happy little brat who sat in the back of the class. Puns led me by the nose. Teach would hold up a fragment of gneiss and out of my poker face would tumble, "Nice, Miss G—gee, that's very NICE!"

"Notice," she would point to crystals in the rock, "in this particular piece of gneiss…"

"Hey, NICE PIECE!" would float out over the heads of my classmates. Hard to tell exactly where the sarcasm originated. As if I were using ventriloquism; although I was actually playing the part of a puppet being worked by quirks bubbling up from inside, as if I were half-awake dream-

Lost in Translation, ink, charcoal & graphite on museum board, 2005, by Paul Flippen

capping every loaded word Miss G spoke.

"We can see on this sample of rose quartz by the cleavage..."

"Not much cleavage anywhere else . . ."

Splutters. Smothered giggles. Thighs slapped in choked hilarity. Not even those in the audience closest knew for sure it was me . . .

"WHO SAID THAT?"

At teach's outburst most of the laughter ceased. A couple titters persisted; died slow, bored deaths. Several adolescents sat up straight. Folded hands on desktops. Faces waxed innocent.

Miss G whipped around. Snatched a stub of chalk. Scratched across the board stiffer homework than usual, color only gradually draining from the back of her buzzard neck.

The dummy, the ventriloquist, the lewd clown, masked my true self—the face I whispered to in the medicine chest mirror locked inside the bathroom late at night. I was a serious student. A scientist. A future astronomer, likely specializing in planetary mechanics.

Last May I had used my paper route money to purchase a six-inch reflecting telescope. I had taught myself the constellations, the names of the stars, and followed under high power the planets. Over the summer I had observed each night Jupiter's four Galilean moons: Io, Europa, Ganymede, Callisto. I had tabulated statistics on their relative positions. Specifically with respect to their occultations and transits— when one of the moons ducked behind Jupiter, or drifted between the giant planet and our perspective from Earth.

I had filled a three-ring notebook with pages and pages of dates and times of ingress and egress of occultation and of transit. On a meter-long sheet of butcher paper I had used colored pencils to draw Jupiter and its tan belts, yellow zones, and Great Red Spot as the planet appeared under 120 magnifications, and had illustrated how the four satellites—first discovered by Galileo Galilei—danced around, behind, and in front of the globe of frozen gases that could hold well over a thousand Earths.

Seventh grade marked the first time we had separate classes with a different teacher for each subject. Since earth science was the only science class, I brought my notebook and butcher paper to Miss G's and laid everything out in the back room, where she stored the mineral samples and the tools for fracturing and examining.

There the project sat for two days and nothing was said. I did not know exactly how these things were done, so on the third day I lingered after the bell, when everyone else had rushed jabbering out into the hall to crowd off to fifth period.

After what seemed several geological eras, Miss G at last squinted up from her desk. "Oh. You're still here. Need tonight's homework clarified? I thought, frankly, my instructions were quite clear."

"Oh, no. I mean, yes: it's obvious we are to explain in essay form the differences between igneous, metamorphic and sediment."

"Sedimen-TARY."

"Yes. That's what I meant. What I thought. The word came too fast. No, I just wondered if you were wondering about my exposition in the back room."

She frowned. Cocked to one side her sunburnt, close-cropped noggin.

"I mean the butcher paper and stuff."

"Oh," she looked back down at the stack of pop quizzes we had deposited on her blotter. "I wondered when you were going to pick that up. You shouldn't leave personal belongings back there. I don't mind for a day or two, but . . ."

"It's the Galilean satellites. For the science fair next week. That's my entry."

"What would you," her gray eyes rolled up, head not budging, "like me to do about it?"

I knew there was something about a sponsor. A teacher who would officially recommend your project. All that meticulous observation faithfully recorded; surely it would win a prize, maybe first; I would be a feather in her cap. She would win, I would win; science would win—this could spark interest in recalibrating the distance between us and Jupiter; because with my accurate to a tenth-of-a-second timings of the eclipses and transits, taken as a whole and averaged out . . . but I stood, dumb as a dummy in a mannikin's lap, staring down at the gray-streaked brown bun atop her occiput.

She sighed. Looked all the way up. "It doesn't stand up. That's the first requirement of any exhibit at the fair: not only is the paper wrong, it lies flat. Nobody could read it."

"Oh."

"That's something to remember if you think you still might want to enter next year. It's a science fair, not a scratch paper party."

"Sure . . . of course." I glanced out the window. Two guys from my Phys Ed class jaywalked across the highway to the Esso station, fishing Camels from their shirt pockets. I didn't know their names. Today still September. So many things still new, still unknown.

My eyes burned. I cleared my throat and deliberately pictured to myself fresh dogshit. I would NOT cry.

I turned away from the window. Stepped toward the door.

"By the bye," her voice tightened. "Did you hear anyone in the back of the room today mispronounce the word SCHIST?"

I cleared my throat. But this time the pipe dry, nothing to clear. The membrane itched. I still had my tonsils. Maybe it was the tonsils itched.

"As if the individual were mocking me. Copying me, only leaving out the word's second *ess*. By the bye—what IS schist?"

She caught my eyes. Her pupils blazed.

"Metamorphic. Medium to large mica flakes." I coughed into a fist. "Often parallel."

"Good. Just be sure always to spell the word correctly." She blinked—Io disappearing behind Jupe. In mythology Jove rapes Io. Myth and science worlds apart. Science finds the answer. Myth makes shit up.

"Sure . . . of course."

"You can leave your scratch work here one more day," she called after me. "Then I need it all out," this last aimed down at her blotter, I could tell by how the sound damped.

Slouching toward the door, I strangled in my throat the itch to sneer, "Ah, who gives a SCHIST?"

Well, I did: I gave a schist.

But because I at that moment struggled to avoid any further dwelling on the trashing of my work, I wondered, as I exited the room to join the crowd flowing down the hall, wondered almost aloud: To fill the Grand Canyon all the way up—into it how much shit would Miss G need to spit? 📖

Blackbird Away

Mary Ellen Talley

The five bones I use for talking
     restrict my repertoire. If all there is to do with speech

is mimic words, then I choose wings. My black plaits wade
     in stagnant breeze, awaiting further

demarcation. They shield my fragile back.
     I perch at the window watching alabaster columns

sway like towering chimneys.
     My bones shift, ligaments stretch, extending

from my obsessive backbone. Gravity holds fast
     but the secret of my keratin

amasses depth and glistens at the peak of sun. Sensory feathers
     alert me to a downwind.

I feel my scapula expand wide to the momentous periphery.
     Intuition yields

as I become contour and direction. I can come to life again,
     manipulate the wind.

Spineless Ecstasy

Willie Smith

Mars blazes in opposition less than a moon-breadth from Antares—Heart of the Scorpion, Rival of Mars. I hallucinate—fixed on the planet kissing the red giant—scorpions—two springs tangled—screwing in the gutter dogstyle. The sole aspect that mars this tableau: no arachnid can blow; nor otherwise pet. But, oh, picture the ritual—the calypso of the dude up on the curb serenading the bird!

He croons the spell her eyes cast. Curses her sting to the heart. Implores the glory of her grease. Worships the venom her skitter stirs. Jitters the truth. While she over her head coils, should he outright lie, death.

The guy coaxes the babe—showing his dope, praising the coke, lauding to the skies the power of his poke, the thrust of his stroke. She, alpha-to-omega slow, relents, losing of face not one iota. Joins him up on the pavement.

Both face-to-face together hop, midair clicking thirteen times thoraxes. He around his love then mazurkas—metasoma uncurling to point at the alley of night between Mars and the scarlet star. After seven revolutions—perfectly executed—the Juliet surrenders of her body all government. Head-to-head, pincers locked, sideways into the gutter they skip.

Where she flips Romeo the length of her exoskeleton. Arches, as his eight legs right ship, her butt to display for delectation the gonopore.

And as he mounts—Scorpius continuing to rise—reflecting the soundless hiss of Earth's rotation—Mars and the giant persisting to blaze—with a lazy back and a sloppy fill, a carload of hopped-up kids crushes all but noiselessly spineless ecstasy. 📖

Vanguardia Interior, painting / mixed media by Vivian Calderón Bogoslavsky

Out their top-down convertible the monkeys hop. Spill onto the trottoir. Stagger, chattering arm in arm, into the night, back to the bar. 📖

That First

Sarah Brown Weitzman

Although I fear death
far less than pain
when my cat brought me
its first small gift of both
proudly in its mouth,
I approached that agony
of loving a killer philosophically.
Later when I heard
the keening of a second
creature, cornered
but not yet taken
slowly, I had a second
chance to separate the sin
from the sinner.
That first I had
to save from pain
was a starling
that no longer fluttered
to please the cat
but when I came close
its eyes flickered
with feeling yet.
In frantic haste
to spare it pain
I struck it with a rock
inexactly. Again,
again that awful botch
of rock before
the clement change.

Yet that sharp black eye
did not change
did not ease into dull peace
nor close nor forgive
as I sank in sickness
at the curled feet
of my own first kill.

Heartline: Diamond Heights, 2017, photograph by Emily Townsend

Chicago

(for Eschikagou)

Angie Trudell Vasquez

Metal sides rise to sky
on banks of water so blue
it hurts eyes.

This water, holy water takes lives,
ships lie at bottom
rice paddies forgotten.

City named after wild onion
now brick, mortar, steel and glass
planted in underpass survive.

Lake slides from river, river
reversed eases merchants,
men don black suits.

Who changes the flow but man?
Ghost river blows hats, winds steal land,
bone people shiver in winter breath.

Fainting Distance

Carter Vance

It always starts with something: that glance across party rooms, an awkward handshake, your mutual friend's introduction, or, increasingly, some popup on a screen. Those smooth bits of digital code hold out a kind of promise when you're in a new and unfamiliar place. It says you've been noticed, it says you're all right enough to someone who is willing to take that most human of jumps and spend an evening of their life with you in hope of something greater still.

London: an internship and foundation grant, ten weeks sharing a Docklands Light Rail Car with seemingly half the population of the world, and a cramped youth hostel with a group of New Labour professional types. I'd switched over the location on my long-unchecked OkCupid profile for the occasion, telling myself that I didn't think much of it, but really holding out a weird kind of hope that everything might just work out this time. Surely, London had everyone, from every land of the dead empire, in its sprawl and, surely, one of them might take that jump with me.

I suppose that now is as good a time as any to mention that, being asexual, my exact form of that "jump" isn't the same as most others. Much of my hesitance in meeting people in the traditional ways, and subsequent general lack of success in this realm, has come from a kind of fear of misperception. Short of wearing a sandwich board reading "no sex, please," the mystification of human interaction makes broaching the subject in bald terms quite a challenge. Online dating, flawed as it might be, at least allows for an accepted degree of upfront discretion about these aspects of preference

David Motel, 2017, photograph by Michelle Brooks

that most of us would be too polite to bring up at the outset of a potential relationship. Even in a city of twelve million, the chance of randomly meeting another of the roughly one percent of the population that is asexual is quite a remote one, so we entrust our fates to the mystery of match algorithms and to the kind of paradoxical honesty that keyboards and screen names allow.

Between work, museums, and concerts, not to mention the unfortunate incident of losing my wallet in a foreign country, I'd managed to schedule a couple of dates for the first five weeks, but both had fallen through in that odd way that makes you believe you did something terribly wrong without knowing exactly what it was. Though I would idly click about a bit whilst waiting for the train and tube, I'd basically given up the serious possibility of finding someone and was halfway resigned to mere fun evenings for the rest of my time in the Great Wen. It was then, though, that one of those hopeful popups came to me.

Being a chronic self-doubter, I suppose I'll always wonder what it was that stuck out for her, but never being one to argue with luck's blessings, I was greatly enthused to meet up. It wasn't the most auspicious of first encounters, involving a number of digital iterations of that London proverb "due to a train fault," a rather bad decision, in retrospect, to run full-tilt to meet-up on a midsummer's noon and culminating in a fainting spell (on my part) in the middle of the standing section of Shakespeare's Globe. What I most remember, though, is her waiting with me in the heat stroke recovery room and the look of utterly genuine concern and empathy she wore. It was then I knew there was something to her, to London, to all of it, something that felt deeper, more real, than what had come before in my life.

From there, I don't think I'd ever seen or wanted to see so much of someone over such a short period of time. It is in that whirlwind of days out in parks, of nights of meetings for tea, that it was possible to believe in those mythologies of what big cities do to young hearts. It wasn't New York, or Paris, or Rome, but then again, maybe I wasn't, maybe we weren't those places.

And, yet, just as quick, it was over; there were conferences in York, PhD theses at King's College, degrees, and bills and lives to go back to for the autumn. The last time we were together, I felt only one thing had lacked resolution: I thought about kissing her, then I thought better of it; more hesitant, I didn't.

Maybe in a former age I would have, not knowing if I'd ever have the chance again, but it is that same force of technological hope that assures us there can always be a next time. We can always message, instantly, and expect a reply within days at most. We can see the evolution of haircuts, event attendance, new victories and defeats at the press of a touch screen. In one sense, what might have been called "flings," or "summer loves," now never have to end. The other person can always be there with us, just a "hey, how are you?" away.

In another sense, though, all things end and there is little sense in trying to deny this. Indeed, it is in the aftermath of sudden things that thought starts to actually focus on their meaning. Being swept up in the dodgy shade of Haringey evenings, of the utter impossibility of meeting someone you feel strongly connected to in perhaps the world's most anonymizing city, plays a funny trick of forever on the mind.

It's easy to believe that "progress" holds our salvation, whether it be from climate change, car accidents, or lonesome nights, but this ignores the fact that technology is crafted by human hands and, moreover, is used by them. New platforms promise us interaction that is more meaningful because it is more advanced, but *what* we share through them is ultimately the same as it ever was. We have pictures and timelines and video and audio, but, in the end, the loss caused by distance still stings; clutching parchment to one's chest in the night is scarcely different than doing so with an iPhone.

It is often said that people of my generation have much of our love lives modulated by the ever-present hum of technology; too much, it is usually concluded. From the sudden ubiquity of Tinder's rightward swipes as a symbolic representation of all that it is to be dating and millennial, the outside observer might conclude that these loves are not so much of another person, but rather of glass and microchips. We are falling in love, lust, or some ever-intermingled combination of the two, not with the person before us but rather with what we perceive them to be in the self-editing funhouse mirror of the digital world. The sort of writing stemming from this hypothesis has a tone of nothing so much as the street corner apocalyptic, foretelling the end of human intimacy writ large and the emergence of purely transactional relationship forms. Though this narrative is convenient, the facts on the ground, in the main, speak to something quite different.

More than anything, technology is a perilous and imperfect vehicle we use in an attempt to transcend those borders which have always made a mockery of deeper plans. As long as human beings have travelled between places without the intent of staying, we have found these affections that have been characterized by a kind of mutually-known impermanence. The best, or rather less neurotic, amongst us, are able to embrace that impermanence as part of the thrill, or at least that is what they say. I often find myself thinking that if all the lost lovers between the invention of the human heart and sufficiently widespread DSL access had the option of adding each other on Facebook, most of them would. The feeling of being forever apart, or at least dependent upon the courage of the local postal carrier to fan a flicker of connection, can drive one mad, or else into the arms of the convenient nearby for comfort. It could be said that knowing these things to have a potential of being but once might have intensified the feelings involved, whereas now we draw back slightly, not wanting to seem uncouth or uncool. This same hesitance, though, impairs our connections. We draw out feelings: a burst of activity, but then rationed over those exchanges of canned reactions and phrases of our favoured digital spaces.

I don't know where, exactly, that leaves us in the wider sense. Perhaps we are doomed to exist in this between-space of lost and found as long as travel and technology hold out the hope of more permanent connection. Perhaps we can reconceive of love as something which requires less of a physical sense of "being there." Perhaps, indeed, we can live again with the spirit of a life of interesting adventures and not hold on too closely to the glancing encounters.

As for myself, when I finally gathered the wherewithal to continue on from that summer, I wrote a letter with an invitation to vacation together. I boxed it up with some particularly tacky emblems of Canadian pride and I sent it by post; the brown paper covering crackled with immediacy. 📖

Rain, digital art by Henry Hu

I've got my finger on
the trigger, too.

(In conversation with Jan Beatty's "Shooter")

Andrena Zawinski

I've got my finger on the trigger.
I'm taking aim
at the teen stalker who left unwrapped Trojans
for my mother to find in my Sherpa pockets /
taking aim
at the old boyfriend who dumped Guinness on my head
in a bar in the middle of winter and stole my peacoat.

I'm looking down the barrel
at a rock band all star who shoved himself inside me
then zipping up said this was about winning—he won /
looking down the barrel
at my ex-husband who grabbed me from behind
at lunch time then blamed me he fell asleep at his job.

I'm staring through the crosshairs
at the cop who wanted to trade a *bj* for not taking me
to #1 Station for walking home at night past curfew /
staring through the crosshairs
at the lifeguard who lifted me onto a bed
raised like an altar with his wingman watching
after dosing my iced tea with a *Roofy*.

I am breathing hard.
My heart is pounding.
My arm has steadied.
I have cocked the hammer.

My eye is on the target
for all my sisters grabbed and groped /
fingered and beaten / raped and murdered /
who suffer daily affronts and shamings
in offices / on elevators / on trains / in streets
just trying to get home.

I am looking at you
who have dared to say
as a woman tells the truth about her life
that she's just overreacting or hysterical.
I am ready
to press my finger to the metal.

This is not a metaphor.
This is righteous indignation.
This is a wound that bleeds
and pulses with pain.

To A Cherokee Poet

(For Marilou Awiakta)

Kristin Camitta Zimet

Awiakta, Eye of Deer, you see best
close up—the under-dance of sprouts,
corn kernels rooting at the Mother's breast;
and where the Mother heartbeat drums within
you plant your hearing.

When you speak, the corn falls from your side,
heaping the same basket Selu filled,
the first Grandmother Corn. Her silk-lined cloak
folds round you like green wings.
Her ground blankets your dreaming.

Me, I am of the pickers-up, the crow people.
They strut the furrows
plucking an arrowhead, a shining shard;
flap off with a husk of story.

Mine are the folk of no patience, the catbird people.
They pick the threads of a thousand seam-ripped songs;
throw off rag-ends of chant
after a single wearing.

I come from the eaters-up, the vulture people,
heads rubbed bald, the better to rummage in the red
ripped drum of the roadkill,
those who get in the way.

I am of a hundred root-torn tribes,
blown overseas; become weeds, unwelcome ones,
stripped of their tasseled histories,
not yet American.

But Awiakta, in your hand
I turn on a parched cob; my people turn—
black, yellow, white, blood-red—
packed side by side, as seed
waiting to be cast.

Teach us to dance in place.
To ripen on the stalk with listening.
To return life for life.
I plant myself in my grandchildren's ground.
I braid a basket for the rising Corn.

"Typical nonsense as I try to write," drawing by Saint James Harris Wood

VIII

RANTS, RAVES & REVIEWS

EUGENIA TOLEDO

MAPTRACES BLOODTRACES

Trazas de Mapa, Trazas de Sangre
Translation by Carolyne Wright

Map Traces, Blood Traces / Trazas de mapa, trazas de sangre

by Eugenia Toledo, Translation by Carolyne Wright
Mayapple Press, http://www.mayapplepress.com
ISBN: 978-1-936419-60-9
2017, paper, 134 pp., $16.95

Reviewed by Rita Sturam Wirkala
Translation by Carolyne Wright

Esta colección de poemas y prosas poéticas son fruto de una visita de la autora a su tierra natal. Quienquiera que haya dejado su país para asentarse en otro lugar del mundo sentirá en carne propia (la nostalgia es una experiencia visceral) lo que transmiten estos versos. Y los que no, tendrán un vislumbre de lo que el exilio, forzado desde afuera o auto impuesto, significa en el íntimo sentir del ser migrante. Porque quien se va, quiéralo o no, no puede cerrar la puerta detrás de sí, como tampoco pudieron las Evas y los Adanes de la historia. Pero algunos, como Eugenia Toledo, tienen la fortuna de poder volver, aunque sea esporádicamente. Ella dice: *"Sé que he vivido varios mundos. Uno es haber sido, otro fue partir, y a veces, como ahora, volver a ti."* ("Nocturno de mis huesos.")

En este viaje de retorno temporario, la poeta subió y bajó por la columna vertebral chilena, así como por su propia interioridad. Y como la marca que el caracol va dejando detrás suyo, ella fue dejando su trazo poético al tiempo que transitaba por la peculiar geografía de su tierra. En más de cuarenta bellos poemas organizados en cinco partes, ha plasmado en versos, a veces tristes y dolorosos, a veces esperanzados y vigorosos, pero siempre evocativos, sus memorias e impresiones de la gente, de los lugares y de los hechos más horrendos de la historia de Chile en tiempos modernos, utilizando un lenguaje a veces realista y las más de las veces altamente metafórico.

En "Entrada al viaje" se nos habla de retorno. Pero la vuelta al Edén siempre sorprende y no pocas veces apena, porque, inevitablemente, las fuerzas entrópicas cambian lo que parecía inmutable: *"esperamos demasiado tiempo para probar la manzana, se nos ha podrido, se nos ha agusanado..."* Entonces, realidad y sueño se encuentran cara a cara y golpean a las puertas del alma de la viajera. El corazón se le parte en dos, en el ayer y el hoy, como las bíblicas *aguas escindidas* a las que alude la voz poética. Pero es de allí, justamente, de donde brota su lirismo.

En este intento de contar el difícil reencuentro con su patria, Toledo dice que le han salido apenas fragmentos. Es, se diría, como si el ente poético hubiera metaforizado las astillas de su corazón, una por una, y formado un todo mayor y elocuente, como la gota de agua que compone el océano, como el segundo que comprende los años de la ausencia.

También dice la poeta que su poema cojea, como su cuerpo, y que así, cojeando, busca el manuscrito del mundo. Pero este se ha perdido. Por eso inicia su labor, y a través de ese poemario teje otro manuscrito, lleno de ansias de esculcar el alma. El lector debe destejer esa escritura, hilo a hilo, para ir entendiendo la trama.

En "Norte," Toledo rinde homenaje a la querida Gabriela Mistral en Monte Grande. En un lenguaje preciso y sucinto nos habla del desierto de Atacama, *"penetrable ocre y almagre / las fisuras de tu suelo/ vítreo trizado..."* del cobre y la vicuña; de esa región donde reina la nada y por debajo de esa nada se ocultan sus secretos. Rememora a los trabajadores que sobrevivieron al derrumbe de las minas; y a otros que, en regiones aledañas y décadas pasadas, sucumbieron bajo la mano asesina de la dictadura. Al fin deja detrás el desierto con rumbo al Sur, y se trae el recuerdo de los sueños que allí se fecundaron.

En "Araucanía," la poeta camina por las calles de su

nativo Temuco, revive sus personajes, recorre sus memorias, algunas dulces y otras manchadas de sangre, de crimen y de silencios y, remontándose a los trágicos onces de septiembre—el uno, afamado; el otro, por muchos olvidado o nomás desconocido—lamenta la violencia. *"Mi mente es un volcán que nunca descansa / impactos de bala en mis recuerdos."* Verso a verso, nos va pintando escenas de esta tierra de terremotos y de poetas, donde conviven lo arcano de un pasado precolombino y lo moderno de un presente postcolonial. La poeta deplora que este presente haya cambiado el rostro de la naturaleza.

Con trazos más impresionistas que realistas, la emoción está siempre presente: pesadumbre por lo que se perdió para siempre, alegría en lo que aún subsiste, esperanza en lo que vendrá. Se detiene a nombrar al indígena destituido, al pordiosero, al pescador pobre, a la mujer sufrida, y tiende una mano en la oscuridad para tomar la mano de los otros poetas de la araucanía que hablaron o hablan su propia lengua.

En "Santiago," cada calle es significativa. Se remonta a los días funestos del 73, se para frente a los edificios, busca la marca de las balas en sus muros, y a cada paso le asalta el recuerdo de la resistencia y de las víctimas: los huérfanos, los torturados, los desaparecidos, los muertos nunca nombrados (*"tu valor es igual al de un gorrión"*); de los funestos centros de detención, y de su propio miedo.

Partir, se suele decir, es morir un poco. Pero volver también, porque quien regresa no se encuentra con una realidad idéntica a la que guarda, congelada, en la memoria. La vieja imagen muere para ser reemplazada por la tangible realidad del presente. Y también aquí en Santiago, el pasado y el presente coliden, el de la ciudad y el de la misma poeta.

"Inventario de mi tierra" es la sección más meditativa de todo el poemario. Ya no se miden las distancias de un mundo al otro en millas náuticas, sino en tiempo y relaciones humanas. Los mapas se desdibujan. Permanencia y cambio se confunden. Pero al menos, ella afirma, las amistades perduran y *"Las distancias son medidas por palpitaciones/ el pulso de las manos de bienvenida."*

La poeta contempla el regreso a su otro mundo y, antes de partir, observa su patria desde arriba, como un pájaro, cuya mirada abarca desde la torre de una iglesia hasta la rugosidad de una montaña, *"más allá de esta primavera hasta donde las aguas nacen."* Pero la brevedad del vuelo es reminiscente de la brevedad de nuestro humano tiempo. Y así, consciente de la imposibilidad de verlo y abrazarlo todo, sus poemas se vuelven más nostálgicos, por lo que vio y por lo que no pudo ver.

Eugenia Toledo nos habla, en suma, de la dicotomía del que se ha ido, pero no del todo. Y esta particular experiencia del que emigró y ahora vuelve y reconsidera y reconcilia, fecunda todos sus poemas.

La precisa traducción de Carolyne Wright no solo es fiel al original sino que mantiene su lirismo en la lengua inglesa.

This collection of poems and poetic prose is the fruit of a visit by the author to the land of her birth. Whoever has left their country to settle in another part of the world will feel in their own flesh (nostalgia being a visceral experience) what these poems convey. Even those who have not experienced such uprootedness will have a glimpse of what exile—whether compelled from without or self-imposed—means in the innermost sensibility of the migrant. Because whoever departs, willingly or no, cannot completely close the door behind herself, just as the Eves and Adams of history could not. But some, like Eugenia Toledo, have the good fortune to be able to return, albeit sporadically. She writes: *"Sé que he vivido varios mundos. Uno es haber sido, otro fue partir, y a veces, como ahora, volver a ti."* / "I know I have lived many worlds. One is to have been, another was to depart, and sometimes, as now, to return to you" (from *"Nocturno de mis huesos"* / "Nocturne of My Bones").

In this journey of temporary return, the poet ascends and descends the vertical spinal column of Chile, as if from within herself. And just like the glistening trail that a snail leaves in its wake, Toledo has laid down her poetic trace upon the time she traveled throughout the unique geography of her native land. In this sequence of over forty compelling poems, organized into five sections corresponding to the geographical regions she traverses, the poet has fashioned—in verse at times sorrowful and dolorous, at times energized and infused with hope, but always evocative—her memories and impressions of people, of places, and of the most horrendous acts of atrocity in the modern history of Chile, employing a language on occasion realistic but far more often highly metaphorical.

The first section, *"Entrada al viaje"* / *"The Journey Begins,"* speaks to us of return. But going back to Eden is always surprising and not infrequently painful because, inevitably, the forces of entropy change what appears immutable: *"esperamos demasiado tiempo para probar la manzana / se nos ha podrido[,]... se nos ha agusanado"* / "we waited too long to taste the apple / it's turned rotten[,]... filled up with worms" (from *"Nocturno de mis huesos"* / *"Nocturne of My Bones"*). Thus reality and dream meet face to face and knock upon the doors of the traveler's soul. Her heart is cleft in two, into past and present, like the Biblical *parted waters* to which the poetic voice alludes. But it is precisely from there that the poet's lyricism springs forth.

In this effort to recount the difficult re-encounter with her homeland, Toledo says that only fragments have emerged. One could say it is as if the poetic self had rendered the splinters of her heart, one by one, into metaphor, and from them formed a larger and more eloquent whole, like the drop of water that comprises the ocean, like the second that encompasses all the years of absence.

The poet also declares that her poem limps, like her body, and thus, limping, seeks the manuscript of the world. But this has been lost. Hence, she undertakes her labors, and by means of this poetic sequence weaves another manuscript, full of the urgency to delve into her soul. The reader must unravel this writing, thread by thread, to reach an understanding of the entire fabric.

In *"Norte"* / "The North," Toledo renders homage to the beloved poet of Monte Grande, Gabriela Mistral (Chile's first winner of the Nobel Prize, in 1945, for Literature). In succinct and precise diction, Toledo speaks of the Atacama Desert, *"penetrable ocre y almagre / las fisuras de tu suelo / vítreo trizado..."* / "penetrable ochre and ferrous ore / the fissures of your ground / shattered glass..." (from *"Ventana en el abierto mundo"* / "Window on the Open World"), of copper and the vicuña; where nothingness reigns and where beneath that nothing its secrets are concealed. The poet recalls the workers who survived the mine's collapse; and others who, in nearby regions, succumbed under the murderous hand of the dictatorship. At last she leaves the desert behind, enroute to the South, and brings with her the memory of dreams engendered there.

In "Araucanía," the poet walks through the streets of her native Temuco, recalling its characters and reliving her memories, some pleasant and others stained with blood, criminality and silence; or, going back to the tragic events of September 11—one of them famous, the other (the September 11, 1973, military coup in Chile) forgotten by many or never acknowledged in the first place—deploring the violence: *"Mi mente es un volcán que nunca descansa / impactos de bala en mis recuerdos."* / "My mind is a volcano that never rests / thud of bullets in my memories" (from *"La emergencia de la memoria"* / "The Emergence of Memory"). Line by line, Toledo depicts scenes of this land of earthquakes and poets, where the ancient, pre-Columbian past co-exists with the modern, post-Colonial present. The poet laments how this present has altered the face of nature.

With traces more impressionist than realistic, emotion is always present: sorrow for what has been forever lost, joy for what still persists, hope for what will come. The speaker pauses to name the destitute indigenous woman, the homeless beggar, the impoverished fisherman, the women who suffer, and she extends her hand in the darkness to take the hands of the indigenous poets of the Araucanía who spoke or who continue to speak in their own language.

In "Santiago," every street resonates with meaning. Harkening back to the grim days of 1973, the speaker pauses in front of the buildings, seeking out the bullet holes in the walls, and at every step she is assaulted by the memories of the resistance and of the victims: the orphans, the tortured, the disappeared, the dead who were never named (from "Relatos de mujeres" / "Stories of Women": "*tu valor es igual al de un gorrión*" / "[your] worth less than a sparrow"), the grim detention and torture centers, and her own fear.

It is often said that to depart is to die a little. But returning is also like that, because the one who returns does not encounter the same reality as the one she preserves, suspended, in memory. The old image dies to be replaced by the tangible memory of the present. And also here in Santiago, past and present—that of the city and that of the poet herself—collide.

"*Inventario de mi tierra*" / "Inventory of My Land" is the most meditative section of the volume. The distances between one world and the other are not measured in nautical miles, but in time and in human relationships. Permanence and change become blurred. But at the very least, the poet affirms, friendships endure and "*Las distancias son medidas por palpitaciones / el pulso de las manos de bienvenida.*" / "Distances are measured by heartbeats / the pulse of welcoming hands" (from "*Lapislázuli*" / "Lapis Lazuli").

The poet contemplates her return to her other world and, before departing, observes her homeland from above, as would a bird whose glance takes in everything from the church tower to the rugged folds of a mountainside, "*más allá de esta primavera hasta donde las aguas nacen.*" / "beyond this springtime to where the waters are born." (From "*Inventario de mi tierra"* / "Inventory of My Land"). But the brevity of this flight is reminiscent of the brevity of our human time. And so, aware of the impossibility of seeing and encompassing everything, Toledo's poems grow more nostalgic for what they have seen and what they have not been able to see.

In sum, Eugenia Toledo speaks to us of the dichotomy of what has come and gone, but not entirely. And this particular experience of the one who emigrated and who now returns, who reconsiders and reconciles, is what produces all her poems.

Carolyne Wright's precise translation is not only faithful to the original Spanish but also sustains its lyricism in the English language.

Here is a poem from Toledo's book:

Colgar la ropa al sol

Eugenia Toledo

La lámpara de mis brazos con que ilumino tu cuerpo se apaga en las lagunas que nos separan. Aún así salto los espacios sin darme cuenta y te alcanzo. Tierra de otras épocas que vive en un viejo mapa colonial tan inscrito en imágenes y tan pensado en versos, tan manchado de café. En tu útero, esqueletos van y vienen por las calles que marcaron la piel de las noches que pasaste en vela. En ti los pobres entierran y desentierran sus muertos, caminan alrededor de una plaza, llevan pancartas con una foto donde se lee "Dónde están" o "Por los hijos caídos, luchamos sin olvido." Bordan *arpilleras* a lo Violeta Parra o bailan la cueca sola. Es necesario aprender un nuevo abecedario y creer en un cambio, empezando por colgar la ropa al sol.

Hanging Clothes in the Sun

Eugenia Toledo

The lamp of my arms with which I illuminate your body
goes dark in the lagoons that keep us apart. Even so, I leap
over the spaces without taking notice and I reach you.
Land from another era that lives on in an old colonial map
so inscribed with images and so thought out in verse, so
stained with coffee. In your womb, skeletons come and
go through the streets that marked the skin of nights you
spent wide awake. Inside you, the poor bury and dig up
their dead, circle the plaza, carry placards with photos and
slogans that read "Where Are They?" and "For Our Fallen
Children, We Will Fight Without Forgetting." They
embroider *arpilleras* like those of Violeta Parra, or dance
the *cueca sola*. We must learn a new alphabet and believe in
change, begin by hanging our clothes in the sun.

Poem translated by Carolyne Wright with the author.

A Japanese Name

An American Story

Suma Yagi

Edited by Victor Yagi
& Frances McCue

A Japanese Name: An American Story

by Suma Yagi, Edited by Victor Yagi & Frances McCue
Published by Victor Yagi, victoryagi@gmail.com
Printed by Third Place Press
2016, paperback, 120 pp., $15.88

Reviewed by Mayumi Tsutakawa

In reading and re-reading Suma Yagi's seemingly short and simple book of poems of a life growing up Japanese American, I could not keep my mind from dwelling on the life of my mother, of similar age but recently deceased. For this book, *A Japanese Name: An American Story*, calmly and sweetly tells the story of damaging racial injustice, incarceration without due process, and the development of a conscience dedicated to telling this story for future generations to remember. These things, my mother also experienced.

In reviewing some numbers, as it has been seventy-five years since Executive Order 9066, forcing 120,000 Japanese and Japanese Americans on the West Coast into concentration camps, I thought about how many of these innocent individuals are still alive and cognizant enough to tell their story. According to Denshō, the Japanese American online encyclopedia, perhaps 20,000 former internees are still alive, but all would be above seventy-one years of age. If you consider that the individuals should have been at least teenagers to recount their stories, they would need to be around 90 years old now, as Mrs. Yagi is.

This makes *A Japanese Name* one of the few new first-hand accounts of war-time Japanese American history. How fortunate I am to have spoken with the lively and sharp Mrs. Yagi, and her son Victor Yagi, who organized the publication of the book.

Born in Seattle in 1927, Suma Yagi showed an early interest in writing. She attended local schools, where Nisei children saluted the American flag, learned the Bill of Rights and portrayed Pilgrims in school plays. She was proud to quote "All men are created equal. They are endowed with certain inalienable rights." But after December 7, 1941, a student at Garfield High School, she was surprised to find herself an "enemy alien."

Her poems provide images of her family's life in the temporary relocation center, Camp Harmony, and in Camp Minidoka, in the barren Idaho desert that became their home for four years. Her words bring observations, such as making mattresses for a home where there was none, to a human level: "They wrestled the straw into the canvas bags . . . the straw scratched back and drew red lines on their skin."

Calling herself a shy and oversensitive teenager, she adroitly describes the horror of latrines and showers without curtains or walls: "We shower in rows. A pipe with tiny holes sprays us like cattle at a trough."

Mrs. Yagi's older brother volunteered for the U.S. Army along with 300 others from that camp. He survived the treacherous European combat zones, bringing much gratitude to his parents' faces, only to see the family had to start over again with nothing after the war. Respect for the Japanese American soldiers who fought for the U.S. while their families were behind barbed wire is a strong theme in the book.

As well, love and praise for her parents, first generation Japanese, for all they endured—under the themes of *gaman* (perseverance), *on* (obligation), and *giri* (duty)—are expressed in a poem: "We children could feel the load of our family on our small backs."

Mrs. Yagi was married in Seattle after the war and, after some education at the University of Washington, went to work at the State Human Rights Commission, and later in the Office of the President at South Seattle Community College.

She says her life was filled to the brim with her four children's activities, church affairs, and golf outings.

But in the 1980s, as her children left home, she felt the need to pursue her writing and record her memories of life in the prewar community and in the camp, so her children also would never forget these experiences. She entered a poetry class taught by the renowned poet Nelson Bentley as a University of Washington extension course. He encouraged her writing, and in 1982, one of her poems was published in the national feminist journal *Off Our Backs*. She published other poems as well.

Around 2001, after retiring from her job and now a widow, she attended a writing class at Richard Hugo House, thus beginning a friendship with the poet and then-director Frances McCue. McCue says she "wanted to help carry this memory capsule home," and helped Mrs. Yagi and her son Victor organize and edit the pieces for a book.

Victor Yagi researched facts and found the book's telling historic photos from Denshō, The Museum of History & Industry (MOHAI), and the Wing Luke Museum. He also got the publisher-printer Third Place Press to handle the publication of the book. With a full-time job as an engineer with the City of Seattle, Victor spent much time over fifteen years completing the project that allowed his mother to tell the family's Japanese American story.

> Barbed wire like corkscrews
> Twisted around the perimeter of the camp,
> lacing the top of a nine-foot fence.

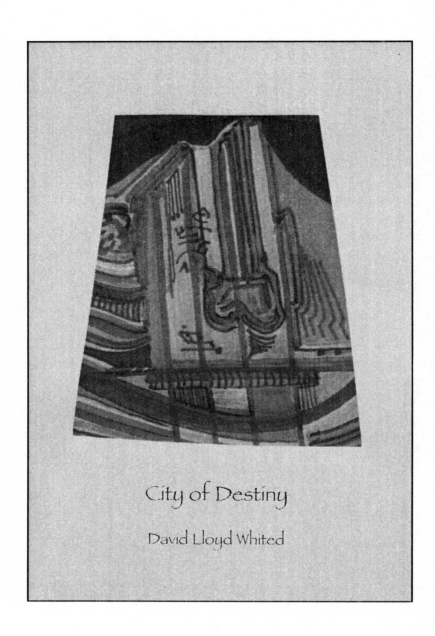

City of Destiny

David Lloyd Whited

City of Destiny

by David Lloyd Whited
nine muses books
3541 Kent Creek Road, Winston, Oregon 97496
ninemusesbooks999@gmail.com
ISBN 978-1878888754
2017, paper, 208 pp., $18.00

Reviewed by Laura Lee Bennett

I knew David Lloyd Whited when he was an MFA (I was a BFA) at Bowling Green State University in northwest Ohio. When I first heard David read, I recognized him as "an elegant beat poet," as his editor dan raphael says. His poems were brazen, prowling, sensual, and he read with jazz in his voice. The lines rolled out in low smokey notes, like a baritone sax; syncopated in short breaths, then swirling, languid, like brushes on a snare drum.

Years later, we met again at a Red Sky Poetry Theatre reading in Seattle. When I visited him on Vashon Island, the first thing he'd do was thrust a manuscript in my hands, demanding to know what I thought of *Billy Bonney*, *The Elevens*, *Pompeii*. In the dim light I pored over the fresh pages. We'd drink red wine, listen to jazz records, and watch Japanese baseball on TV. It was a heady time.

We connected once again in 2012, during the planning for the release of *Olde Man Coyote Goes to Towne*. David jumped at least two ponds to read in Redmond, Washington, and elsewhere locally. That coyote, that trickster, that alter ego. I was happy to witness the fruition of the work. Coyote had a developed persona, and it worked at readings. A voice so sly, so ironical, practiced, unfettered, and true. The clear, evolved voice of a scholar, a mathematician, a poet, a myth maker. Coyote. Still brazen and yet embraced in awe, with tinges of love, anger, and sorrow. A mature voice. An elegiac voice. And there was still jazz.

And then he left us.

And now, this book, *City of Destiny*. The poet's life and longing captured in the gritty city streets, the violence of the weather, the seasons, the island and the sea.

We are graced with this book through the efforts of family and friends: the poet's widow, Marian Whited, who envisioned the project; dan raphael, another BGSU alum, who arranged the poems for publication; margareta waterman, who designed the book with dan raphael; and James Grabill, another BGSU alum, who provided the cover art.

City of Destiny is a compilation of eras and places—the poet's life on the island he loved, his critter companions, his lovers/mates—and his work in the city, his commingling with the people on the streets of Tacoma (the city once thought to be the western terminus of the Northern Pacific Railroad in the late 19th century, hence the moniker). For decades, he was a planner for the Puyallup Tribe, and that experience also galvanized his poetry.

In his observations of the weather, flora and fauna, the stars, the news, politics, the night sky—the reader's senses are bombarded. The poet uses his gifts to impart deep emotion. The poems read like interior monologues, impressionistic and shimmering, poems that sing a bright, fierce, sorrowful song, an elegiac ditty, as he lopes through—and comments on—the daily life of commuting by ferry and bus from island to city and back again.

In Part I, "On the Avenue," the poems are stories of loss. The poet tells us, in "Seventy percent of the dust in a house is human skin," using repetition to assuage grief:

...
A flight of geese lost in the fog navigating
a wing and a honking while the water slaps

geese lost in the fog navigating
wing and a honking while the water slaps
fresh down to the sea. taking finally the long
slow way home. skirting the beach along this low sky
that breaks its knees crawling across the island.

  Later in the poem, we get the full story:

Overlooking the flooded fields, the reported
disproportion, a city's desolation does not sleep.
Crossed by the moon & the city planning office
though endorsed by the mayor. government works
through and itch and squirm day. scant breakfast
quavering at the lip of the grave. still dancing.

morning kittens, half-grown tigers, chattering
to the loggy slow early spring fly at the morning bath.

the forest is a lost myth. the forester a jailer.
the logger disappearing, tracking the far trees.
snags of firs, like soldiers bent lower by the guns.
tools, heroes, and marines. the owls taking the fall
the salmon mourning their losses, like fishermen.

out at the end of wind knuckle loop drive
lost continents are harbored in her eyes.
the scant ceremonials are still secret sins. frog noise
early afternoon at the swale. the island, like the
jungle eats its dead. spring buds swell to blossom
the multiple uses of bitterness. the morning muse
of coffee. Half-light & bird songs. late last
night she held the light as I buried that road-kill tiger.
this morning there is coffee, and it rains.

The poet gives a nod to literati past and present, his heroes: Virgil, Rimbaud, Baudelaire, John Ashbery, Herman Hesse, Dylan Thomas. Bukowski. There are many ironies, many layers. The book has an extensive table of contents—divided into seven sections; every poem has a corresponding page number. That is, every section except in Part II, the series "Rimbaud Left Uncollected." If you look at the poem titles here, all italicized, they themselves can be read as a poem:

suffering and pleasure; black moons, white moons.
a shivering song which chants its measure
the wallpaper mildewed, the room filled with distractions
beneath a coraled archipelago of stars
the early morning avenue is cold & vacant
this astonishing chicken, astonished chicken announcing
"I called up executioners in order to bite
ankle deep in grass the star show falls

In Part III, "Trees Are Tangled," we see the poet angered. His tongue turns to acid, but still ironical, still true. In "The Unemployment Line on Venus," he gives us a sharp reckoning: the "mental desolation" of the "person creatures" waiting in line:

The unemployment line on Venus has no shadows
because each one in it becomes a shadow.
Line up here enough times & even your pride &
what's left of it disappears. But the line holds.
Not even a shadow of these shadows standing in the line
waiting in this unemployment line on Venus.

This can't be the earth, this city, downtown, the City
of Destiny. These are only shadows. This can't be the /
  earth
the sky is not right, but this is the only line in town.

The bureaucracy is not, has never been, modest.
If this is how it is. If this is our destiny. Then we want /
    another
line. (We want something quite else.) in which
we can cast our own shadows. Without this waiting line
we want our shadows back.

In another poem in this section, "Sprinkling blossoms on the floor," we see the poet healing. Recovering from illness, he reclines in the night, addressing his beloved fellow travelers, the crow and the owl, in a kind of lullaby:

thunder frozen in my heart, starlight gone brittle
& wavering. even for the blackberries the memory of /
    summer
is growing old & spring is some pure far dream.
there is a secret strength in the island & always the
lonely bird-borne cry of dawn, a cup of anguish for the /
    heart.
trembling, whispering bright magic moon & planet star.
the always rain. moon & star & rain & distance the same.

The crows remain & my illness too passes away
The spike of fever weaker each cycle down
The sound breaks against the island
The salt diluted by the soft mouth of my creek
The geese exercising the endless vee of their daily flights
There is spring & lavender in my eyes. I heal
The wilderness returns. A tree's shadow broken by the /
    wind.

lonelily at dawn the owl whimpers his territorial /
    imperative
the moon & its star turn only to listen as
the crushed mint blows through my windows in the /
    dusk.

crows have brave hearts, fear nothing in a flock, in /
    murder
they fear nothing but perhaps the owl, & this only
when they are alone & near the dark of sleep.

There is a richness to this work, a luminosity. It is a lovely,
gritty pastiche that apologizes for nothing. In the end, we
have the poet's voice, and his voice lives on.

In Part II, "Island of Destiny," the poet tells us his reasons.
In "Following the Equinox," he quotes Octavio Paz:

"I do not write to kill time
nor to revive it
I write that I may live and be revived,"

And we close with the stanzas that follow, the poet is
longing in love:

ashes, dust, & dirt in love, profoundly in love
& lost in the desire to forget death, gravity, & time.
does my memory yet burn in your body?

The breaker wave-crashing sound of the freeway
throbbing in my temples. her name is high tide
in a small sheltered harbor. clawed lightning
scratched across the sky. her knees half open
she drinks her lazy coffee, adjusts her skirt
turns back to her desk. it is her legs that draw
my eyes. "the mouth of moss." nakedness is ancient.

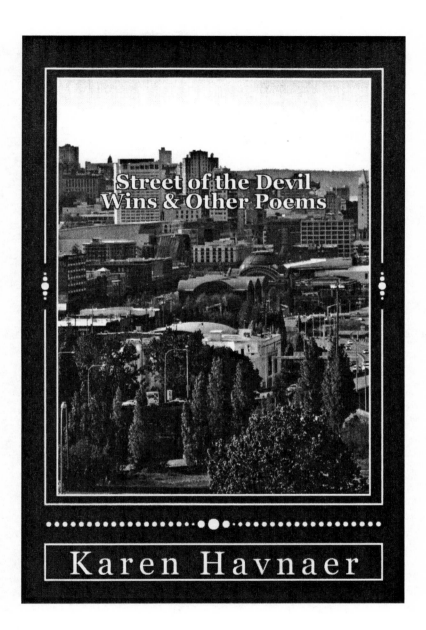

Street of the Devil
Wins & Other Poems

Karen Havnaer

Street of the Devil Wins & Other Poems

by Karen Havnaer
G StreetPress
ISBN-978-1-546439462
2017, paper, 48 pp., $7.00

Reviewed by David Fewster

At the age of seventy-nine, Karen Havnaer has finally published her first book, *Street of the Devil Wins & Other Poems*. In this slim volume, the kaleidoscopic impressions of a life are presented like a montage shot by a mad 1920s Soviet film director, starting from early childhood in Yakima (where Karen was a high school classmate of Raymond Carver, although they didn't hang out—even then he was probably one of the bad boys), a brief idyll in the tropics where she worked as a governess (do they still do that?), and on to a career in social work and political activism—all the while being a mainstay in the poetry and theater communities in Tacoma, which she surveys from her perch in the parlor of Captain Olaf's Double House in the Hilltop neighborhood, where she has lived for four decades.

Havnaer is not a confessional poet, and she changes poetic forms and personae like characters in the plays she performed in and directed. This stance is given a near-manifesto form in the second poem in the collection, "Have You Seen Me?" In "In Response to Your Question, This Is How I Am," she answers the query with quasi-surrealistic goofiness mixed with extreme historical improbability: "Emma Goldman helps me hem / in the living room drapes / Anais Nin tells me what it was like / with Gore Vidal, / we all laugh and pour more gin; / Sylvia Plath comes in with a perfectly / matched set of Samsonite luggage / (the set she carried with her to Cambridge), / tells us she is happy now / but still writing well." However, in "Cinema Verite", a scathing satire of pop culture in the era of late-stage capitalism, the poetic narrator unfortunately meets her doom.

The meat of the book, though, lies in the series of poems Havnaer has dedicated to the disenfranchised of Tacoma (which is never mentioned by name). She is a well-situated observer of such a scene, by benefit of her professional capacity and also by the close proximity of her home to Guadalupe House, the Tacoma chapter of the Catholic Worker founded by the late Fr. William Bichsel—the activist Jesuit priest for whom Havnaer was both friend and biographer. Even in some of these poems Havnaer's humor is evident, whether of the gallows variety, like in the title poem ("He claims his brain was stolen / and his watch. He slumps in doorways. / He sizzles like cold meat on a hot griddle. / / He isn't ready for high tech."), or the sheer farce of what looks like a "found" poem of a client's monologue, "The Viet Nam Vet Considers Darwin" ("but a monkey? Never. / Can you see the difference? / Why not a dog? / Who knows what happened back then? / They couldn't even write!"). In "The Bag Lady" this sense of absurdity becomes, ultimately, heartrending, and "Nativity House" (the name of Tacoma's drop-in daytime homeless shelter, now-defunct) is a vision of the Inferno, pure and simple.

Of course, there are many more things included in these pages. Poems for family, friends, (ex)lovers. Political poems. Silly drinking songs. A crazy poem, which may or may not be true, set in Red Square that for some reason Nelson Bentley particularly liked (I've seen the note!). The book ends with a couple of wry, beautiful poems infused with Havnaer's love of gardening ("Morning Glory" and "Five Hearts"). Karen was a prime mover (with copious donations of money and time) in the creation of Gallucci Learning Garden, a community garden located on G Street in Tacoma's Hilltop neighborhood, dedicated to teaching young people the basics of urban farming. Along with that legacy, we can now add this volume of poetry. And you don't even have to water it!

Seven Parts Woman

Poems by Marjorie Power
WordTech Editions
https://www.wordtechweb.com/power.html
ISBN-978-1-625492012
2016, paper, 102 pp., $19.00

Reviewed by Julianne Seeman

First off, I love the cover image: a lovely side view of a sensuous, long-legged woman—slim and graceful with a cap of artfully arranged white hair. *Seven Parts Woman* indeed!

Let me say up front too, I love the poems in this eighth collection by Marjorie Power (six chapbooks and one full length collection). These are important, necessary poems that deal with difficult subjects: aging, death, poverty, the loss of a breast through cancer. The poems are quiet, layered with nuance and meaning. They are Plain Chant: the music of a small women's choir in a darkened sanctuary, the wind off the sea, the call of a Raven at dusk . . . "rare delicacies filled with color and song," writes fellow poet Judith Skillman, "poised against fragile landscapes of eroding beaches and ruined haciendas." Poems, in Power's words, that stand "at the edge / of the world, at the young edge of old, / watching the old disappear. ("Mountains that Block Sunrise")

The collection begins with "On Cape Perpetua," a lyric mediation on place that invites the reader to follow the lush trail past a "*shell midden*, meaning / waste heap, summer place, / monument, memory, grave," and "across the highway and" down to the beach where we

> . . . sit [with the poet] by the sea . . .
> its waves turquoise, lazy, slack,
> as if the ocean floor
> couldn't possible slip.

This opening poem offers the natural world as a constant of beauty and refuge establishing the intimate tone of personal journey the poet takes as she struggles to face and survive the diagnosis all women fear.

In "Why Am I Unable to Ask?" the poet writes, "We women have an uneasy time." (That's putting mildly!)

We get biopsied for what we fear,
surrender breasts to virtual strangers.
Still, I'm grateful for the help.

When she gives her surgeon some of her poems, "He says / they'll help others, and wants more."

I'm flattered of course. But how
does he plan to use them? I still don't know
exactly what he did with my breast.

Exactly is the right word in the right place; the words that follow hit the reader like a compressed explosion.

Cancer happens to both partners in a long and loving marriage. In "Still Life with Husband," his "right arm wraps me, its hand with nothing to hold." She wonders "what the absence of my breast is like for him."

In time the prosthesis is made. Its creation is detailed in the title poem, "Seven Parts Woman, One Part Art." Seven is the archetypal number for creation: the perfect balance of earth / body (4) and intellect (3).

The poet dispassionately observes the "sculptor of human flesh," as he takes weeks to manipulate her skin "to receive a new breast— / a synthetic object, shaped / to match, cool to the touch. / He wore the face of a soul at work . . . / / its focus on creation." Artist to artist. Cool, objective, skilled control. "That gaze gave her full confidence," and ". . . After his work was done / and she returned to the day, / she found her desires intact, / a flock of Harlequin Macaws." These first generation hybrids, a cross between a Blue and Gold Macaw, are rarely found in the wild; still they are beautiful and enjoy a long, raucous life.

Although healed from surgery and with the new prosthesis, her body is irrevocably changed and the woman with it. In "The Deaf Percussionist," the poet speaks of the change with restraint, honesty and candor:

> After a women surrenders a breast to cancer,
> after she lets a doctor install an imitation,
>
> she finds her perception of beauty
> has changed. She feels akin to the blind
>
> who see with fingers, ears, noses and tongues.

She longs for comfort and direction. "Her Shawl, Removed" recalls a high school music teacher who conducted the choir when the poet was a teenager. Miss Warner was a "typical teacher," until at graduation, the girl noticed her teacher's "withered" right arm, "bent, / up against her chest / in an ironed white sleeve. // How had she led us? / How did she face the world?" the poet now asks. How could the girl she was have missed seeing such "a glaring flaw? / . . . one's right arm / was the way through life." The poet feels kin to her former teacher. The questions she asks apply as well to her own wounded body and soul. I love the raw emotion in the ending lines: "Winter's coming, Miss Warner, and I am lost // Sing to me. Please. / Sing anything."

The poems recount losses as the poet journeys with her husband from place to place where homes, that have been abandoned or destroyed, echo the poet's personal loss and struggle to survive. Beside a hot springs in "Rio Caliente," a woman speaks of her "southern California childhood;" a man "grasps his cane" to help himself up out of the steaming water, recalling his forty-five years in Alaska. A stretch of coast becomes real estate in "Green Rope." Condos take over in "Shaded by Sitka Spruce" (love the alliteration). Houses spring up on "Oceanfront Property." In "Approaching Milepost 85," the land where cattle once roamed is now "packed, barren dirt, / zoning squabbles, sprayed-out / paint cans, graffiti." She doesn't need to say: without art. There is no art or beauty here. In the "Day Before the Fire" an old woman's little house and yard, once filled with grass and "Daffodils, azaleas, / a climbing rose, daisies, dahlias, asters. . . ." is "purchased by someone called Kit" and, later, her "shrubs began to tangle and blur"; in the garage, "chaos thrives, complete with mattresses," and noise from "amplifier, drums, and a guitar . . . could strangle someone." Next to the rubble and discord the natural world brings wild beaches, lush terrain, and cultivated gardens the poet clearly loves. Color dominates like the undertow of powerful emotion in Northwest Coast grays, blues, and greens. One of my favorites, "In a Bruise Blue Hour" (l love the sound of the title), is a meditation on the sheer beauty of place, as is "Raven Triptych" and "On Cape Perpetua."

The rhythm and repetition of the beautifully executed "Ivy," captures the constant cycles of time passing: "Time comes unmoored when we approach a porch," and so much is gone: "no one's neighbor's ghost . . . no gardener with shears." Plywood has replaced the front door. Nature has taken over the site emptied of human habitation: "A volunteer maple. A wild young ash. / The giant oak's roots more under, press on." Each beautiful in their own way. "Here the world begins and ends."

Aging itself, which the poet is facing, is a time of dust and dusk and slant afternoon light. In "Karen's Song," old women croon "under the vast oak" in "end-of-summer sun" listening to "a bluesy piece that floats / sadly on and on // till it becomes a shawl / that can be gathered up, / carried home and arranged / around the shoulders / in winter." The quiet beauty of the metaphor is stunning in its simplicity, reflecting not only the poet's skill but the place of knitting in her life. In "Why I knit" she explains, "Because I delight in spring / but belong to autumn." Knitting is its own art—not unlike writing poetry, or making a life out of the new or of what is left.

In one of my favorite poems, "Gone Crone," age has its own kind of beauty: Stark, bleached, washed clean, without embellishment or mess. "An elk bone / found clean and dry. / Found hiking. Carried home." Everything is empty, open, waiting, expectant, full of primary color. "White bed sheets." "A cobalt blue vase. // Sunbeams. / A picture window" that we assume looks out into the world. "Afternoon light / spread all the way out. / An open door. Sand under-/ foot. Bare, dry sand / where there used to be slime, . . ." I love the sensuous, spare images in this poem, the assured voice declares the changes aged wisdom brings: "Yes, I've changed," the poet says, "I did warn them."

A world in which children are killing children needs this voice. In "Designing a Necklace for Nicole," ordinary craft—the simple act of making a graduation gift for the daughter of a friend—becomes a vehicle for social commentary. "Because of the massacre / at the high school close to yours. . . . Because my mother has passed away . . . Because my mother was spared this news / your grandmother hears." The repetition of *Because* expertly contains, controls and expresses the poet's—and our—horror at children equipped with military-type weapons killing other children.

In "Virtual Candles," the poet fights NRA propaganda supporting gun rights by claiming that recent "Headlines" are the result of "aberrant" acts: "*This is a case of evil, / someone who's an aberration / of nature. If it weren't one / weapon, it would be another.*" The poem counters:

Does anyone who's *not* aberrant
pull down blinds and fill his apartment

with bullets, bombs, an assault rifle
purchased with the click of a mouse?

In "a world that is ending in fire" ("Minding Our Business"), her poem, "Dreaming That the M.C. Is a Raven," delivers the answer: "One at a time I will swallow you whole / and release your spirits — ghostly lunatics / awhirl in the void. At last without choice / you'll begin to love me. You'll begin / to love. / You'll begin." Lines so blatant, so true, we take comfort and hope.

And find moments of sheer joy. In "Resting on the Couch," one of the last poems in the collection, the intellect and the heart come together in a lovely scene: the poet's granddaughter, dozes "comfortably / atop my reconstructed breast. / I've been thinking of it / as an art purchase / that's wearing well."

Still there is "Fear." In this penultimate poem, early February brings the promise of spring, yet the poet is unable to fully embrace it. To fear is "to stand at a window / and watch the snow melt, / then go on watching."

"December Coastline" ends the collection where it began, on the Pacific Northwest Coast. We have come full circle, traveling the seasons of grief from the lush spring at Cape Perpetua, to where the "roar of the wind / is the roar of the surf / is the aria of December," where the poet concludes: "There's something / I wanted to tell you. / The wind must have taken it."

There is music, power, and wisdom in these poems. I echo Judith Skillman when I say this collection is, "A must read."

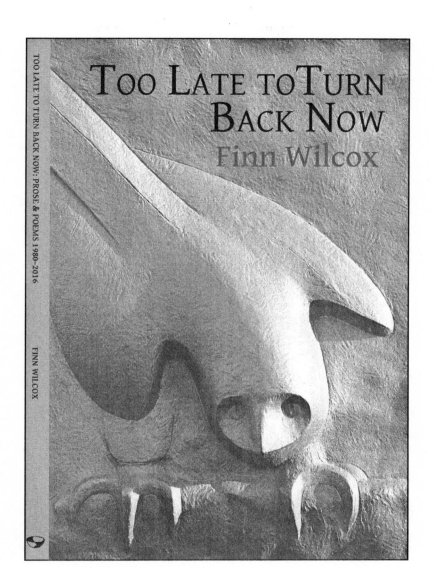

TOO LATE TO TURN
BACK NOW
Finn Wilcox

TOO LATE TO TURN BACK NOW: PROSE & POEMS 1980–2016

FINN WILCOX

Too Late To Turn Back Now: Prose & Poems 1980 - 2016

by Finn Wilcox
Empty Bowl Press, 201 West 89th St., New York, NY 10024
Order info: www.pleasureboatstudio.com
ISBN 978-0912887524
2017, paperback, 151 pp., $18.00

Reviewed by Larry Laurence

There is so much to be happy about, as well as grateful for, in *Too Late To Turn Back Now,* Finn Wilcox's new and selected works spanning some thirty-six years. First, to have *so much* of his work available in one volume when much of his work is either out-of-print or only available in limited edition chapbooks or small press anthologies. And then, of course, there's the work itself. Whether in journals, stories, poems, Wilcox is always accessible, passionate, sometimes serious, sometimes funny and sometimes seriously funny, instructive in the ways of living a good life, a life of conscious choices, without being preachy or pedagogical.

Wilcox's major influences clearly include classic Chinese and Japanese poetry, Kenneth Rexroth, Beat prose and poetry, particularly Jack Kerouac's and Gary Snyder's, along with the many writers, poets, artists, Chinese scholars / translators from Northwest Washington's Ish River Country (lands bordering the Salish Sea). And there is, of course, Wilcox's friend and mentor, Robert Sund, whom Wilcox calls the "unofficial poet laureate of the Pacific Northwest and patriarch of the Ish River poets"—but more on that later.

Too Late To Turn Back Now begins with a complete reprint of Wilcox's first book, *Here Among The Sacrificed,* Empty Bowl Press, 1984—a journal of prose and poems chronicling his "riding the rails" along the West Coast from the Pacific Northwest to Southern California. Included in this section are photos by Steven R. Johnson, Wilcox's rail-riding companion and gifted photographer. We have written and photographic portraits of hobos, i.e., "the sacrificed," done with respect and compassion. Here's a snippet from "Goodnight Crummy Willy." Crummy Willy is speaking:

". . . there's two things in my life I've never missed: a meal is one and a freight train is the other. Now I ain't sayin' I haven't put that meal off a day or two, an' them trains left more'n once when I wasn't ready ta go, but I ain't missed either of 'em yet."

Too Late continues its travels in its second section, a selection of poems from the chapbook, *Nine Flower Mountain*, Tangram Press, 2002. Wilcox accompanies Bill Porter, aka Red Pine, scholar / translator of ancient Chinese literature and Buddhist thought, "tramping through the sacred mountains of China." Here's a taste, from "Hard To Believe":

Hard to believe only
yesterday
we stood on the cliffs
of Cold Mountain

watching swallows
  sweep and skip
a drifting
cloudless
sky.

The third section of *Too Late To Turn Back Now* is a selection of love poems from the chapbook, *Lesson Learned*, Tangram Press, 2008. Here are two, both dedicated to Pat Fitzgerald,

Wilcox's "wife, partner and love of my life of forty years":

EXTRA ROOM
for Pat

So it's decided.
Roads are frozen.
Too much too drink.
Forty-five minute drive
back to Mount Walker.
Just stay here tonight.
You can sleep in the extra room.

Never made it there.

But by morning,
you asleep in my arms,
I found extra room
in my heart.

LOVE POEM WITH JERRY IN IT
for Pat

I finish the poem
and read it to you.
I see in your eyes
a tear beginning.
It's beautiful you say.
Maybe one of your best.
But you love all my poems,
how can I trust someone
who would take a bullet for me?
You roll your eyes:
show it to Jerry then.

But he loves me too.

The last section, *Not Letting Go*, is new work, both prose and poems. Here's a quick taste:

OUTDOOR WORK

The one time
I experienced what my Buddhist friends
call enlightenment,
that recognition, sharp and clear
as a shot of whiskey,
was packing my tree bag
on a landing pooled in drained skidder oil
in a clear-cut
big as the town I lived in,
understanding
finally and fully,
the rotting extravagance of greed.

And lastly, back to Robert Sund. Wilcox has several moving pieces regarding Robert Sund (1929-2001). This is from "FOR ROBERT SUND *In Memoriam*":

. . . A fierce defender of beauty in all its myriad forms—his poetry and art became standards by which many of us measure our own.

Recently a friend said to me, "I've known a handful of people who write good poems, but Robert was the only poet I ever met."

Shortly before his death he was talking with my wife and me about all the haywire things he'd done to scrape by as a poet. After a long pause in the conversation he looked up at us smiling and said, "I've had some ridiculous ideas in my life and only failure has saved me." A hearty amen to that, brother Sund. We will miss you.

Guiding a stray bee
    out of the house—
Enough work for one day!

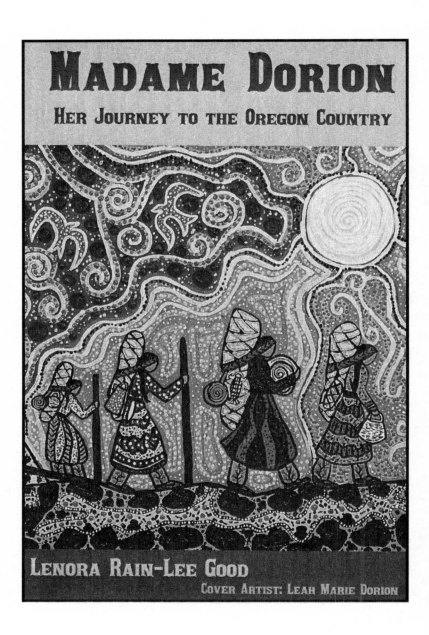

MADAME DORION

HER JOURNEY TO THE OREGON COUNTRY

LENORA RAIN-LEE GOOD

COVER ARTIST: LEAH MARIE DORION

Madame Dorion, Her Journey to the Oregon Country

by *Lenora Rain-Lee Good*
S & H Publishing, Inc.
http://sandhbooks.com/story/madame-dorion/
ISBN 978-1633200050
2014, paperback, 236 pp., $14.99

Reviewed by Thomas Hubbard

This historic novel traces the travels and travails of Madam Dorion, a woman of the Ioway tribe of the midwestern Ho-Chunk peoples. Author Lenora Rain-Lee Good takes us back, with her well-researched story, to the time of the Oregon Trail and the beginnings of Astoria, and to the founding of a mission near the fort that would become Walla Walla, Washington.

In the years following Lewis and Clark's expedition, parties of French fur trappers and their native guides made the long trek from around Saint Louis, across North America's western mountain ranges to the verdant lands of the Pacific Northwest. Recorded historical documents and personal journals that have been preserved all these years tell us that one of these Frenchmen, John Baptiste Dorion, and his tribal wife served as guide and interpreter for such a group.

In the ten years this story describes, Madam Dorion births three children, travels thousands of miles on foot, by canoe, and sometimes on horseback. She cooks, makes camps, doctors sick or injured party members, and cares for her children while suffering mountain snowstorms, attacks by hostile tribes, and periods of extreme hunger and thirst.

The book, fictionally presented as Madame Dorion's journal, includes Good's extensive bibliography, plus an epilogue in which Good follows Madame Dorion and some of the other characters after the journey. Good also explains the fictive aspects of how she combined official documents, journals, old correspondence, and peripheral research to tell this captivating story.

Some of the necessary liberties Good allowed herself in the characterization of Madame Dorion and her children may crowd a reader's "suspension of disbelief." One example is Madame Dorion's second son, Paul, who appears as a toddler demonstrating surreal abilities of a medicine man almost from birth. And a wilderness cabin is built in a day or so. But the story, overall, is strong enough to carry on without loss of the reader's interest.

Overall, this book provides an enlightening picture of early nineteenth century reality on the Oregon Trail. Lenora Rain-Lee Good shows us the grit and strain, and the dangers of real life on America's extreme frontier. And the cover, by Leah Marie Dorion (a direct descendant of Madame Dorion) is a beautiful piece of art that seems to lend credibility to Good's work. It will surely become dog-eared in my personal library, and perhaps in yours.

The

DEEPEST ROOTS

FINDING FOOD AND COMMUNITY
ON A PACIFIC NORTHWEST ISLAND

KATHLEEN ALCALÁ

The Deepest Roots, Finding Food and Community On A Pacific Northwest Island

by *Kathleen Alcalá*
A Ruth Kirk Book
University of Washington Press
ISBN 978-0295999388
2016, hardcover, 344 pp., $28.95

Reviewed by Jim Cantú

Much more than a casual drive by, Kathleen Alcalá's book delivers on the title's promise of *The Deepest Roots*. As Alcalá notes:

"Because foodways form the heart of any community, I have spent the last few years exploring those of the many communities on Bainbridge Island. My conversations focused on two questions: 'If we had to, could we support our current population with food grown on the island?' and 'What would it take to do so?' These two questions seemed to encapsulate how we think about the land and our relationship to it. They get beyond the easy answers ('I'm for preserving the environment') to what lies at the heart, our hearts, when we talk about land."

She explores the land of Bainbridge Island by talking to its people and telling their stories, both present and past. Alcalá introduces us to the Suquamish, the original indigenous inhabitants of the island. She provides historical integrity as she recounts how the Suquamish land was taken, and sacred sites, such as the "Old Man House," were burned by the United States government. How fishing, hunting, and natural plant habitation have been impacted by new inhabit-ants, and what the current Suquamish are doing.

I enjoy reading historical information and found her periodic dives into different time-periods to be informa-tive and insightful. I had done some reading on Executive Order 9066 and the imprisonment of U.S. citizens (Japanese Americans) in concentration camps during the Second World War. Alcalá's use of the concentration camp administrator's journal entries provide a new view into this disgraceful time in our country's history, and sheds new light on the valor of our imprisoned fellow citizens.

We meet butchers, bakers, farmers, and neighbors who have come from all over the world to help mold a special way of life on the island. Alcalá also shares glimpses of her own history and heritage that have helped frame her world view. She provides new topics of discussion and even some cooking suggestions, and she ends it all with over a dozen pages of notes and references for additional exploration.

Some say that reading a book is like taking a journey. It has the magic to transport you to a different place and time, as the author's words paint a picture in your mind. Some authors can make you forget about today's troubles. You don't want to leave the special place they've conjured up with word magic. When you travel into Kathleen Alcalá's book, *The Deepest Roots*, be sure to pack extra socks for your trip. It is well worth the read and the journey.

The White Crow, detail of collage by Anita Endrezze

IX

RAVEN NOTES

LIST OF ARTISTS AND ILLUSTRATORS

Pages art/illustrations appear on:

Daniel Ableev, Germany: 135
David Anderson, Nebraska: 17
Anna Bálint, Seattle: 24, 31, 39, 106
Phoebe Bosché, Seattle: 179
Michelle Brooks, New Mexico: 223, 251
Vivian Calderón Bogoslavsky, Colombia: 146, 153, 245
Alexander Chernavskiy, Russia: 195
Anita Endrezze, Washington: 20, 304, 340
Paul Flippen, Colorado: 161, 239
Jeannie Grisham, Washington: cover artwork
Jeff Niles Hacking, Washington: 32
Henry Hu, Australia: 169, 183, 209, 255
Doug Johnson, Washington: 41, 44
Sarah E.N. Kohrs, Virginia: 127, 175
Megan Magill, Illinois: 104, 193
Rudy Hansen Murray, Washington: 185, 189
Ndubueze Okonkwo, New York: 203
Bridget Reweti, New Zealand: 56, 69, 70
David Rodríguez, Spain: 75, 76, 91, 92, 98, 102
Judith Skillman, Washington: 47
Marilyn Stablein, Oregon: 235
Emily Townsend, Texas: 199, 201, 231, 248
Andrew Wesner, Seattle: 116, 139
Saint James Harris Wood, California: 261

NOTES, PERMISSIONS, AND PUBLICATION CREDITS

Kathleen Alcalá: "When The Tide Is Out," an edited excerpt from *The Deepest Roots: Finding Food and Community on a Pacific Northwest Island* © 2016. Reprinted with permission of the University of Washington Press.

Anita Endrezze: "Raven In Eden," was used as cover art for the online magazine *Star*Line, Fall 2017, Vol. 40.4,* a magazine of Science Fiction & Fantasy Poetry, edited by Vince Gotera. Reprinted by permission of the author.

Fiona Farrell: novel excerpt from *Decline and Fall on Savage Street*, Penguin Random House, New Zealand, 2017. Reprinted by permission of the author.

Jill McCabe Johnson: "Raptor" was previously published online by *Page & Spine*, 2017. Reprinted by permission of the author.

Nic Low: "Ear to the Ground," first published in longer form in *Griffith Review 35: Surviving*, January, 2012 (https://griffithreview.com/articles/ear-to-the-ground/). A version also appeared in *The Press*, February 23, 2012. Reprinted by permission of the author.

JT Stewart: "Left To My Own Devices" was previously published in *Love On The Rocks, Yet Again*, by JT Stewart, Lamaya Press, Seattle, 2011. Reprinted by permission of the author.

Eugenia Toledo: "Colgar la ropa al sol": *Colgar los trapos al sol* es una expresión que significa contar la verdad. Las *arpilleras* son cuentos elaborados en género que hacen testimonio a las vidas de los más afectados por los años del régimen militar. Durante las casi dos décadas de dictadura militar, fueron creadas miles de *arpilleras*. Marjorie Agosín escribió un libro seminal sobre este tema titulado *Tapicería de la esperanza, hilos del amor: el movimiento arpillera en Chile, 1974-1994. La cueca sola* es una metáfora. Mujeres chilenas cuyos maridos e hijos fueron desaparecidos durante la dictadura bailan este baile folclórico popular chileno—representado tradicionalmente por un hombre y una mujer—solas en las calles. El compositor-cantante inglés Sting las inmortalizó en una canción llamada "They Dance Alone" en 1987.

Eugenia Toledo: "Hanging Clothes in the Sun": To hang rags in the sun (*colgar los trapos al sol*) is an expression that means to tell the truth. Chile's *arpilleras* are patchwork stories that bear testimony to the lives of those most affected by the years of military rule. During the almost two decades of military dictatorship, thousands of *arpilleras* were created. Marjorie Agosín wrote a seminal book about this subject titled *Tapestry of Hope, Threads of Love: The Arpillera Movement in Chile, 1974-1994. La cueca sola* is a metaphor. Chilean women whose husbands and sons were disappeared during the dictatorship dance this popular Chilean folk dance—traditionally performed by a man and a woman—by themselves in the streets. The English singer-songwriter Sting immortalized them in a song called "They Dance Alone" in 1987. Reprinted by permission of the author. (Poem Notes translated by Carolyne Wright with the author.)

BIOGRAPHICAL NOTES
Artists / Illustrators

Daniel Ableev is a certified strangeologist and Selectronix engineer from Bonn, Germany. He is co-editor of *DIE NO-VELLE — Zeitschrift für Experimentelles*, and has publications in German and English, print and online (*Born to Fear: Interviews with Thomas Ligotti*, Ann and Jeff VanderMeer's *The Big Book of Science Fiction, Alu*, etc.). See his work at: www.novelle.wtf; www.wunderticker.com; www.soundcloud.com/proegressor; www.proegressor.bandcamp.com.

David Anderson is an artist and historian from Omaha, Nebraska. He dwells in a brick house that was built in 1926. He lives with his best friend, and five little people. The five do not pay rent, but they do provide laughter. He enjoys swimming, writing, baseball, and playing chess. The photograph in this issue [pg. 17] was inspired by experiencing winter in Omaha, and the feeling that there can be a profound element of joy that can exist with sadness and the past.

Anna Bálint "The theme for this issue inspired me to notice and photograph places in my day to day life where urban development and infrastructure intersected with green spaces in interesting ways. However, the pea patch in Budapest [pg. 39] came as a complete surprise. On a recent visit to Hungary, I was wandering District 8, historically the poorest neighborhood in the inner city, known for its high concentration of Roma residents. Indeed, members of my own family lived there prior to WWII. In recent years, gentrification has resulted in many old and neglected residential buildings being torn down, leaving behind empty lots with new construction everywhere. I came across this small lot beneath towering cranes where people had planted vegetables. Now the area is fenced off by barbed wire, and thistles and sun-flowers have sprung up."

Vivian Calderón Bogoslavsky is a native-born Colombian, born to Argentinian parents. She holds a BA in anthropology with a minor in history, and a postgraduate degree in Jour-nalism from Universidad de los Andes in Bogota, Colombia. She has studied art for over thirteen years with a well-know Argentinian art master, abroad in Florence, Italy, and in the USA. Vivian has spent the last few years investigating "The Prints of the Earth."

"During this investigative process I have come to the realization that these prints [pgs. 146, 153, 245] reflect my most intimate and profound feelings, emotions, wishes, sad-ness, and life experiences. My intention behind my paintings is to create magical worlds that move people, that make them look within and explore their feelings when confronted with my work. The prints are related to an extraordinary universe, filled with dolor, texture, sand, and ashes. I try to translate my own path onto the canvas and in the process a print is left behind, filled with all of what makes me me." Website: www.ArteCalderon.com

Michelle Brooks: "My photography seeks to capture the quotidian details of people and places in a way that forces the viewer to experience them in an emotional way. My process is one not of discovery as much as rediscovery. I juxtapose the natural world with the man-made one to create a tension between what has always existed and what has been created or discarded. As a writer I have a narrative sensibility. My photographs [pgs. 223, 251] attempt to give a glimpse of a story that allows the viewer enough room to bring their own story to the image as well.

"Part of my process is not to stage photographs. I work with objects as they are. I seek to photograph people on the street from a distance or ask strangers if I can photograph them. I've never been refused a photograph. I've been surprised and delighted by the variety of poses my subjects assume. As with objects, I offer no directives, as I believe the essence of a person, object, or place reveals itself when it is as undisturbed by the viewer as possible."

Alexander Chernavskiy was born in 1981, in Moscow, Russia. He is a Magister of Sociology (Moscow Psychologic-Social University), and is working as a freelance photographer and artist. He has worked with Corbis, Demotix, DAD, and TASS news agencies in recent years. He is a member of the Union of Russian Photo Artists (since 2009). In 2015 and 2016 he was a recipient of scholarships from the Ministry of Culture of Russia. His first photo book, *Alpha*, was published in 2015 by Dostoevsky Publishing, Amsterdam. His works have been published by privateonline.com, *The Sonder Review*, *Snapdragon*, and *The Ocotillo Review*.

[pg. 195] "The parable of the Law was told a long time ago. Proverbs about Judges can always be told. Or vice versa. We all came to court. Or the court thought of us. Perhaps we decided to meet with the Judges. Or vice versa. Who are these Judges? Many people think of fear and death. Some people think that these are dreams of a troubled conscience. Some— that they are companions of intellect and special punishment for it. All of them are right. Probably. This Book of Judges is written about them and for us. Or vice versa."

Anita Endrezze has a quiet sense of humor. She laughs a lot inside her head where her main audience is. When she isn't cracking herself up she does collaborative art with other women. A recent altered-book project was archived in the Smithsonian. She also writes fiction and poetry. Her chapbook of poems and art, *A Thousand Branches*, Red Bird Press, 2014, was a poetry postcard project.

"Originally I created over forty poetry postcards for a month-long event. Along with over three hundred people around the world, I created and sent thirty-one poem cards, one for each day of August, 2013. Each poem had to be succinct in order to fit the size limitations of the cards. In a couple of cases, though, I made a pocket on the message side of the card, typed and folded the poem on a piece of paper, and then sealed it in the pocket. The art was a little easier in that I could reduce the images to fit the format. I called this book *A Thousand Branches* because I imagined the words and imagery reaching out to people all over the world."

Paul Flippen was born in Berlin, Germany, and, as an Army Brat, bounced around between Germany, Texas, and California at the whim of the Pentagon. He earned a BFA in Painting and a BA in Art History, both from the University of Texas at Austin. He completed his studies at Pratt Institute, New York, receiving an MFA in Painting and an MS in the Theory, Criticism, and History of Art.

"I create visual puzzles. My paintings communicate through several languages simultaneously by incorporating a variety of applications and techniques. Crisp-edged patterns and representations overlay, and comment on, the central image. Images of telephone poles [pgs. 161, 239] are layered with abstract representations of sound and speech—an attempt to communicate. These modes build and over-lap—circles of intent that clarify their meaning through the accumulation of implications, to impart a density of meaning."

Jeannie Grisham [cover artist] received her education at Washington State University and Burnley School of Professional Art in Seattle, Washington, with advanced studies at Lyme Academy of Fine Art in Lyme, Connecticut. An award-winning watercolorist, her works have been included in major exhibitions at The National Academy in New York, the Palette and Chisel Club, Chicago, and numerous National Watercolor Exhibitions. She is President Emeritus of both the Northwest Watercolor Society and Women Painters of Washington, and she teaches at the Winslow Art Center. She has had a long association with the Bainbridge Arts and Crafts Art Gallery on Bainbridge Island, Washington.

"The joy in painting for me lies in the process of creating. As soon as I dip my brush in water, load it with the pigment and introduce it to paper, I'm in a different world. The painting starts with transparent watercolor and continues developing darks while managing to keep the lights. During this process I usually end up adding gouache to the work. It is great fun to manipulate and adjust the textures until the results are pleasing. The painting is considered finished only when it feels just right. Any medium, as long as it is water soluble, is fair game, and any tool I can think of to help create textures on hot press paper is a welcome find." Visit her website: www.jeanniegrisham.com.

Jeff Niles Hacking was raised in Utah by a pack of excommunicated Mormons. He graduated from the University of Utah with a degree in Geophysics, hence his love of rocks. In prison, he learned to draw [pg. 32], paint watercolors, and found a love for writing.

Hong Kong-bred, Sydney, Australia-based, **Henry Hu's** artworks are personal, intentional, with a focus on storytelling. He strives to assemble a full body of work, forming a series piece by piece. Each series consists of multiple pieces, grouped by specific concepts or stories [pgs. 169, 183, 209, 255]. By experimenting with digital tools, Henry creates something fresh, alternative yet familiar, and then frames the work in traditional forms. A variety of visual styles can be seen across his collections; through recurring structure and language—the heart of each series stays consistent.

Doug Johnson: "Art is what I breathe. My efforts have three foci. 1) As a poet, novelist, and ghostwriter, I use words. 2) As a musician and composer I concentrate on the piano and the symphonic metaphor. 'Obama's Prelude' gained a kind 'Thank You' from the president. An anthology of African Folk Music was produced in collaboration with Dr. David Akombo. I am currently working with the Secretary of Culture of Morelia, Michoacán, Mexico, who is a symphony conductor. 3) As a visual artist I concentrate on honing skills in pen and ink [pgs. 41, 44]. All three foci inform each other, and I try to explore the tensions we all experience in power and weakness, joy and tragedy. I love collaborating most of all, so contact me at cavemoonpress.com."

Sarah E. N. Kohrs is an artist and poet. Having earned a BA in Classical Languages and Archaeology from The College of Wooster in Ohio, as well as a Virginia State teaching licensure endorsed in Latin and Visual Arts, Sarah infuses her art with a love of languages and antiquity. American poet Langston Hughes said: "Let the rain kiss you. Let the rain beat upon your head with silver liquid drops. Let the rain sing you a lullaby."

Kohrs: "Rain mimics our weeping. Sometimes, it's filled with joy; often, with sombre unrest; always, with emotion. The series 'Rain on Glass' [pgs. 127, 175] turns the spotlight onto water as it falls from the sacred space created by rain clouds. Sometimes the dense emotion of a rainy day erupts into the beauty of fog or flashes with lightning or ends in a rainbow, but it always creates an ominous space—one that seems to mimic the dimension within our very selves."

Megan Magill is a visual artist based in Chicago and Maine. She received her BA in Humanities at the University of Colorado, her Masters from Northwestern University, and her MFA from Maine Media College. In 2017, her work was published in *American: Authors, Interpreters and Composers*, a book series created by Patricio Binaghi of Paripé Books, and designed by Matt Wiley of the *New York Times Magazine*. Megan experiments with a variety of photo and printmaking processes. In her most recent project, "My Business is Circum-ference," [pgs. 104, 193] she pushed dry mediums, such as powdered graphite and chalk pastels, through a photographi-cally-exposed silkscreen onto printmaking paper, resulting in one-of-a-kind works on paper. "I make work to rebel against absolute answers; to visually question the things we take as given; and ultimately, to reassure myself that I can be OK and find meaning from within the uncertainty of life."

Ndubueze Okonkwo is a high school student. He is a young and ambitious artist, and spends the majority of his free time drawing comics. Art is a passion of his which he has pursued since a very young age. He hopes to continue learning and improving his drawings. "Modern Angel," [pg. 203] was heavily inspired by mainstream Japanese manga style. "The main focus of this piece, as the title suggests, is that anyone can be an angel. People don't need to go to extremes to be noticed for good works, but, rather, should live their lives doing little good deeds here and there. Though people may not realize it, it's the little things in life that can make the most difference; through kindness to others one can attain the title of an angel in our modern world."

Bridget Reweti is an artist from Ngāti Ranginui and Ngāi Te Rangi in Tauranga Moana, Aotearoa, New Zealand. Her lens-based practice explores landscape perspectives and contemporary indigenous realities. Currently living in Wellington, Bridget holds a Masters in Māori Visual Arts from Toioho ki Āpiti, Massey University, and a Postgradu-ate Diploma in Museum and Heritage Studies from Victoria University of Wellington. Bridget is part of Mata Aho Col-lective, a collaboration between four Māori women artists who produce large scale textile works, commenting on the complexity of Māori lives.

"These photographs [pgs. 56, 69, 70]—from a wider

series called 'What are you looking at?'—reference the narrative of Tamaahua and his chase across country in search for Waitaiki and Poutini. The narrative is an oral map of important geological deposits, highlighting significant sites for numerous hapū and iwi. The photographs are taken from inside a camera obscura tent, reminiscent of late 1800s surveyor tents, and simulating the three-legged taipō, a surveying tool Māori referred to as a goblin."

David Rodríguez is thirty-nine, and was born and lives in Spain. "From an early age, I have always been attracted to the art world, but my love for photography didn't start until 2013, the year I bought my first reflex camera. I like to photograph people; I feel very comfortable doing portraits, but I always try to go a little further. That is the reason why I try to look for risky compositions, with a touch of surrealism. Each person inspires in me a different sensation, so before I do a shoot, I imagine how I would like to portray him or her. Then, I create a concept and imagine a story. I do not like to get attached to reality. Instead, I like to transform it, challenging the model with unusual situations. I play with the model, making each session a culture encounter, but also an enriching and surprising experience for both of us.

"Memories" [pgs. 75, 76, 91, 92, 98, 102] is a series composed of several black and white photographs that show memories of a summer love—each photo being a different memory. The photos are full of symbology and the protagonists of the story appear blurred—representing the memories that with time are fading. The rocks symbolize the pain that remains after separation."

Judith Skillman is interested in feelings engendered by the natural world. She strives to capture the interplay of light in borders between land and water. Her usual medium is oil on canvas or oil on board; her works range from representational to abstract. She has studied at the Pratt Fine Arts Center and the Seattle Artist's League under the mentorship of Ruthie V. Visit her website: jkpaintings.com.

Marilyn Stablein is the author of fourteen books, including *Splitting Hard Ground: Poems, Sleeping in Caves,* and a collection of environmental essays set in the Northwest, *Climate of Extremes: Landscape and Imagination.* She received degrees in Creative Writing from the University of Washington and the University of Houston, where she was a Cullen Fellow.

"Discarded and recycled cultural artifacts, found objects, shamanic tools, ritual objects, and green and ecological specimens from nature are all found in my work. Object Poem, a term borrowed from the surrealists, may describe some of my assemblages and still life photographs. I'm attracted to old, discarded, worn, chipped, dented, scratched, and outdated objects that evoke the past and reflect the passage of time. "Crow Balance Scale Seesaw" [pg. 235] joins other crow still life photographs that use vintage typewriters, books, mannikin heads, and clocks. By using recycled materials— ninety-five percent of my materials are recycled—I actively embrace and support recycling and green awareness." Visit her website: marilynstablein.com.

Emily Townsend is a graduate student in English at Stephen F. Austin State University. Her works have appeared in *Superstition Review, Thoughtful Dog Magazine, The Bookends Review,* and others. She was a 2017 AWP Intro Journals Award nominee, and a creative nonfiction finalist for Pen 2 Paper's Creative Writing Contest. She is currently working on a collection of essays in Nacogdoches, Texas.

"I lived with my brother in Eugene, Oregon, this past summer, and we traveled along the West Coast. The Pacific Northwest has always been home to me. These photographs [pgs. 199, 201, 231, 248] are nostalgic reminders that I was alive once, standing exactly where I could finally breathe. Any ferry in Puget Sound is my absolute favorite place; the postcard fog is a recollection of my childhood in Issaquah, Washington. There's a romantic, cinematic quality to the atmosphere of the Pacific Northwest that I've always loved, and I hope to return there permanently when I'm done with school."

Andrew Wesner is a professional print photographer living in Seattle. His work is displayed in commercial buildings and private residences. He believes in the principles of traditional film photography and image development as they can be applied to digital capture. Edits are minimal and limited to work that can be performed in a darkroom. He distributes his work in print format only to preserve the integrity of classic photography. Examples of his work can be seen at www.apwesner.smugmug.com, or by appointment.

"Allium" [pg. 139]: "I should have clicked the shutter again after taking that picture. I framed the shot in the viewfinder, clicked the shutter and then looked up. There was nothing but a nub where all of the seeds had been. A wind gust had taken them all away. In 1/250 of a second, all that I had captured was gone. I remember smiling and reflecting on my own impermanence. It was a cool Zen moment . . ."

Saint James Harris Wood was on the road with his psychedelic punk blues band, The Saint James Catastrophe, when he picked up the heroin-smoking habit. This inevitably led to a California high desert penal colony where he reinvented himself as a writer of the darkly absurd. His poetry, fiction, and essays have been published in *Confrontation, Meridian, Tears In The Fence, On Spec, Lynx Eye, The Sun,* and other less reputable literary gazettes.

BIOGRAPHICAL NOTES
WRITERS

Avis Adams lives in the Puget Sound area of Washington State on a small farm, where she loves to garden and write. She teaches English courses at a local community college, and her poems have won awards and been published online and in various literary journals. She also writes for children.

Kathleen Alcalá is the author of six books of fiction and nonfiction, including *The Deepest Roots: Finding Food and Community on a Pacific Northwest Island*, from the University of Washington Press, 2016. Along with Phoebe Bosché and Phil Red Eagle, she co-founded *The Raven Chronicles* on her dining room table. More of her thoughts can be found on her blog, "The Clueless Eater, " www.kathleenalcala.com.

Luther Allen writes poems and designs buildings from Sumas Mountain, Washington. He facilitates SpeakEasy, a community poetry reading series in Bellingham, Washington, and is co-editor of *Noisy Water*, a poetry anthology featuring local Whatcom County poets. His collection of poems, *The View from Lummi Island*, can be found at http://othermindpress.wordpress.com. His work appears in three recent anthologies: *WA 129* (an anthology of poems from Washington poets, edited by Tod Marshall), *Refugium*, and *Poetry of the American Southwest, Volume 3*.

Anna Bálint edited *Words from the Café*, an anthology of writing from people in recovery. She is also the author of *Horse Thief*, a collection of short fiction spanning cultures and continents, and two earlier books of poetry. Anna is an alumna of Hedgebrook Writers Retreat, the Jack Straw Writers Program, and has received awards and grants from the Seattle Arts Commission and 4Culture/King County. Currently, she teaches adults in recovery from the traumas of homelessness, addiction, and mental illness. She is a teaching artist with Seattle's Path With Art, and the founder of Safe Place Writing Circle at Recovery Café in Seattle.

Janée J. Baugher is the author of two ekphrastic poetry collections, *The Body's Physics* and *Coördinates of Yes*. Her non-fiction, fiction, and poetry have been published in *The Writer's Chronicle, Boulevard, NANO Fiction*, and *Nimrod*, among other publications, and she's held nonfiction residencies in Pennsylvania, Alaska, Idaho, Vermont, and California. Her nonfiction was nominated for the *2017 Best of the Net Anthology*.

Kyce Bello earned an MFA in poetry from the Institute of American Indian Arts. Her poems have appeared in *Taos Journal of Poetry, Anomaly, Heron Tree*, and *Sonora Review*. She lives beneath a very old apple tree in Santa Fe, New Mexico, with her husband and two young daughters. Her occasional blog is "Old Recipe for a New World," oldrecipe.wordpress.com.

Laura Lee Bennett received her MFA in creative writing from the University of Oregon in 1982. In the 1990s, she discovered Red Sky Poetry Theatre in Seattle, and was embraced by that community. She is a past president of the Redmond Association of Spokenword (RASP), a local literary arts organization in Redmond, Washington. In 2016, she collaborated with poets Elizabeth Carroll Hayden and Chi Chi Stewart on *I Am Not Cursed*, a voice play retelling the Demeter myth. She channels Persephone on a daily basis.

Eleanor Berry lives in rural western Oregon. She has two full-length poetry collections, *Green November* (Traprock Books, 2007) and *No Constant Hues* (Turnstone Books of Oregon, 2015). A former college teacher of English, she is President Emerita of the National Federation of State Poetry Societies and the Oregon Poetry Association.

Danielle D. Billing holds a BA in Education of the Deaf and Hard-of-Hearing from Augustana University, South Dakota. She teaches English Language Arts and Drama to Deaf and hard-of-hearing students at the Idaho School for the Deaf and the Blind, where she focuses on critical literacy and arts integration in a bilingual setting. Her poetry reflects her relationship to land and family, finding the gaps between her homes in North Dakota and Idaho. Her work has appeared in *Revolt*, the Augustana University literary magazine, and she has performed by invitation at Poetically Correct, a spoken word gathering of local artists. She entertains the masses in improv and theatre groups, gaining notoriety for her Fargo accent and Norwegian flair. She is the proud poultry mama of Yakko, Wakko, and Dot.

Michelle Brooks has published a collection of poetry, *Make Yourself Small* (Backwaters Press), and a novella, *Dead Girl, Live Boy* (Storylandia Press). She has just finished a book of photographs titled *Illusion Warehouse*. A native Texan, she has spent much of her adult life in Detroit, Michigan.

Thomas Brush: "I published my first poems in *Poetry Northwest* in 1970, and over the years have had work in *The Indiana Review*, *The Iowa Review*, *Prairie Schooner*, *The North American Review*, *The Cimarron Review*, *The Texas Observer*, *Nimrod* and other magazines. My most recent books are from Lynx House Press: *Last Night*, 2012, and *Open Heart*, 2015. I have just completed a new manuscript."

Jim Cantú has penned poems, prose, and personal essays. His written work has appeared in *Raven Chronicles* (2017), *Seattle Poetic Grid* (2017), the online *Whirlwind Magazine* (2016), and 4Culture/King County Metro's "Poetry on the Buses" project (2015). In August, 2016, he was the Writer-In-Residence for the month-long "La Cocina," a Pop-Up Latinx Artists' Salon hosted by La Sala and held in conjunction with the Seattle Art

Fair. He is a graduate of the Artist Trust 2016 Literary Edge program. Jim is also a news producer at Bellevue College's KBCS.FM Radio (91.3), and his community volunteer activities in Seattle include La Sala, *Raven Chronicles,* and Seattle City of Literature.

Sarah Capdeville is currently pursuing an MFA in creative writing at Chatham University in Pittsburgh, Pennsylvania. She graduated from the University of Montana with a BS in resource conservation and a BA in Spanish. A proud Montanan, she has worked as a wilderness ranger, ranch-hand, construction-hand, field instructor, and in other odd jobs across the West and internationally. Her work has been published in *Camas Magazine* and *Montana Naturalist,* as well as forthcoming in *Bright Bones,* an anthology of contemporary Montana writing.

Daniel Carter is from Seattle. Drawing inspiration from the rich Arabian tradition, he has made a career of helping others to make stepping stones out of stumbling blocks inside the Washington State prison system. He is the editor of the *I Hope* Newsletter at Larch Corrections Center in Yacolt, Washington.

Nancy Christopherson lives and writes in eastern Oregon. She is the author of one full-length collection of poetry, *The Leaf* (2015). Recent work is published or forthcoming in *Hawaii Pacific Review, Helen, Peregrine, Third Wednesday, Verseweavers, Willawaw Journal,* and *Xanadu.* She is currently immersed in four full-length manuscripts-in-progress: "Canyon Poems," "While the Moon Floats Ranch," "Lungfish Swallow Me Whole," and "Confessions and Conversations." Visit www. nancychristophersonpoetry.com.

Ng Yu Ci lives in Singapore, a dot on the map at the tip of the Malay Peninsula. She has been published in anthologies such as *ASINGBOL: an Archaeology of the Singaporean Poetic*

Form and *Eye On The World: Tomorrow's Cover*. She was also the recipient of the top award for poetry at the National Poetry Festival. As she navigates the currents of the world, she writes in an attempt to resist and remember.

Deborrah Corr grew up in the Yamhill Valley of Oregon, and moved to Seattle in 1969, where she currently lives and writes. After twenty-eight years of teaching kindergarten, retirement has given her the freedom to dive deeply into her love of poetry. She has studied with several teachers at Richard Hugo House in Seattle. The poem that appears in this issue, "Eating the Earth," is her first published work. She is excited and grateful!

Mary Eliza Crane is a native of New England who migrated to the Pacific Northwest three decades ago and settled into the Cascade Foothills east of Puget Sound. A regular feature at poetry venues throughout the Puget Sound region, she has read her poetry from Woodstock to Los Angeles. Mary has two volumes of poetry, *What I Can Hold In My Hands* (Gazoobi Tales Publishing, 2009), and *At First Light* (Gazoobi Tales Publishing, 2011). Her work has appeared in *Raven Chronicles, The Cartier Street Review, Tuesday Poems, Quill and Parchment, The Far Field, Avocet,* and several anthologies, including *The LitFUSE Anthology,* and *WA 129,* an anthology of poems from Washington poets, edited by Tod Marshall, 2016-2018 Washington State Poet Laureate.

Sharon Cumberland's poems have been published in many literary journals, including *Ploughshares, Iowa Review, Image,* and *Beloit Poetry Journal*. She has been awarded *Kalliope's* Sue Saniel Elkind Award, Pacific Northwest Writer's Association's Zola Award for Poetry (2001, 2013), and the Writer's Haven Press Bright Side Award. *Peculiar Honors,* a full-length collection of poems, was published by Black Heron Press in 2012. Her chapbooks are *The Arithmetic of Mourning,* Green

Rock Press (1998), and *Greatest Hits 1985-2000*, Pudding House Press (2002). She has been a resident artist at Yaddo, New York, the Jack Straw Foundation in Seattle, and the Grünewald Guild, in Plain, Washington. She is also the founder (2005) and a member of the Greenwood Poets at the Greenwood Senior Center in Seattle. Her poetry collection, *Strange with Age*, was published by Black Heron Press in 2017.

Doc Drumheller was born in Charleston, South Carolina, and has lived in New Zealand for more than half his life. He has worked in award-winning groups for theatre and music, and has published ten collections of poetry. His poems have been translated into more than twenty languages, and he has performed in Cuba, Lithuania, Italy, Hungary, Bulgaria, Romania, Japan, India, Nicaragua, USA, Mexico, El Salvador, and widely throughout New Zealand. He lives in Oxford, New Zealand, where he edits and publishes the literary journal *Catalyst*.

Anita Endrezze is an author and artist. Her short story collection, *Butterfly Moon*, was published in 2012 by the University of Arizonia Press. Anita's Red Bird Press Chapbooks include *Breaking Edges* (2012), and *A Thousand Branches* (2014). Her work has been translated into ten languages and taught around the world. She won the Bumbershoot/Weyerhaeuser Award, a Washington State Governor's Writing Award, and a GAP Award for her poetry. She collaborates on art projects with a small group of women. An altered book project on the value of art in Latin America is archived at the Smithsonian. She has also worked on an altered book about Don Quixote. She is half-European (Slovenian, German, and Italian), and half Yaqui (a nation native to Mexico). She has MS and is housebound.

Chris Espenshade: "I have been a professional archaeologist for thirty-two years. During my career, I have written one book, several chapters for edited volumes, numerous journal articles, and more than 1,000 technical reports on archaeological subjects. As I approach retirement, I am branching into creative writing. I have had a creative nonfiction piece published by *The RavensPerch*, and another has been accepted by *The Dead Mule School of Southern Literature*. My creative nonfiction work, "The Big Fish Swagger," will be published in February, 2018, by *Georgia Outdoors News*. I work in Pittsburgh, Pennsylvania, and live in Corning, New York."

Fiona Farrell publishes nonfiction, fiction, poetry, and plays, for which she has received numerous awards, including the New Zealand Book Award for Fiction, the 2007 Prime Ministers Award for Fiction, and, in 2012, the Order of New Zealand Merit for Services to Literature. Her most recent work, twin volumes of fiction and nonfiction prompted by the earthquakes that struck her home town, Christchurch, in 2010 and 2011, has been greeted as a major work "destined to become a classic of New Zealand literature."

David Fewster's work has appeared in the anthologies *Revival: Spoken Word From Lollapalooza 94* (Manic D Press, 1995) and *Thus Spake the Corpse: An Exquisite Corpse Reader, 1988-1998, Vol. 2* (Black Sparrow Press, 2000). His poetry collection, *Diary of a Homeless Alcoholic Suicidal Maniac & Other Picture Postcards* (2003), funded by an Artists Initiative Project Grant from the Tacoma Arts Commission, would never have come to fruition if not for Karen Havnaer's friendship, encouragement, and advice.

Anne Frantilla was born and raised in Seattle. After fifteen years in Michigan, she was happy to return to the left coast. She cares for voices from the past in her job as City Archivist for the City of Seattle, and works to connect them with people in the present. She has published previously in *Hippocampus* and *Raven Chronicles*.

An Indigenous daughter of the West, **CMarie Fuhrman** was born in Southwest Colorado, and has lived in various rural towns all along the Rocky Mountains. She has earned degrees in Exercise Physiology, English, and American Indian Studies, and is currently an MFA candidate at the University of Idaho where she is an Advisor for Native students and is Associate Poetry Editor for *Fugue Magazine*. CMarie's poetry has been featured in Broadsided Press's NoDAPL compilation, two anthologies, and several literary journals, including *Cutthroat: A Journal of the Arts*, and *Whitefish Review*. She is a recipient of the Burns Award for Poetry and multiple fellowships. Her current project, "The Problem of My Body," focuses on the forced sterilization of Native women. CMarie divides her time between Moscow and McCall, Idaho.

Rafael Jesús González, Professor Emeritus of literature and creative writing, was born and raised biculturally / bilingually in El Paso, Texas, and Ciudad Juárez, Chihuahua, Mexico. He taught at the University of Oregon, Western State College of Colorado, Central Washington State University, University of Texas El Paso (Visiting Professor of Philosophy), and Laney College, Oakland, California, where he founded the Department of Mexican & Latin-American Studies. His collection of poems, *La musa lunática / The Lunatic Muse,* was published in 2009, with a second printing in 2010. He received the 2012 Dragonfly Press Award for Outstanding Literary Achievement, and was honored by the City of Berkeley with a Lifetime Achievement Award at the Berkeley Poetry Festival in 2015. He was named the first Poet Laureate of Berkeley in 2017. Visit http://rjgonzalez.blogspot.com/.

Edward Harkness is the author of two full-length poetry collections, *Saying the Necessary* and *Beautiful Passing Lives,* both from Pleasure Boat Studio Press. His poems can be found online in *2River, Atticus Review, Cascadia Review, The Good Men Project, Hinchas de Poesia, The Humanist, Rat's Ass Journal, Salt*

River Review, Split Lip Magazine, Switched-On Gutenberg, and *Terrain.Org.* Recent publications in print journals include *Chariton Review* and *Miramar.* His most recent chapbook, *Ice Children,* was published by Split Lip Press in 2014. To hear Ed read "Union Creek in Winter," (and published, not incidentally, on Jan. 21, 2017, the day of the inauguration of #45), go to Terrain.org at http://www.terrain.org/2017/poetry/letter-to-america-harkness/. He lives in Shoreline, Washington.

Alicia Hokanson, retired from forty years of teaching, now devotes her time to reading, writing, and political activism in Seattle and on Waldron Island, Washington. Her first collection of poems, *Mapping the Distance,* was selected by Carolyn Kizer for a King County Arts Commission Publication Prize. Two chapbooks from Brooding Heron Press are *Insistent in the Skin* and *Phosphorous.*

David D. Horowitz founded and manages Rose Alley Press, which primarily publishes books featuring Northwest formal poetry. His latest collections are *Cathedral and Highrise* (2015), and *Sky Above the Temple* (2012). David's poems have appeared in many journals and anthologies, including *The New Formalist, The Lyric, Candelabrum, The Smoking Poet,* and *Here, There, and Everywhere.* His essays regularly appear in the online journal, *Exterminating Angel.* David frequently organizes and hosts readings in the Seattle area, and maintains a website: www.rosealleypress.com.

Thomas Hubbard, a retired writing instructor and spoken word performer, authored *Nail and other hardworking poems,* Year of the Dragon Press, 1994; *Junkyard Dogz* (also available on audio CD); and *Injunz,* a chapbook. He designed and published *Children Remember Their Fathers* (an anthology), and books by seven other authors. His book reviews have appeared in *Square Lake, Raven Chronicles, New Pages* and

The Cartier Street Review. Recent publication credits include poems in *Yellow Medicine Review, I Was Indian,* editor Susan Deer Cloud, *Florida Review,* and short stories in *Red Ink* and *Yellow Medicine Review.* He serves editorially with *Raven Chronicles* and *The Cartier Street Review,* and still performs spoken word in and around Seattle, and at other venues around the country.

Jill McCabe Johnson is the author of two poetry books, *Revolutions We'd Hoped We'd Outgrown* and *Diary of the One Swelling Sea,* winner of a Nautilus Book Award, and the nonfiction chapbook *Borderlines.* Honors include an Artist Trust grant, an Academy of American Poets Award, the Mari Sandoz/Prairie Schooner Prize in Fiction, and Scissortale Review's Editor's Prize in Poetry; plus the Deborah Tall Memorial Fellowship from Pacific Lutheran University—where she completed her MFA in Creative Writing—and the Louise Van Sickle Fellowship in Poetry from the University of Nebraska—where she received her PhD in English. Johnson teaches Creative Writing and English at Skagit Valley College, and is the founding director of Artsmith, a non-profit to support the arts.

Susan Johnson writes in Roslyn, Washington, her home of thirty-nine years, where she met her husband, raised their family, taught in K-12 and university classrooms, hikes the trails, and is grateful to be a part of a vibrant writing community. Her work has appeared in *Poets Unite! LiTFUSE @10 Anthology, Yakima Coffeehouse Poets Twenty-Second, Rise Up Review, Cirque Journal, Windfall,* and is forthcoming in *Digital Washington 129* and *Yakima Coffeehouse Poets Twenty-Third.*

Barbara Johnstone's poems have appeared or are forthcoming in *Hummingbird: Magazine of the Short Poem; Peregrine;* and in a juried exhibit at the University of Puget Sound and the book by the same title: *Dirt? Scientists, Book Artists and Poets*

Reflect on Soil and Our Environment. She is currently working on a book of essays, "Love Lessons," learned from forty-one years as a couple's therapist in Seattle.

Erik Kennedy is the author of the chapbook *Twenty-Six Factitions* (Cold Hub Press, November, 2017), and his first full-length book of poetry will be published by Victoria University Press in New Zealand in 2018. His poems have recently been published in (or are forthcoming in) places like *3:AM Magazine, LEVELER, Poetry, Powder Keg Magazine*, and *Prelude*, and his criticism has appeared in the *Los Angeles Review of Books* and *The Times Literary Supplement*. He is the poetry editor for *Queen Mob's Teahouse*. Originally from New Jersey, he lives in Christchurch, New Zealand.

Eugenia Kim's debut novel, *The Calligrapher's Daughter*, won the 2009 Borders Original Voices Award, was shortlisted for the Dayton Literary Peace Prize, and was Best Historical Novel and Critic's Pick by *The Washington Post*. Her work has appeared in *Asia Literary Review* and elsewhere. Kim teaches fiction in Fairfield University's MFA Creative Writing Program. She lives in Washington, D.C.

Sarah E. N. Kohrs is a visual artist, whose poetry can be found in *Poetry from the Valley of Virginia, Crosswinds Poetry Journal, From the Depths, Virginia Literary Journal, Horn & Ivory, Claudius Speaks*, and *Adelaide Literary Magazine*. Kohrs has a BA from The College of Wooster, and a Virginia State teaching license. She lives in the Shenandoah Valley, where she homeschools three sons, manages *The Sow's Ear Poetry Review*, directs The Corhaven Graveyard, and works to kindle hope, where it's needed most. Visit: http://senkohrs.com.

Larry Laurence's books are a full-length volume of poems, *Life Of The Bones To Come*, Black Heron Press, chosen as a National Poetry Month selection by NACS, the National

Association Of College Stores; a chapbook, *Scenes Beginning With The Footbridge At The Lake*, Brooding Heron Press; and an e-chapbook, *Successions Of Words Are So*, E-Ratio Editions. His poems have appeared in the anthologies *How Much Earth: The Fresno Poets*, Roundhouse Press, and *Jack Straw Writers*, Jack Straw Productions, and in journals including *CutBank, Floating Bridge Review, Poetry Northwest, POOL, Raven Chronicles*, and *Southern Poetry Review*. Laurence earned an MA in English at California State University, Fresno, studying poetry under Philip Levine.

Daniel Lee is a near lifelong resident of Spokane, Washington, where he currently lives with his wife. He has been published in *Rock & Sling*, and anthologized in *Railtown Almanac*. He studied at the Inland Northwest Center for Writers at Eastern Washington University, and works as an English Instructor.

Nic Low is a writer, installation artist, and arts organizer of Ngāi Tahu Māori and European descent. He divides his time between a hyper-social Melbourne sharehouse, and an anti-social bush retreat. His first book is *Arms Race*, a collection of fierce, playful short stories published by Text Publishing. His second, a literary walking expedition through New Zealand's Southern Alps, comes out in 2018. Nic has published essays and short fiction in multiple publications, including *Griffith Review, The Big Issue, Overland, The Lifted Brow, Australian Book Review,* and various suspect anthologies. He was runner-up in the 2013 Overland Short Story Competition, shortlisted for the 2012 Commonwealth Short Story Prize, and received a 2011 GREW Prize for nonfiction. He recently participated in Lit Crawl Seattle (October, 2017) as part of the Christchurch-Seattle Sister City exchange.

David Lukas lives in New York City where he works for Planned Parenthood and trains as a competitive marathon runner. His debut poetry collection, *Barstools and Nightstands*, was recently featured by *2 Elizabeths*.

Jamie McGillen was born in Alaska and currently resides in Washington State. She holds an MA from Northern Arizona University. Her work has been published in *Marathon Literary Review*, and online in *Rust + Moth*, Winter 2017.

Frankie McMillan is the author of four books, the most recent of which, *My Mother and the Hungarians, and other small fictions* (Canterbury University Press, 2016), was longlisted for the 2017 New Zealand Ockham awards. In 2005, she was awarded the Creative New Todd Bursary. Other awards include winner of the New Zealand Poetry Society International Poetry Competition in 2009, and winner of the New Zealand Flash Fiction Competition in 2013 and 2015. In 2014, she held the Ursula Bethell writing residency at Canterbury University, and in 2017, the University of Auckland's Michael King writing residency.

Heather McQuillan is a writing teacher, and her novels for young readers have won several awards, including the Tom Fitzgibbon Award (2005), and recognized as Storylines Notable Books in 2006 and 2012. In 2016, Heather won the New Zealand National Flash Fiction Day Competition and the Micro Madness Award, and placed third in the Sunday Star Times Short Story competition. Her flash fiction appears regularly online at *Flash Frontier*, and can also be found in *Best Small Fictions 2017* (US), *Bath Flash Fiction Vol 2* (UK), and *Sleep is A Beautiful Colour* (UK). She also writes a few poems. Heather is currently a Masters of Creative Writing student at Massey University of New Zealand, and associate director of The School for Young Writers.

Jayne Marek's poetry and art photos appear, most recently, in *Women's Studies Quarterly, Amsterdam Review, About Place*

Journal, Chroma, Bombay Gin, Sin Fronteras, Notre Dame Review, Forage, River Poets, and *New Verse News.* She has provided color cover art for several journals and for her two full-length poetry books—*In and Out of Rough Water* (Kelsay Books, 2017), and *The Tree Surgeon Dreams of Bowling* (Finishing Line, 2017). Twice nominated for a Pushcart Prize, she also was a finalist for the David Martinson–Meadowhawk Prize, the Ex Ophidia Poetry Book Prize, and the Ryan R. Gibbs Photography Contest. A former literature professor and Indiana Master Naturalist, she has now begun learning about the natural history of the Olympic and Quimper Peninsulas.

Gigi Marks lives on the western edge of Cayuga Lake, in the Finger Lakes region of New York. Her most recent book of poems, *Territory,* is forthcoming from Silverfish Review Press.

Ruby Hansen Murray is a writer and photographer, whose work appears in *World Literature Today, The Rumpus, As/Us,* and *American Ghost: Poets on Life after Industry.* Winner of the 2017 Montana Prize in Creative Nonfiction, she's a Jack Straw and VONA fellow; and was awarded residencies at Ragdale, Hedgebrook, Virginia Center for Creative Arts, and the Sitka Island Institute. She received an MFA from the Institute of American Indian Arts in 2017. She is a citizen of the Osage Nation, with West Indian roots on her mother's side, living in the Columbia River Estuary.

Jed Myers is author of *Watching the Perseids* (Sacramento Poetry Center), *The Marriage of Space and Time* (MoonPath Press, forthcoming), and two chapbooks. Recent honors include the *Prime Number Magazine* Award for Poetry, *The Southeast Review's* Gearhart Poetry Prize, and the McLellan Poetry Prize. Poems are forthcoming in *Poetry Northwest, Southern Poetry Review,* and *Natural Bridge.* He's Poetry Editor for the online magazine *Bracken.*

Michael Terence O'Brien is a poet, playwright, songwriter, and artist. He currently resides in Chesterfield, New Jersey. He has a BA in Political Science from Richard Stockton College, and a MA in Special Education from The College of New Jersey. Michael is a special education teacher, and works with students with Autistic Spectrum Disorder.

John Olson is the author of numerous books of poetry and prose poetry, including *Echo Regime, Free Stream Velocity, Backscatter: New and Selected Poems, Larynx Galaxy,* and *Dada Budapest* (2017). He was the recipient of *The Stranger's* 2004 Genius Award for Literature, and in 2012 was one of eight finalists for the Washington State Arts Innovator Award. He has also published four novels, including *Souls of Wind* (shortlisted for The Believer Book Award), *The Nothing That Is, The Seeing Machine,* and *In Advance of the Broken Justy.*

Anna Reaney: "Nelson Bentley encouraged me when I attended his workshops at the University of Washington, and invited me to read at the Castalia Reading Series a few times. I also studied fiction with Lois Hudson. Later, I attended Pesha Gertler's women's poetry workshops. I had a number of poems printed in alternative magazines. I started writing fiction in the 1990s, and published one story, but fiction began to seem irrelevant. I resumed it again a few years ago. *Raven Chronicles* will be my first major publication."

Luisa Kay Reyes has had pieces featured in *Fire In Machines*, Hofstra University's *The Windmill, Halcyon Days, Fellowship of the King, Enchanted Conversation: A Fairy Tale Magazine, Route 7 Review, The Foliate Oak, The Eastern Iowa Review,* and other literary magazines. Her piece, "Thank You," is the winner of the April, 2017, memoir contest from *The Dead Mule School of Southern Literature.* Her Christmas poem was a first place winner in the 16th Annual Stark County District Library Poetry Contest. She lives in Tuscaloosa, Alabama.

Mary Lou Sanelli has published six collections of poetry and three works of nonfiction, *Among Friends, Falling Awake,* and her latest, *A Woman Writing.* Her regular columns appear in Seattle's *City Living Magazine, Art Access,* and *Lilipoh Magazine.* She has written for National Public Radio, Seattle's NPR affiliate KUOW.FM, *The Seattle Times, Seattle Metropolitan Magazine, Crosscut,* and many other publications. She works as a literary speaker and is booked at regional and national conferences, and other venues, including Town Hall Seattle. An instructor of Contemporary Dance, she teaches Master Classes and workshops throughout the world. She lives with her husband in Seattle.

Heidi Seaborn starting writing poetry in 2016. Since then her work has appeared in over thirty journals, including *Nimrod International Journal* (2017 Pablo Neruda Prize for Poetry semifinalist), *Timberline, Gravel, West Trade Review,* and *American Journal of Poetry;* in five anthologies; as the political pamphlet *Body Politic* (Mount Analogue Press); on a Seattle bus; and in her forthcoming chapbook, *Finding My Way Home* (Finishing Line Press). She is on the editorial staff of *The Adroit Journal* and lives in Seattle. Visit: www.heidiseabornpoet.com.

Julianne Seeman's first book, *Enough Light to See,* was chosen by Charles Wright for the Anhinga Award and published by the University of Florida Press. She is published in many periodicals, and has recently retired from teaching at Bellevue College in Washington State.

Dave Seter is a civil engineer and poet. Originally from Chicago, he currently lives in Sonoma County, California. His poetry and critical works have recently appeared in *Paterson Literary Review, Evansville Review, Palaver, Confluence,* and other journals. He received his undergraduate degree from Princeton University, and is currently enrolled in the Masters in Humanities Program at Dominican University of California, where he is studying ecopoetics. His poetry chapbook, *Night Duty,* was published in 2010 by Main Street Rag Publishing Company.

Judith Skillman's recent book is *Kafka's Shadow*, Deerbrook Editions. Her work has appeared in *LitMag, Shenandoah, Zyzzyva, FIELD*, and elsewhere. Awards include an Eric Mathieu King Fund grant from the Academy of American Poets. She is a faculty member at the Richard Hugo House in Seattle, Washington. Visit: www.judithskillman.com.

T.J. Smith is a poet in New York. Originally from Jacksonville, Florida, he studied German and Creative Writing at Princeton University, and he's currently completing an MFA at NYU, where he's the Web Editor of *Washington Square Review*. His work has appeared or is forthcoming in *Gyroscope Review, Split Rock Review, Red Flag Poetry, Drunk Monkeys, Stoneboat Literary Journal,* and *Nassau Literary Review*.

Willie Smith was born in Greenbelt, Maryland, sometime in the last century, and is a long-time resident of Seattle. His writing has appeared in *Poetry Motel, Thieves Jargon, The American Drivel Review, Cherry Bleeds, Bewildering Stories, Litvision, The Ragged Edge, Lost and Found Times, Raven Chronicles, Libido, Word Riot,* and *Zygote in my Coffee*. His collection of short stories, *Nothing Doing* (Honest Publishing, 2012), is "An ode to misspent childhood, lost innocence and creeping depravity, blowing apart the American ideal of life spent in pursuit of wholesome activity. Written over a period of thirty years, these stories anatomize America's most vivid perversions . . . signalling underground legend Willie Smith's perfectly executed return to the literary world."

Joannie Stangeland is the author of *In Both Hands* and *Into the Rumored Spring,* both from Ravenna Press in Edmonds, Washington, and three chapbooks. Her poems have also appeared in *Prairie Schooner, Mid-American Review, The Southern Review*, and other journals. Joannie has been a Jack Straw Writer, and she is currently enrolled in the MFA program at Rainier Writing Workshop. Visit her website at joanniestangeland.com.

Scott T. Starbuck's new book of climate change poems is *Hawk on Wire* (Fomite, 2017), about which UC Berkeley poetry professor John Shoptaw noted that no one writes about "unsustainability [. . .] more compellingly," and John Keeble added, "This is a wonderful, bracing, and searching book." Starbuck's ecoblog, *Trees, Fish, and Dreams*, has a video of his book launch at riverseek.blogspot.com The book was a July 12, 2017 "Editor's Pick" (along with *The Collected Stories of Ray Bradbury*) at Newpages.com, and will be featured at The Yale Center for Environmental Communication's Climate Connections, which will distribute an interview about it to 340 radio stations and online via podcast and internet radio.

JT Stewart (poet, writer, playwright, public artist, editor, teacher) co-founded the Clarion West Writers' Workshop, now in its thirty-second year. As a public artist, JT considers the following as representative of her work: poetry broadsides placed at the Seattle Art Museum, the Washington State Convention Center Galleries, and the Allen Library (University of Washington). She was Poetry Editor for *Seattle Poets & Photographers: Millennium Reflections* (Seattle Arts Commission, 1999). JT has received grants from Artist Trust, 4Culture, and the NEH. Viewers can see her poetry broadsides in the permanent installation "Raven Brings Light To This House Of Stories" (Allen Library, University of Washington). She currently serves as a juror (one of eighty from five countries) for the yearly SOVAS Awards [Society of Voice Arts & Sciences].

Mary Ellen Talley's poems have recently been published in *Cirque, U City Review,* and *Ekphrastic Review,* as well as in the anthologies, *The Doll Collection* and *Raising Lilly Ledbetter:*

Women Poets Occupy the Workspace. Mary Ellen worked for many years with words and children as a Speech-Language Pathologist (SLP) in Seattle public schools.

Eugenia Toledo was born in Temuco, Chile, grew up in the same neighborhood as Pablo Neruda, and came to the U.S. for doctoral studies after the 1973 military coup. Her award-winning, bilingual poetic sequence is *Trazas de mapa, trazas de sangre / Map Traces, Blood Traces* (translated by Carolyne Wright, Mayapple Press, 2017), the story of an exile's return to her homeland after the military coup that sent her away for decades. With her husband, she divides her time between Temuco and Seattle.

Mayumi Tsutakawa is an independent writer and editor. She is a lecturer with the Humanities Washington Speakers Bureau on the topic of the one-hundred-year history of Japanese Americans in Washington State. She co-edited several multicultural literary anthologies, one of which, *The Forbidden Stitch: Asian American Women's Literary Anthology* (Calyx Books, 1990), received the Before Columbus Foundation's American Book Award.

Carter Vance, a student and aspiring poet from Cobourg, Ontario, currently studies at Carleton University in Ottawa, Canada. His work has appeared in *The Vehicle* (parenthetical) and *F(r)iction*, amongst others. He received an Honourable Mention from *Contemporary Verse 2's* Young Buck Poetry Awards in 2015. His debut chapbook, *Songs About Girls*, is now available from Urban Farmhouse Press.

Angie Trudell Vasquez received her MFA in poetry from the Institute of American Indian Arts in May, 2017. In 2016, she was a poetry panelist at Split This Rock! Her poems have been published most recently in *Cloudthroat, Yellow Medicine Review, Raven Chronicles,* the *San Diego Poetry Annual 2015-*

2016, *Subtle Forces,* and *Return to the Gathering Place of the Waters.* She has work forthcoming in the *Taos Journal of Poetry.* She was nominated for a Pushcart in 2014 for her essay, "The Making of the Latina Monologues." Her short stories have appeared most recently in *The Rumpus* online, and *Basta! 100+ Latinas Against Gender Violence.* She has her own press, Art Night Books, and will resume publishing other people's work in 2018.

Sarah Brown Weitzman, a past National Endowment for the Arts Fellow in Poetry and Pushcart Prize nominee, has been published in hundreds of journals and anthologies, including *Rosebud, The New Ohio Review, Poet & Critic, The North American Review, Rattle, Mid-American Review, The MacGuffin, Poet Lore Spillway, Miramar,* etc. A departure from poetry, her fourth book, *Herman and the Ice Witch,* is a children's novel published by Main Street Rag, 2011.

Rita Wirkala is an Argentine writer residing in Seattle, whose work has been published in Europe and the United States. She writes novels, poetry, literary essays, and school textbooks. Her doctoral thesis, about *The Book of Good Love* by Juan Ruiz, the Archpriest of Hita, reflects her deep interest in the rich tradition of storytelling. Her novel, *El Encuentro,* and its English edition, *The Encounter,* won the International Latino Book Award and the Books into Movies Award. After twenty years of teaching at the University of Washington, she is now helping other Spanish writers at Seattle Escribe workshops.

Carolyne Wright's latest book is *This Dream the World: New & Selected Poems* (Lost Horse Press, 2017), whose title poem received a Pushcart Prize and was included in *The Best American Poetry 2009.* Her ground-breaking anthology, *Raising Lilly Ledbetter: Women Poets Occupy the Workspace* (Lost Horse, 2015), received ten Pushcart Prize nominations and was a finalist in the *Foreword Review's* Book of the

Year Awards. Her latest volume in translation is *Trazas de mapa, trazas de sangre / Map Traces, Blood Traces* (Mayapple Press, 2017), a bilingual sequence of poems by Seattle-based Chilean poet, Eugenia Toledo [reviewed in this issue]. She teaches for Richard Hugo House, for the Antioch University Los Angeles MFA Program, and for national and international literary conferences and festivals. She is a Contributing Editor for the Pushcart Prizes and an Advisory Board member for *Raven Chronicles*.

Andrena Zawinski is an award-winning educator and poet from Pittsburgh, Pennsylvania, who has made her home in the San Francisco Bay area, where she founded and runs a Women's Poetry Salon. Her latest collection of poetry is *Landings*, and she has two previous award-winning collections: *Something About*, a PEN Oakland/Josephine Miles Literary Award recipient, and *Traveling in Reflected Light*, a Kenneth Patchen Poetry Prize winner. She is also Editor for *Turning a Train of Thought Upside Down: An Anthology of Women's Poetry*. Her poems have received accolades for lyricism, form, spirituality, and social concern. Visit: www.poetrymagazine.com/zawinski.

Kristin Camitta Zimet is the author of *Take in My Arms the Dark*, a full-length collection of poetry, and the editor of *The Sow's Ear Poetry Review*. Her poems appear in many journals, including *Poet Lore, Salamander,* and *Natural Bridge*. She is also a Reiki healer and leads nature walks as a master naturalist.

Horse of the mists, collage by Anita Endrezze

BIOGRAPHICAL NOTES
EDITORS

Anna Bálint (Words From the Café): edited *Words from the Café*, an anthology of writing from people in recovery. She is also the author of *Horse Thief*, a collection of short fiction spanning cultures and continents, and two earlier books of poetry. Anna is an alumna of Hedgebrook Writers Retreat, the Jack Straw Writers Program, and has received awards and grants from the Seattle Arts Commission and 4Culture/King County. Currently, she teaches adults in recovery from the traumas of homelessness, addiction, and mental illness. She is a teaching artist with Seattle's Path With Art, and the founder of Safe Place Writing Circle at Recovery Café in Seattle.

Phoebe Bosché (Managing Editor): is a cultural activist, and has been managing editor of The Raven Chronicles Literary Organization / Raven Chronicles Press since 1991. She is a full-time editor and book designer. Her favorite poet is Archy, the cockroach, whose muse is Mehitabel, the alley cat.

Paul Hunter (Poetry Editor): has published fine letterpress poetry under the imprint of Wood Works Press since 1994. His poems have appeared in numerous journals, as well as in seven full-length books and three chapbooks. His first collection of farming poems, *Breaking Ground*, 2004, from Silverfish Review Press, was reviewed in *The New York Times*, and received the 2004 Washington State Book Award. A second volume of farming poems, *Ripening*, was published in 2007, a third companion volume, *Come the Harvest*, appeared in 2008, and the fourth, from the same publisher, *Stubble Field*, appeared in 2012. He has been a featured poet on *The News Hour*, and has a prose book on small-scale, sustainable farming, *One Seed to Another: The New Small Farming*, published by the Small Farmer's Journal. His new book of prose poetry,

Clownery, In lieu of a life spent in harness, was published in 2017, by Davila Art & Books, Sisters, Oregon.

Matt Briggs (Fiction Editor): is the author of eight works of fiction including *The Remains of River Names* and *Virility Rituals of North American Teenage Boys*. His first novel, *Shoot the Buffalo*, was a finalist for the 2006 Washington State Book Award, and won the 2006 American Book Award. The Italian edition of *The Remains of River Names* was released in 2017, by ad est del' equator (Napoli), and a new collection of prose will be released by Dr. Cicero Books in 2018. His stories have appeared in *The Chicago Review, Word Riot, BULL, Opium Magazine, ZYZYYVA*, and elsewhere. His fiction has won a number of prizes including The City Artist Award from the City of Seattle, The Nelson Bentley Prize in Fiction from *The Seattle Review* and The Stranger Genius Award. He has an MA from the Writing Seminars at Johns Hopkins University, and lives near Seattle. You can find him online at: http://mattbriggs.com.

Doug Johnson (Nonfiction Editor): lives in Yakima, Washington with his family. He founded Cave Moon Press, in 2006, to try to connect poets and artists to community. His book of short stories, *Frank's Diary* (Mary Celeste Press, Australia), was nominated by the Pacific Northwest Bookseller's Association as a finalist for their book award. His feature-length novel, *The Golden Years: First Half* (Bennett and Hastings, Seattle), debuted in 2014. His artwork was featured in collaboration with artist Alfredo Arreguín in a show entitled, *In the Shadow of a Master: The art of Alfredo Arreguín*. In 2016, he co-edited a book of poems with Paul Nelson to help homeless veterans. He most recently acted as the guest poet for Yakima's TEDx salon entitled "Breaking Barriers." He loves to collaborate so feel free to contact him at cavemoonpress@gmail.com.

ACKNOWLEDGMENTS

Raven is indebted to our 2017 co-sponsors for partial funding of our programs: the Seattle Office of Arts & Culture (Civic Partners); 4Culture/King County Lodging Tax (Arts Sustained Support Program); the Washington State Arts Commission/ArtsWA, with National Endowment (NEA) funding (Project Support); and all Raven subscribers and donors. Special thanks to Jack Straw Cultural Center for office space and support of our reading series. And many thanks to the generosity of Rachel **Beatty**, Carletta Carrington **Wilson**, Larry **Laurence**, Alfredo **Arrequín**, and Kevin **Miller** for their generous donations in support of Raven ongoing programs.

Founded in 1991
Vol. 25, Winter 2017-18
www.ravenchronicles.org

PUBLISHER
Raven Chronicles Press,
501(c)(3) Organization

MANAGING DIRECTOR
PHOEBE BOSCHÉ, SEATTLE

FOUNDERS
KATHLEEN ALCALÁ
PHOEBE BOSCHÉ
PHILIP RED EAGLE

EDITORS, VOL. 25
ANNA BÁLINT
PHOEBE BOSCHÉ
MATT BRIGGS
PAUL HUNTER
DOUG JOHNSON

COPY EDITORS:
KATHLEEN ALCALÁ, PHOEBE BOSCHÉ,
PAUL HUNTER, ANNA MOCKLER

HOPVINE PUB 2017 ART SERIES, CURATOR:
SCOTT MARTIN AKA LES MORELY

ALL QUERIES
THE RAVEN CHRONICLES

MAILING ADDRESS:
15528 12TH AVENUE NE
SHORELINE, WA 98155

STREET ADDRESS:
JACK STRAW CULTURAL CENTER
SUITE 205
909 NE 43RD ST.
SEATTLE, WA 98105-6020

TEL: 206.941.2955
WWW.RAVENCHRONICLES.ORG
EDITORS@RAVENCHRONICLES.ORG